IMAGES
of America

DETROIT AREA TEST TRACKS

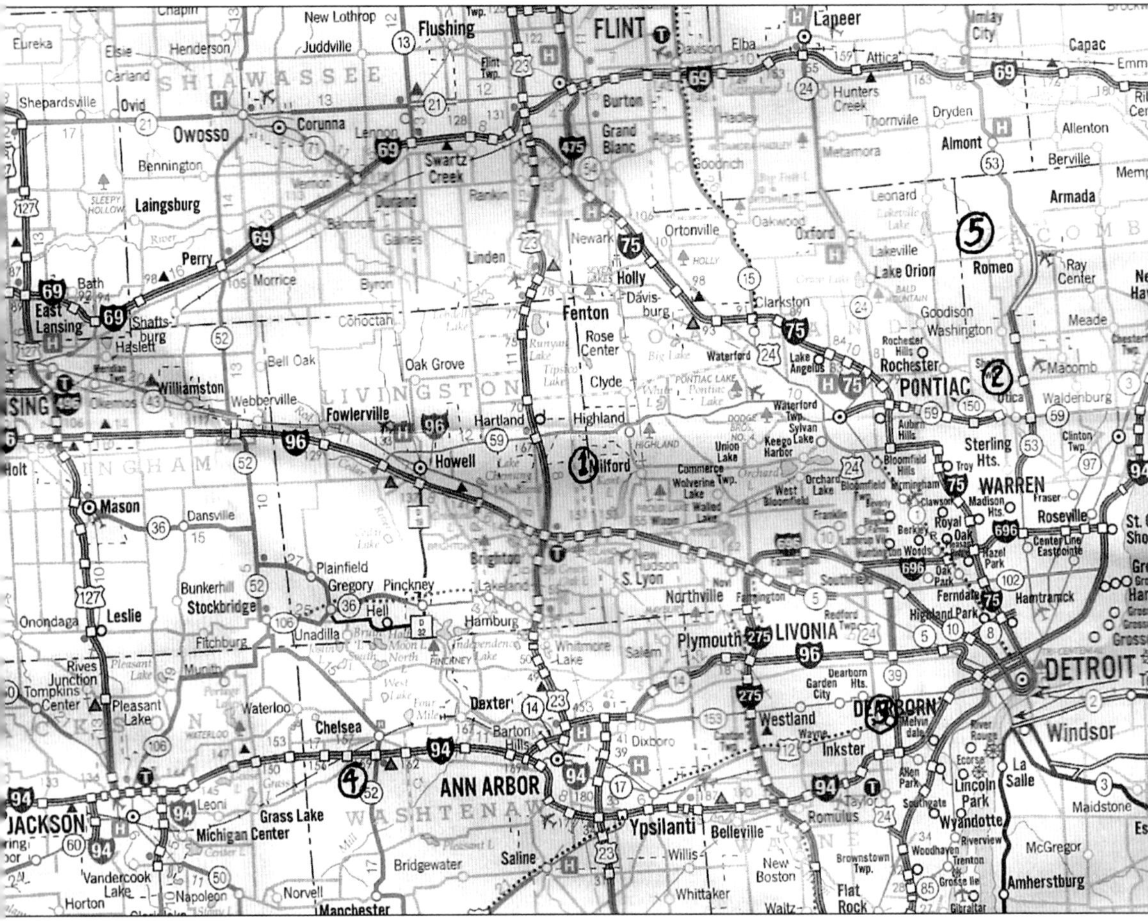

This map shows the location of the five main automotive test tracks, more formally called proving grounds, in the Detroit area of southeastern Michigan. In the order of their opening, they are General Motors Proving Ground, two miles west of Milford, in 1924 (1); Packard Proving Ground, two miles north of Utica, in 1927 (2); Ford Dearborn Proving Ground, formerly Ford Airport, now called Dearborn Development Center, located adjacent to Greenfield Village in the middle of Dearborn, in 1937 (3); Chrysler Proving Ground, one mile southwest of Chelsea, in 1954 (4); and Ford Michigan Proving Ground, two miles northwest of Romeo, in 1956 (5). (Author's collection.)

On the cover: The hill-climbing ability of a new 1939 Chevrolet is tested on an 11.6 percent grade on the General Motors proving ground near Milford, 40 miles northwest of Detroit. This was a common test at a time when climbing hills in "high," or third gear, was a challenge with the relatively low-compression engines then in use in the industry. A 1938 Chevrolet trails the new model, while engineers clock the elapsed time for the climb. (Courtesy of General Motors Media Archives.)

IMAGES
of America

DETROIT AREA TEST TRACKS

Michael W. R. Davis

ARCADIA
PUBLISHING

ISBN 978-0-7385-6022-9

Published by Arcadia Publishing
Charleston, South Carolina

Printed in the United States of America

Library of Congress Control Number: 2009925354

For all general information contact Arcadia Publishing at:
Telephone 843-853-2070
Fax 843-853-0044
E-mail sales@arcadiapublishing.com
For customer service and orders:
Toll-Free 1-888-313-2665

Visit us on the Internet at www.arcadiapublishing.com

Contents

ACKNOWLEDGMENTS

The idea for this book on automotive test tracks began with an afternoon I spent in October 2008 as a volunteer sorting old photographs at the National Automotive History Collection (NAHC) at the Detroit Public Library. Hence a majority of the images herein originated in that collection, and I am particularly indebted for the assistance given me by the following library personnel: Barbara Thompson, Gina Tecos, Carrie Pruett, India Davis, Mark Patrick, and John Gibson.

Next I would like to acknowledge the time and effort granted me by Larry Kinsel of the General Motors Media Archives. Greg Wallace of the GM Heritage Center also provided me with helpful information.

Others assisted me either as part of their jobs or, for the most part, simply as knowledgeable and helpful friends: Ray Day, Said Deep, and Beth Jenkins of Ford Public Affairs; Jim Dunne; Howard Freers; Joe Gormley; Charles K. Hyde; Bob Lees; Ken Ratkovich; John Sanderson; Del Schroeder; and especially Jim Wagner.

And I am once again grateful for my wife Karen's patience during her long periods of enforced solitude while I was researching test tracks and at my computer.

A guide to the photographs is as follows: D, author's collection; H, Howard Freers; G, General Motors Corporation Media Archives; J, Jim Dunne; and N, National Automotive History Collection, Detroit Public Library.

INTRODUCTION

In effect, this book is both a photo album and a history of automotive testing in America. In the process, it tears down the test track walls, showing what happens unseen, which for decades has drawn legions of the curious, especially males.

The first automotive testing took place on the streets of Stuttgart, Germany, where in 1885 Karl Benz unleashed the first gas buggy, a three-wheeler. The best-known test-drives, though, took place on Detroit streets, first by pioneer Charles B. King on March 6, 1896, and then by Henry Ford three months later.

However, testing of motorcars was preceded by centuries of development for man-, horse-, mule-, donkey-, ox- and even dog-drawn wheeled vehicles, and decades of experience with bicycles. Breakdowns were corrected by experience and new developments, a matter of tryout and correct. This history paved the way for the development of automobiles and trucks.

As the auto industry boomed in the early decades of the 20th century, engineering development was carried out in garages and on public roads. There were no templates, handbooks, nor reference bases—so practical and trained engineers alike had to learn by cut-and-try methods how engines and transmissions worked and, importantly, how to improve their function, reliability, and durability.

Early carmakers also depended on public performance events like oval-track racing, hill climbs and cross-country endurance trials to wring out problems, open therefore to public and competitive eyes—and mockery when things went bad. The first auto show in New York City in 1901 featured a test structure for car demonstrations on the roof of Madison Square Garden where the show was held. After its 1914 inception in Hamtramck, Dodge built a modest test course with an artificial wooden hill adjacent to its assembly plant, where each new car could be driven to insure it worked before being shipped to a dealer. Assembly-plant functional testing has been common among manufacturers right up to the present.

The advance to modern, scientific automotive proving grounds—known informally as test tracks—resulted from one of the industry's historical flops: the copper-cooled Chevrolet of 1923. This was one of the few bad ideas of genius Charles F. Kettering, who patented the first electric starter. What seemed like a brainstorm by Kettering to eliminate radiators and their problems of freezing and boiling over turned into a disaster for the rejuvenated General Motors Corporation (GM) after World War I. Alfred P. Sloan Jr., then new president of GM and later architect of the modern automobile company, recounted how a handful of the flawed copper-cooled Chevrolets were delivered to some 100 customers before the industry's first known recall was ordered by horrified GM executives in 1923. The problem was that the concept had never been tested fully, and further that there were no standardized procedures in GM (or anywhere else in the mass production auto industry) for such testing.

"Cars then were being tested on public roads," Sloan recalled in his 1964 classic, *My Years With General Motors*, "and there was no easy way of telling whether the test driver had pulled up at the side of the road, taken a nap, and then driven faster than the test schedule called for to make up the necessary mileage. Once one of our engineers discovered a test car jacked up outside a dance hall with the engine running up the required mileage on the odometer.

"The most important step we took to standardize and improve test procedures was the establishment in 1924 of the General Motors Proving Ground, the first of its kind in the automobile industry." The pioneering GM test track was located at Milford, Michigan, in hilly open country 40 miles northwest of the GM headquarters in midtown Detroit.

"The thought," Sloan continued, "was that we would have a large area [originally 1,300 acres, it grew to 4,000], properly protected, and entirely closed to the public. . . . It would be provided with roads of various types representing all the various demands on the motorcar. There we would be able to prove out our cars under controlled conditions both before and after production, and we could also make comprehensive tests on competitive cars."

Packard soon followed GM in 1927 with its own somewhat less ambitious test track and engineering garages near Utica, some 20 miles north of its Detroit office and manufacturing complex. Studebaker likewise built a proving ground west of South Bend, Indiana, also in 1927. A decade later, Ford Motor Company converted its small 360-acre Tri-Motor air field in Dearborn, which had concrete runways capable of adaptation to high-speed straightaways, to its first test track, long called Dearborn Proving Ground. At the end of World War II, Nash (later American Motors) established a test track at Burlington, Wisconsin, west of the Nash manufacturing center at Kenosha.

Apparently Hudson, Willys (Jeep), and Kaiser-Frazer never developed large-scale, dedicated test tracks. And even Chrysler's legendary engineering team likewise deemed it unnecessary to have such a facility until the Chelsea Proving Ground west of Ann Arbor was opened in 1954. GM established a desert proving ground near Phoenix, Arizona, in 1953, and three years later Ford opened its 3,900-acre Michigan Proving Ground near Romeo, north of Detroit, and the 3,800-acre Kingman Proving Ground in northwestern Arizona.

In addition to these large facilities, Detroit's big three operated a number of special test facilities around North America: test stations measuring high altitude performance at Pike's Peak, Colorado; cold weather in northern Minnesota, western Canada, and Michigan's Upper Peninsula; and facilities for evaluating upholstery trim, paint, and plastic in the heat and high-humidity of Florida. Major auto suppliers, especially tire companies, likewise developed proving grounds to test various requirements of vehicle components.

Environmental testing—desert, altitude, cold, etc.—began to be seriously needed in the postwar years as air flow to radiators was increasingly restricted by "lower and wider" body designs. Then came air conditioning, which became a popular option from the early 1950s. A third factor driving proving ground construction were longer new car warranties beginning with Ford's 12/12 (12 months or 12,000 miles, up from the industry standard before of three months/3,000 miles) for 1961 models (24/24 for Lincoln), and Chrysler's 5/50 powertrain warranty of 1963.

Meanwhile, special purpose engineering laboratories and test facilities spread rapidly, with an array of cold rooms, wind tunnels, light rooms, safety crash test set-ups, indoor suspension testing, engine dynamometer and transmission labs, and automotive pollution testing sites. California emission control requirements from the early 1960s, Federal safety regulations in the late 1960s, and environmental controls in the early 1970s made both the specialized test facilities and extensive durability tests a necessity, not merely a choice for auto engineers. Emissions and fuel economy rules imposed minimum 50,000 mile tests for every vehicle/engine/transmission combination—some later extending to 150,000 miles. Testing became a growth industry in itself.

In recent years, test tracks have been threatened by expanding suburbia, especially near Phoenix, where land values for subdivision development have trumped land for automotive testing. Computer simulation has grown progressively.

Michael W. R. Davis
June 2009

One

Vehicle Testing before the Motorcar

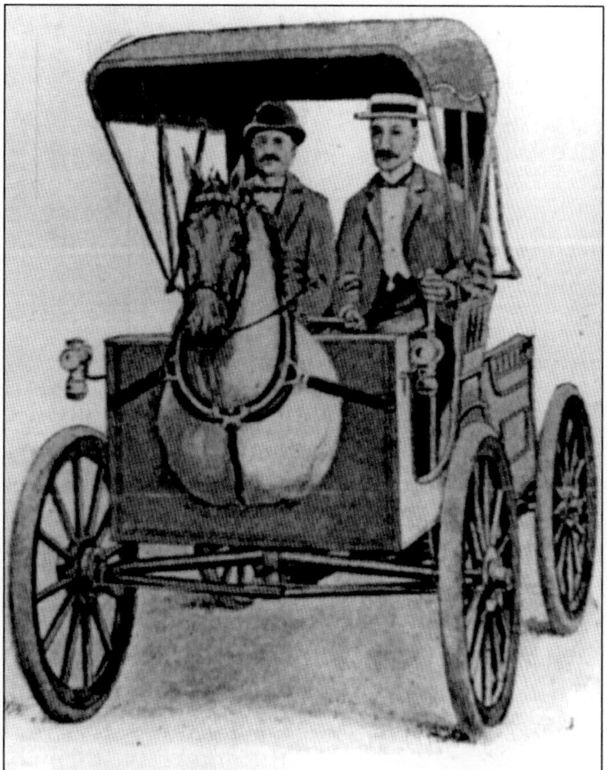

At the dawn of the automotive age in 1899, *Horseless Age* magazine printed this illustration, reporting that Uriah Smith of Battle Creek thought having a false horse's head on the front of a motor carriage would fool a real horse into believing another horse-drawn vehicle was approaching and not one of those frightening motorcars. The infant automobile industry learned much from both horse-drawn vehicles and bicycles. (N.)

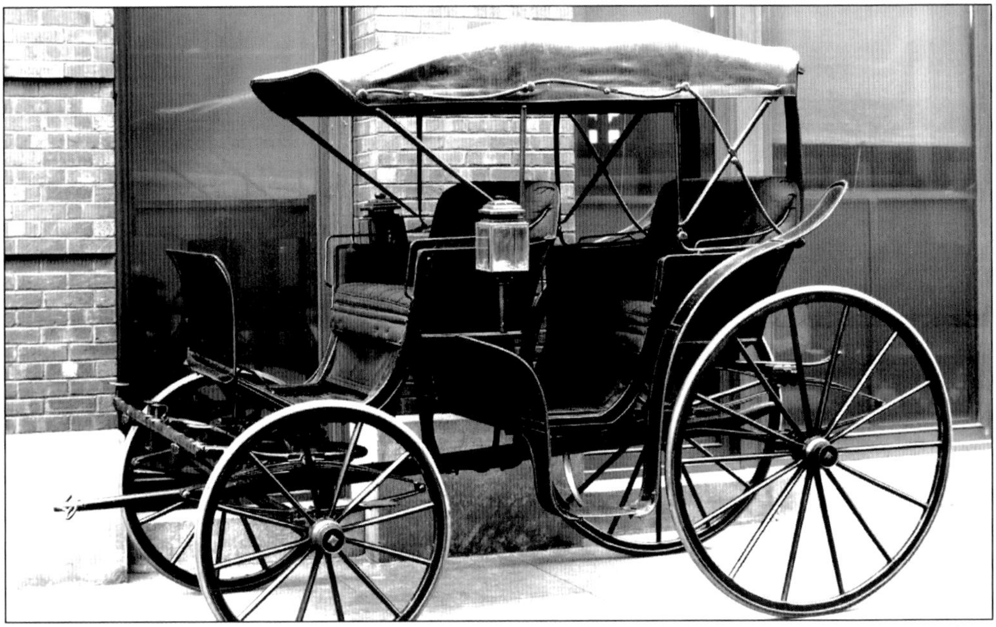

In this Studebaker carriage, Pres. William McKinley rode from his home in Canton, Ohio, to catch a train in September 1901 to Buffalo, New York, where anarchist Leon Czolgosz assassinated him. Note the fore-and-aft leaf springs, wheels, hubs, axles, and fenders that carried over to early automobiles, as well as the comparatively lightweight construction for a vehicle meant only to carry passengers. (N.)

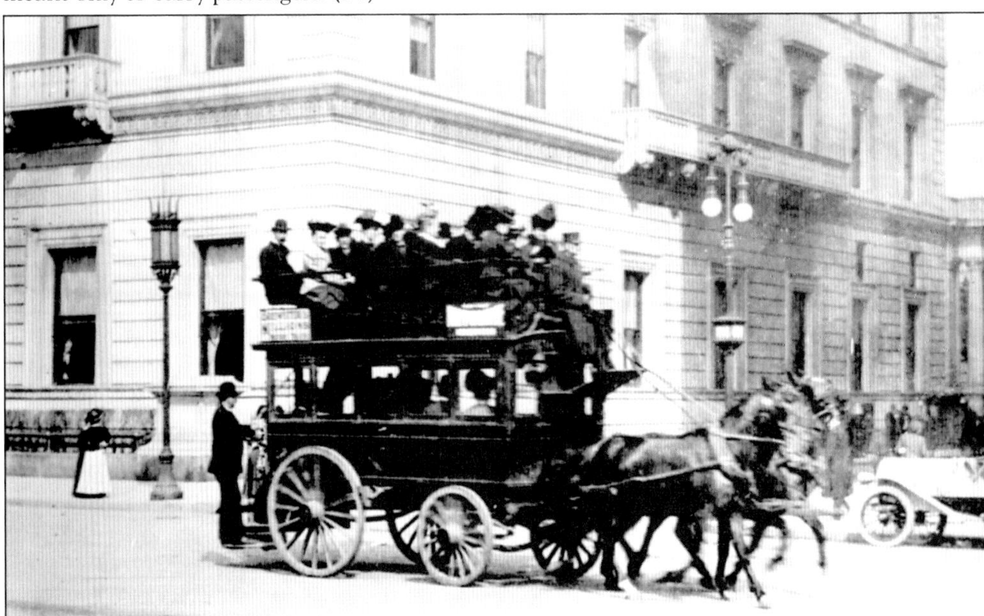

In 1904, before the advent of motor buses and where electric streetcars were not available, people in New York City still commuted in horse-drawn stages, as shown here on Fifth Avenue. Compared to the lightweight carriage at the top, the wheels and axle hubs and the body are much stronger to account for the weight of many passengers, the result of generations of experience with building such vehicles. (N.)

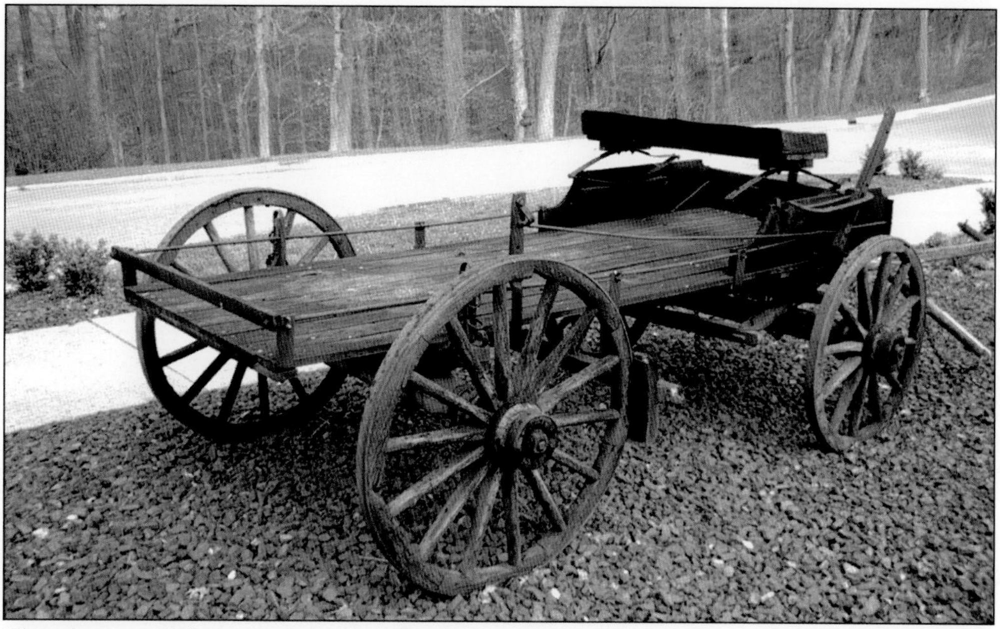

This shows a 19th-century version of today's pickup truck, built for carrying loads of goods or farm produce, hence the heavier axles, hubs, wheels, and spokes compared to the carriage opposite. Over the ages, wagon builders had learned the requirements for different purpose vehicles through "on the road testing." Note the leaf springs beneath the seat and the hand brake lever to actuate a friction pad against the rear wheels. (D.)

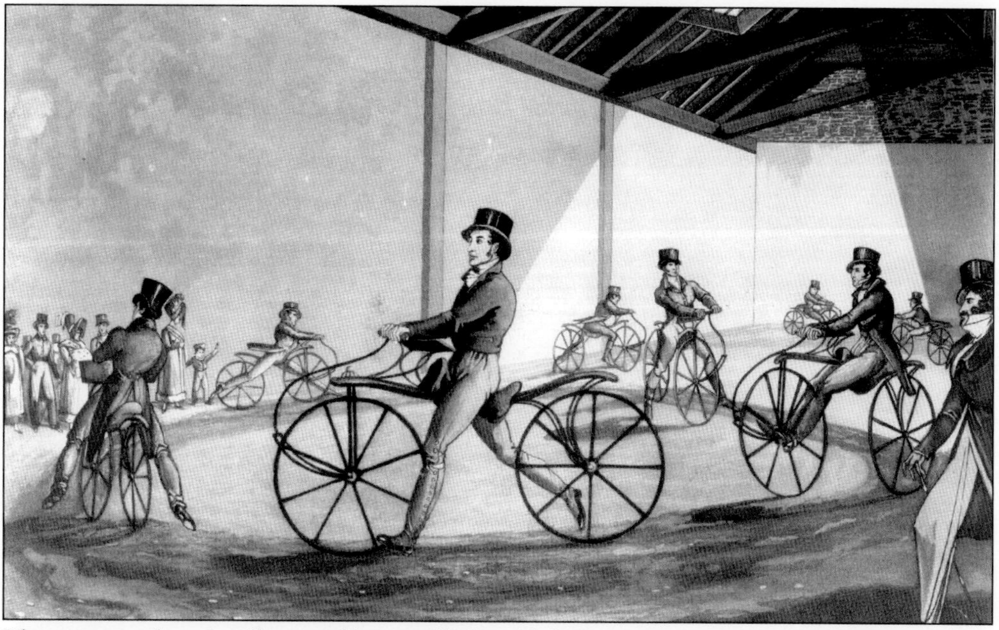

The primitive bicycles illustrated here, called pushbikes, were invented around 1820 in Europe. As can be seen, they were propelled by the feet but could be steered and coasted upon by resting feet on the front axle extensions. Over several decades, experience and refinement—road testing in effect—led to pedal power and the development of a host of technologies useful for motorcars at the end of the 19th century. (N.)

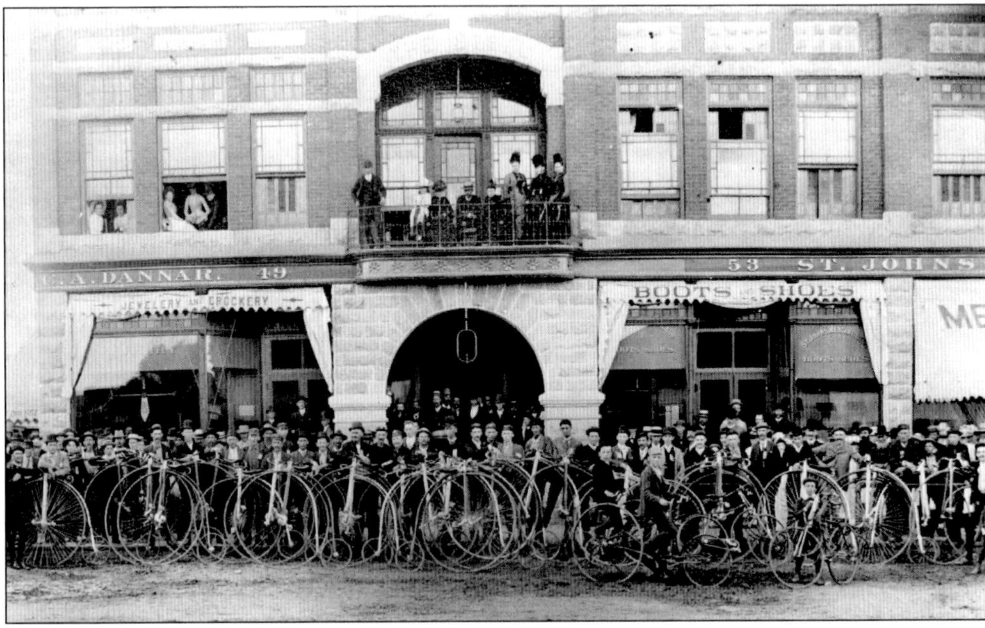

Around 1860 in France, high wheeled crank-driven bicycles evolved, as shown here at a late-19th-century "meet" in the United States. They had many practical drawbacks but presented humans with an alternative besides walking to animal-based transportation. The problems with these highwheelers inevitably led to further developments in only a few decades, as shown below. (N.)

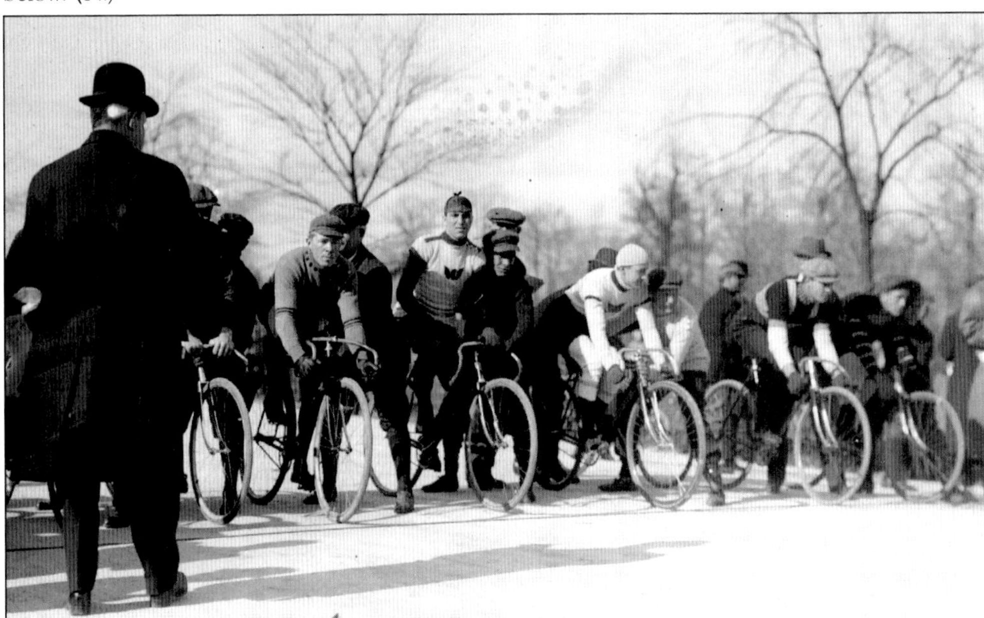

By the 1890s, bicycles had reached a high stage of development, with many improvements adaptable by motorcar inventors, such as ball bearings, pneumatic tires, chain-driven sprockets, and spoke-tensioned wheels. Sporting bicyclists on the new safety bikes shown here were part of a powerful public movement demanding smoother road surfaces, literally paving the way for automobiles. (N.)

Two

EARLY AUTOMOBILE TESTING

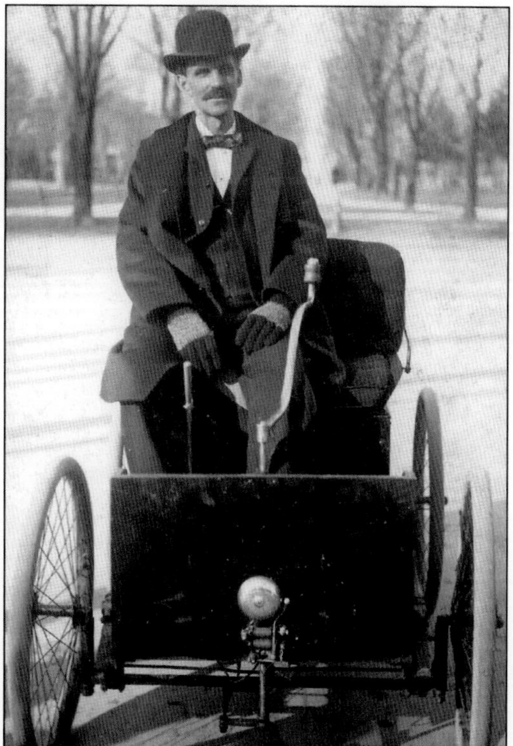

Henry Ford's first motorcar, this 1896 Quadricycle, was essentially a motorized four-wheeled bicycle, using bicycle wheels and tires and steered by a tiller adapted from small boats. The suspension came from buggies and body from a carriage maker. Still, he tested his vehicle by driving it on Detroit streets. The pattern of testing motor vehicles on public roads lasted for nearly 30 years until private test tracks were developed. (D.)

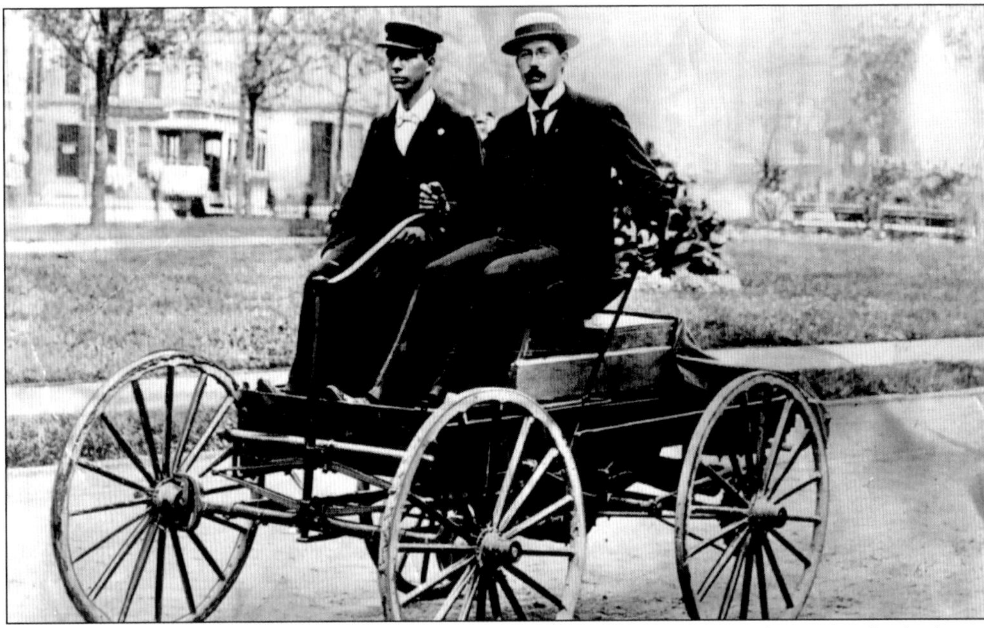

In contrast to Henry Ford's first automobile, the earliest gasoline-powered motor vehicle driven on Detroit streets was this buggylike car invented by Charles B. King (right), shown on its maiden voyage in Detroit on March 6, 1896, three months before Ford's. Note its resemblance, including the platform body and wooden wheels, to the horse-drawn wagon pictured at the top of page 11. (N.)

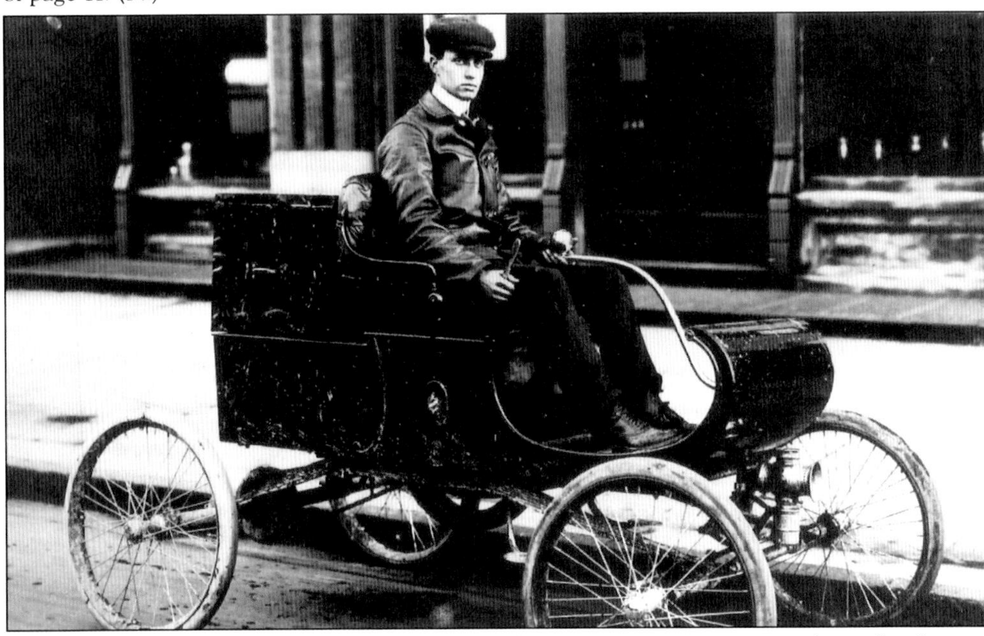

In 1901, Roy Chapin—a future founder of the Hudson Motor Car Company—drove this "curved dash" Oldsmobile with its bicycle-like wheels from Detroit to the New York Auto Show. The trip took seven and a half days but the road test demonstration of its reliability over primitive highways brought 750 orders to the pioneering automobile company. Manufacture of this first Oldsmobile model had begun two years earlier in Detroit. (D.)

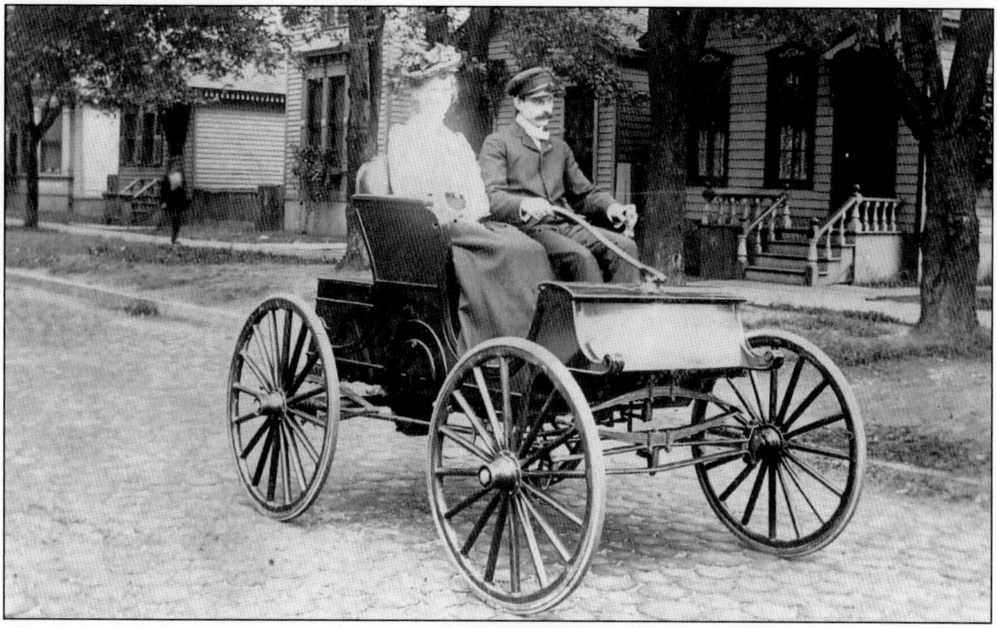

This first experimental Buick was built in Detroit between 1898 and 1901 with wooden wagon wheels. David Buick, a plumbing manufacturer, also built boat engines before venturing into motorcars. Walter Marr, Buick's chief engineer, is photographed here in 1901 with his wife in the pioneer automobile. Early vehicle manufacturers were leaning toward wagon rather than bicycle wheels because experience showed they supported the greater weight of the motors. (D.)

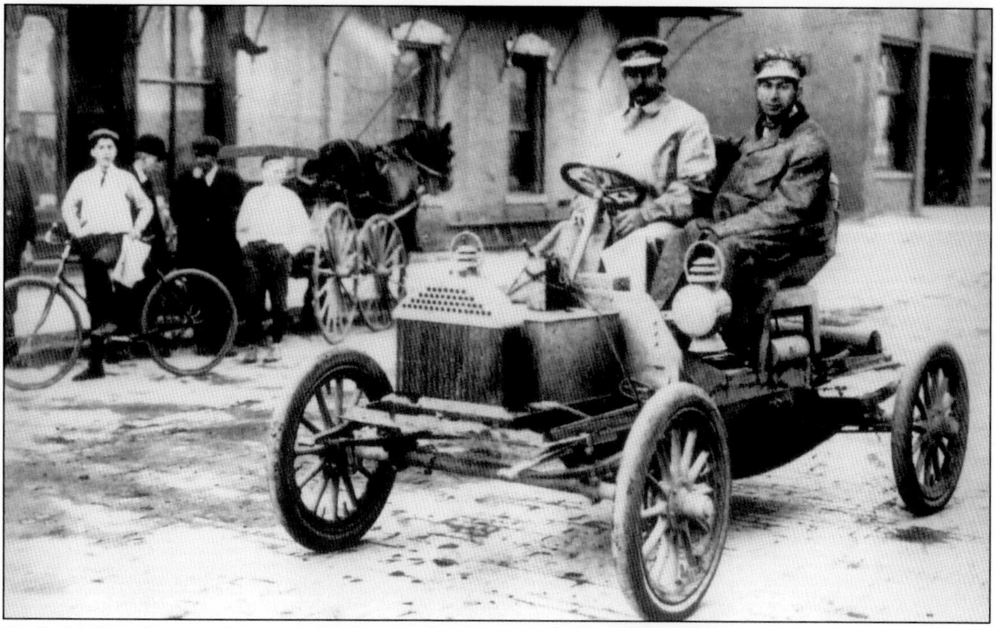

By 1904, Buick manufacturing had moved to Flint and the design of the car had been completely changed, as seen in this prototype when it completed a 110 mile round-trip demonstration test between Flint and Detroit. Note the front engine (rather than under the seat, as in earlier cars shown above and on previous pages), a steering wheel in place of the tiller, and stronger wooden wheels of smaller diameter than the buggy in the background. (D.)

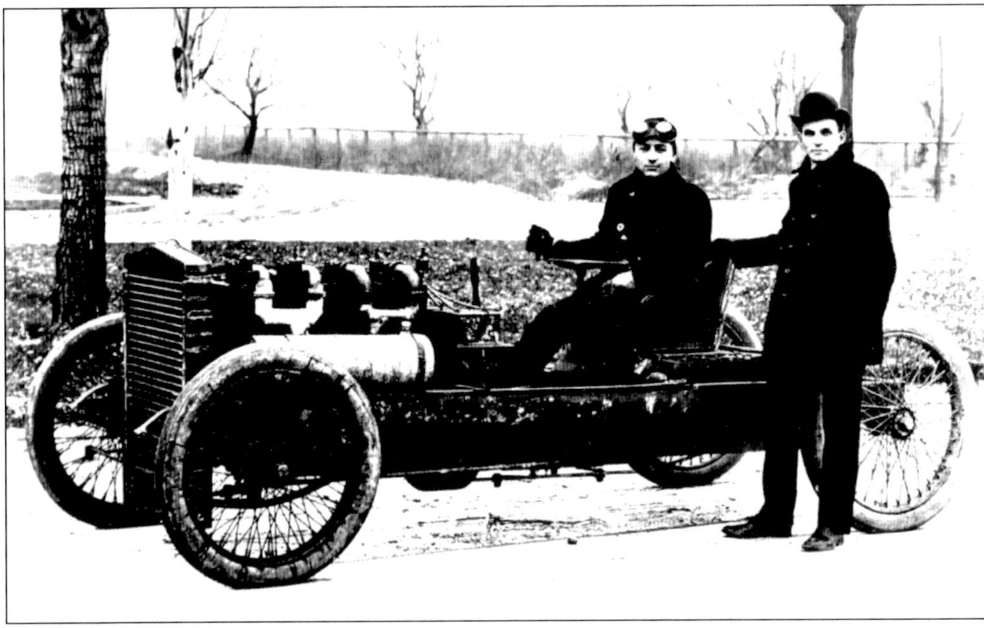

In addition to testing newfangled motorcar inventions with cross-country demonstrations over primitive roads around the beginning of the 20th century, automotive pioneers turned to racing and speed events to attract investors and wring out their designs. This is Henry Ford's famous 999 in which he achieved a speed record of nearly 92 miles per hour over the ice in 1904. Ford is standing at right. (N.)

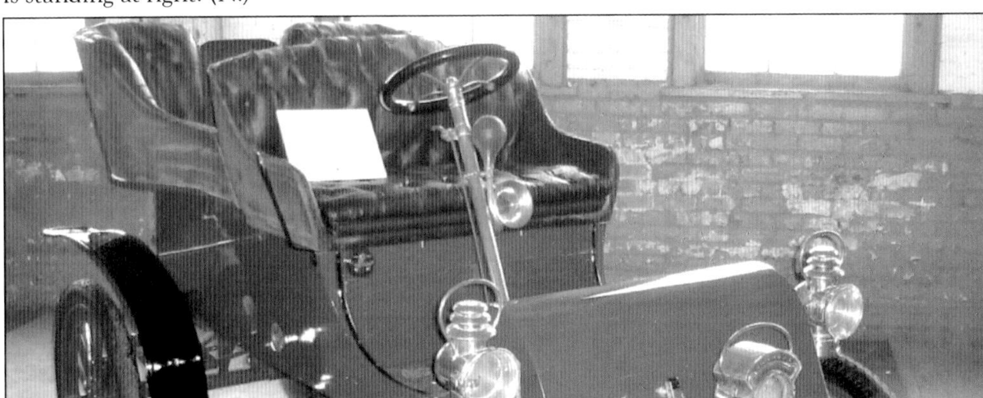

After a couple of false starts, one of which became Cadillac, Ford incorporated Ford Motor Company in 1903 with this Model A as its first production vehicle. Note that he switched from bicycle wheels to buggylike wheels of smaller diameter, which was similar to Buick and doubtless due to elemental testing and feedback from street use. The Model A also has a steering wheel, lights, a horn, fenders, and leaf springs. (D.)

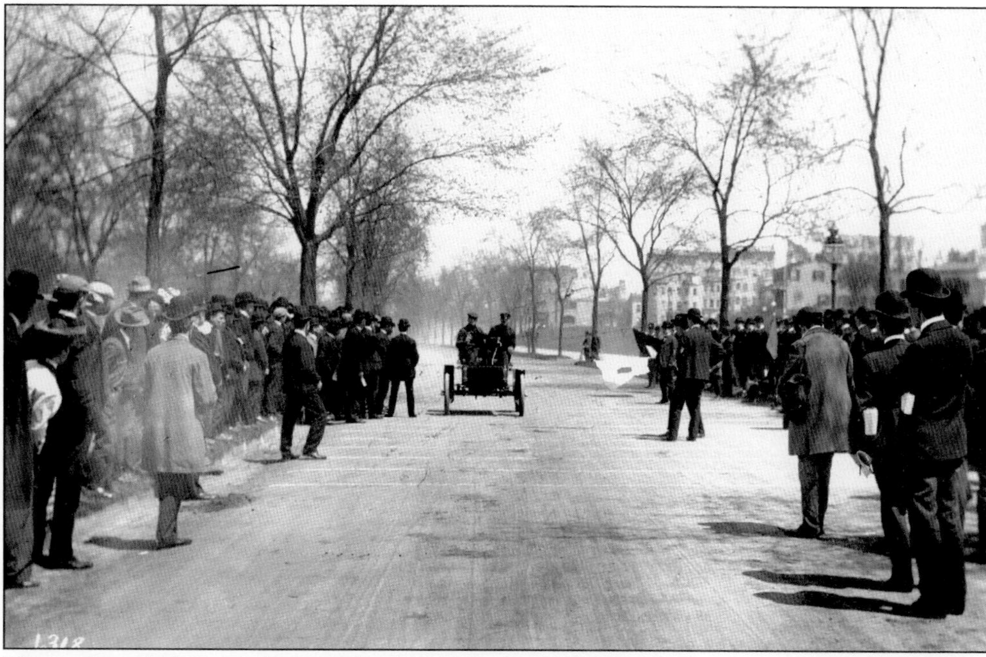

This is the only known photograph of early automobiles identified as "testing." Handwritten on the reverse of the original in the National Automotive History Collection are only the words, "brake testing on Riverside Drive," without a date, city, or make of car identified. It likely was taken before 1905. Clearly it was a public event as opposed to a private test. (N.)

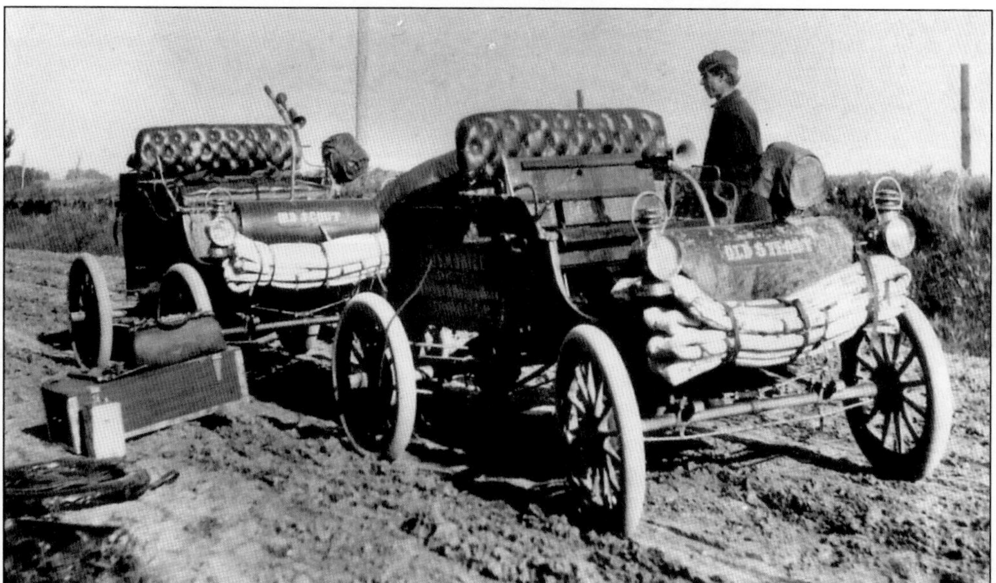

Competition between pioneering American automakers increased in the first decade of the 20th century, leading to evermore-adventurous test demonstrations of a design's reliability and dependability. Here is a pair of Oldsmobiles in 1905 on a staged "first transcontinental race" from New York City to Portland, Oregon, which took 44 days. Note that wagon wheels have replaced bicycle wheels, but the car is still steered by a tiller. (D.)

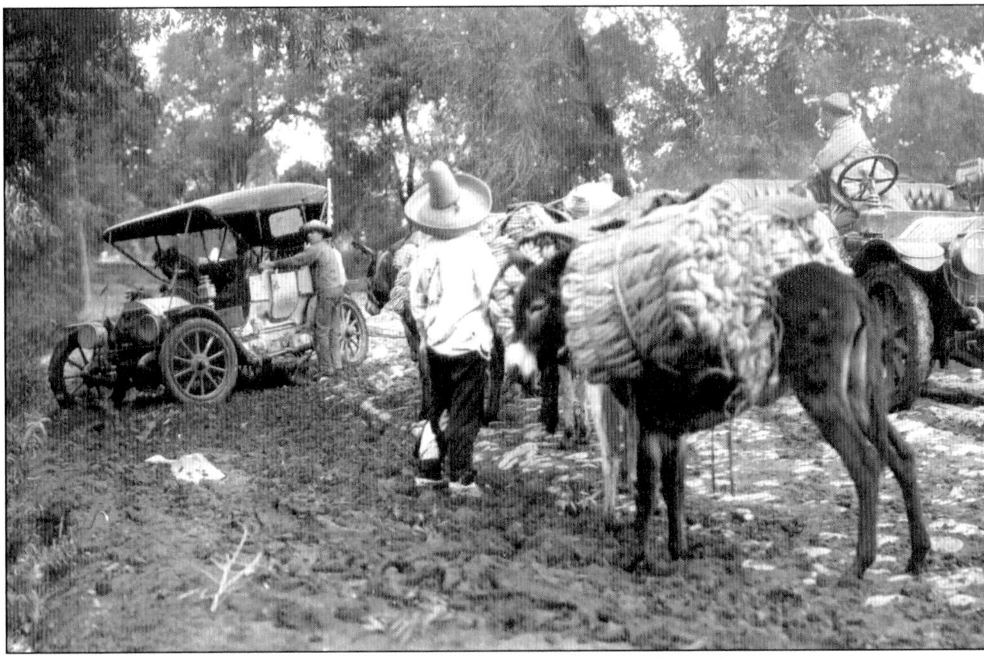

By 1909, automobile manufacturers were tackling international test demonstrations to promote their cars. Here a Chalmers-Detroit (one of several predecessors of Chrysler) has gone off a Mexican road in a run from Denver, Colorado, to Mexico City. While such tests could, and did, stumble with product breakdowns, the public recognized them as unimportant in the growing freedom the motorcar offered. (N.)

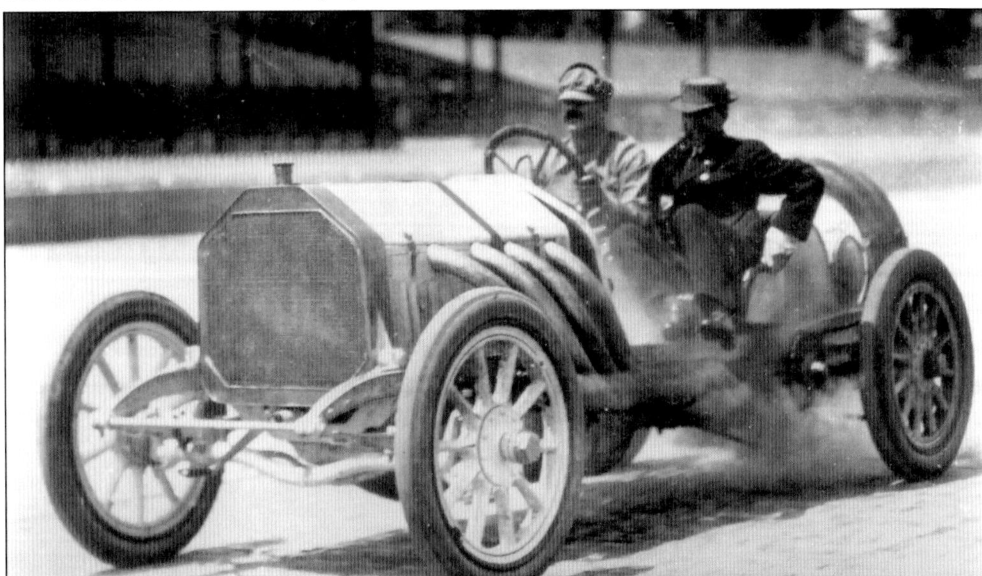

Competitive automobile racing with both amateur and professional drivers became a popular sport in place of individual speed trials by automakers. Here a 1910 Buick Model 10, driven by Louis Chevrolet, participates in a race at an unidentified track, probably a fairground because such arenas already had ovals for horse racing. The demands of such racing provided road laboratories for a number of automotive improvements, including windshields, for example. (D.)

Three

Laboratory Testing

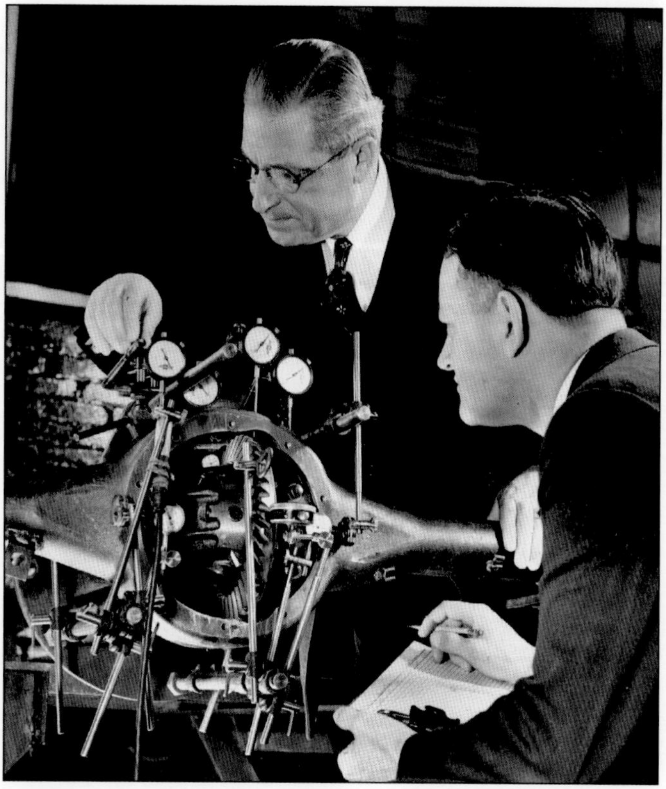

From this unique laboratory test on a rear axle, set up in Detroit's Chevrolet Gear and Axle Plant in 1938, engineers determined optimum mounting of bearings to prolong axle life. Henry Ford's kitchen in his rented row house on Detroit's Bagley Avenue served as his laboratory while he was developing his first gasoline engine in the 1890s. The controlled conditions and test rigs in laboratories supplemented road testing from the automobile industry's beginnings. (N.)

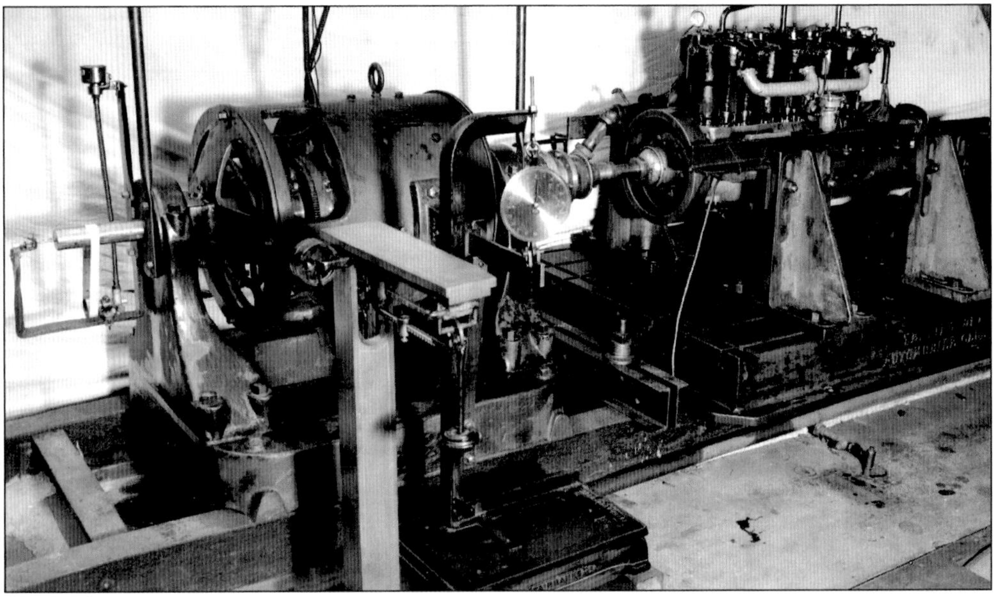

Shown here in an early automotive laboratory is this 1911 view of a six-cylinder engine dynamometer test, place and make unknown. In such a test, common in the industry even in the 21st century, an engine bolted to a test stand is connected to an external power source such as an electric-powered generator to simulate the road load of the transmission, axle, and road conditions, including hills. Instruments measure engine performance as it goes through various load scenarios. (N.)

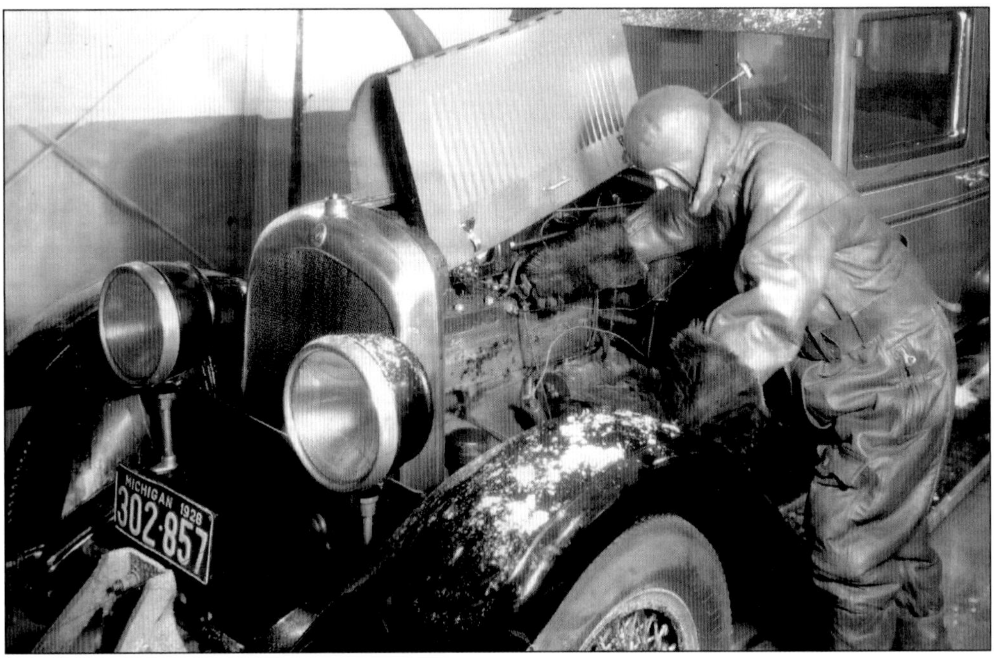

Another step in laboratory testing was to bring extreme climate conditions inside the engineering garages, such as this cold weather test of a Chrysler in 1928. The technician had to wear heavy winter clothes to continue adjustments under the hood while he worked. Note the frost on the fender, headlamp, and sun visor. (N.)

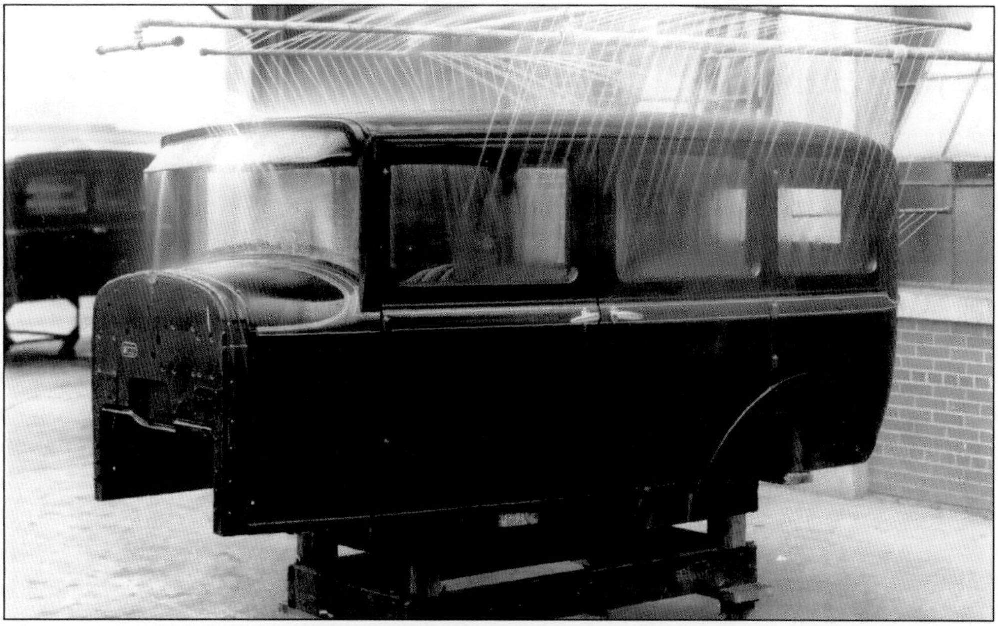

The caption pasted on the back of this 1929 photograph reads as follows: "This device which throws water with the effect of a driving rain storm is used to test the 'waterproofness' of De Soto bodies. Many streams of water under high pressure are driven at various angles over the entire body and particularly around the windshield, doors, side windows and rear windows. The body must be waterproof before it can pass final inspection." (N.)

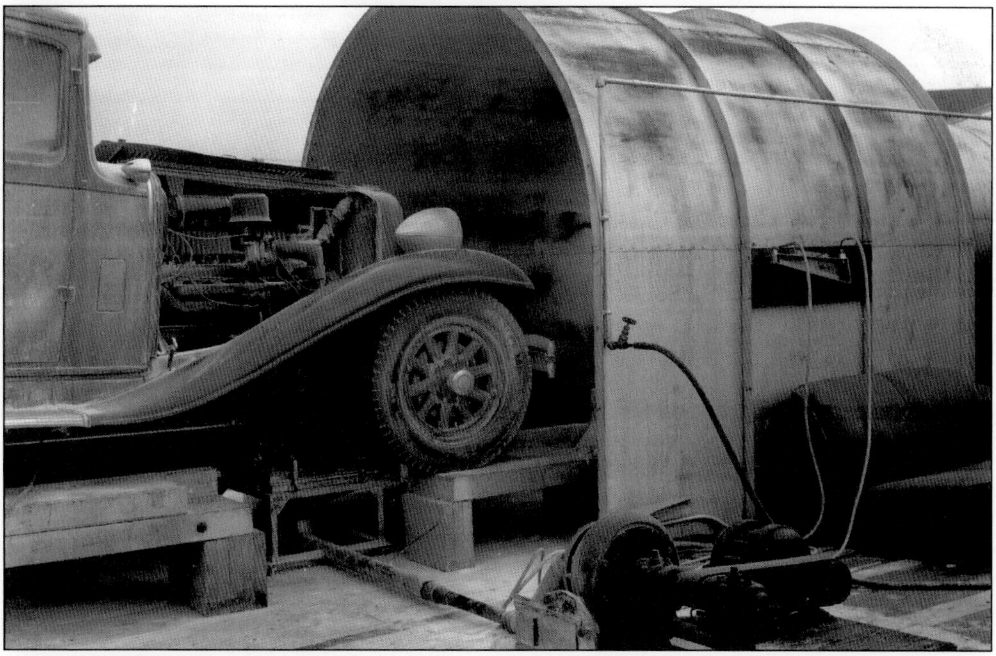

In the laboratory test shown here, dust and sand were blown by an aircraft motor against the front of a 1931 Chrysler to simulate certain conditions of the undeveloped roadways of the time. Thus engineers could evaluate the adequacy of air cleaners and gasoline and oil filters to test modifications before they were put into production. (N.)

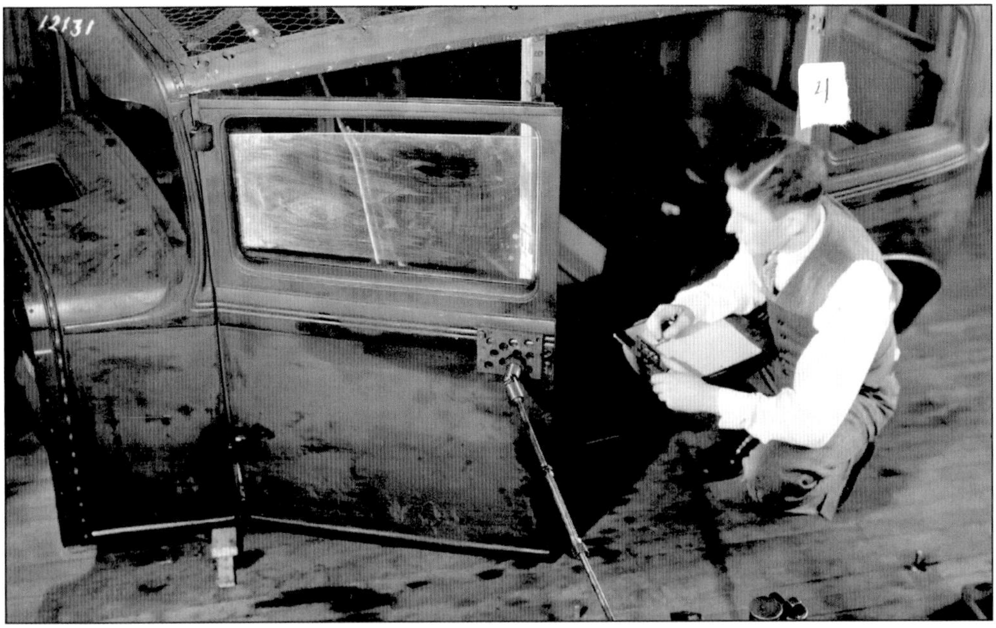

At Studebaker laboratories in 1930, the test rig shown here opened and closed the door 100,000 times to assess the reliability and durability of door latches, locks, window glass, handles, and hinges. According to the information accompanying the photograph, Studebaker periodically pulled cars off the production line to test them in this fashion and insure customer satisfaction. (N.)

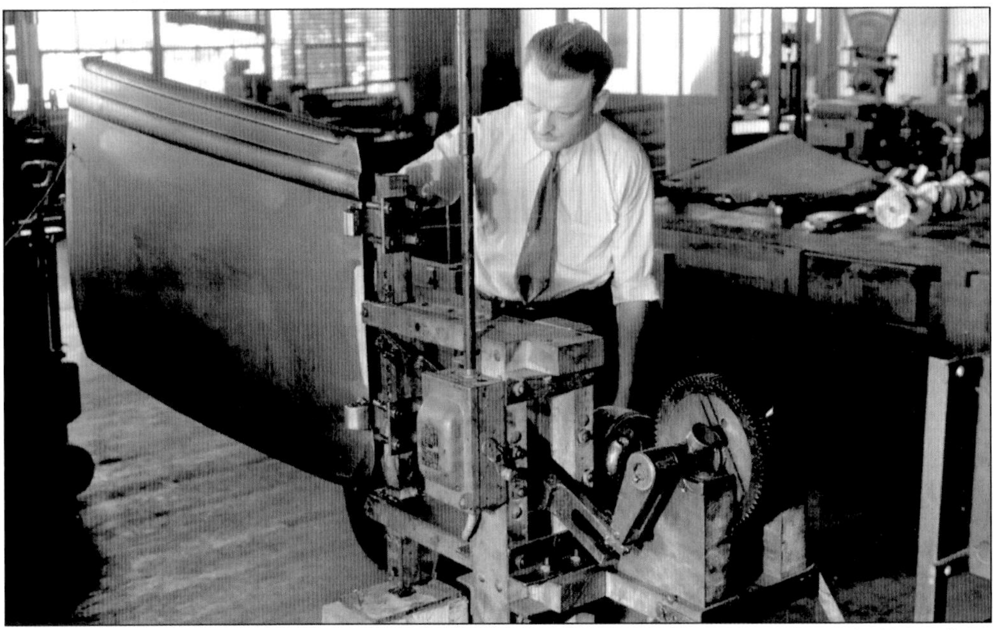

Another laboratory test at Studebaker, this one in 1932, swung the door more than half a million times to ensure hinge durability and freedom from sag, especially important when bodies and door frames were largely made of wood. Studebaker engineers believed the test was more severe than customers would encounter over the life of the car, but fundamentally this was still all in the realm of guesswork. (N.)

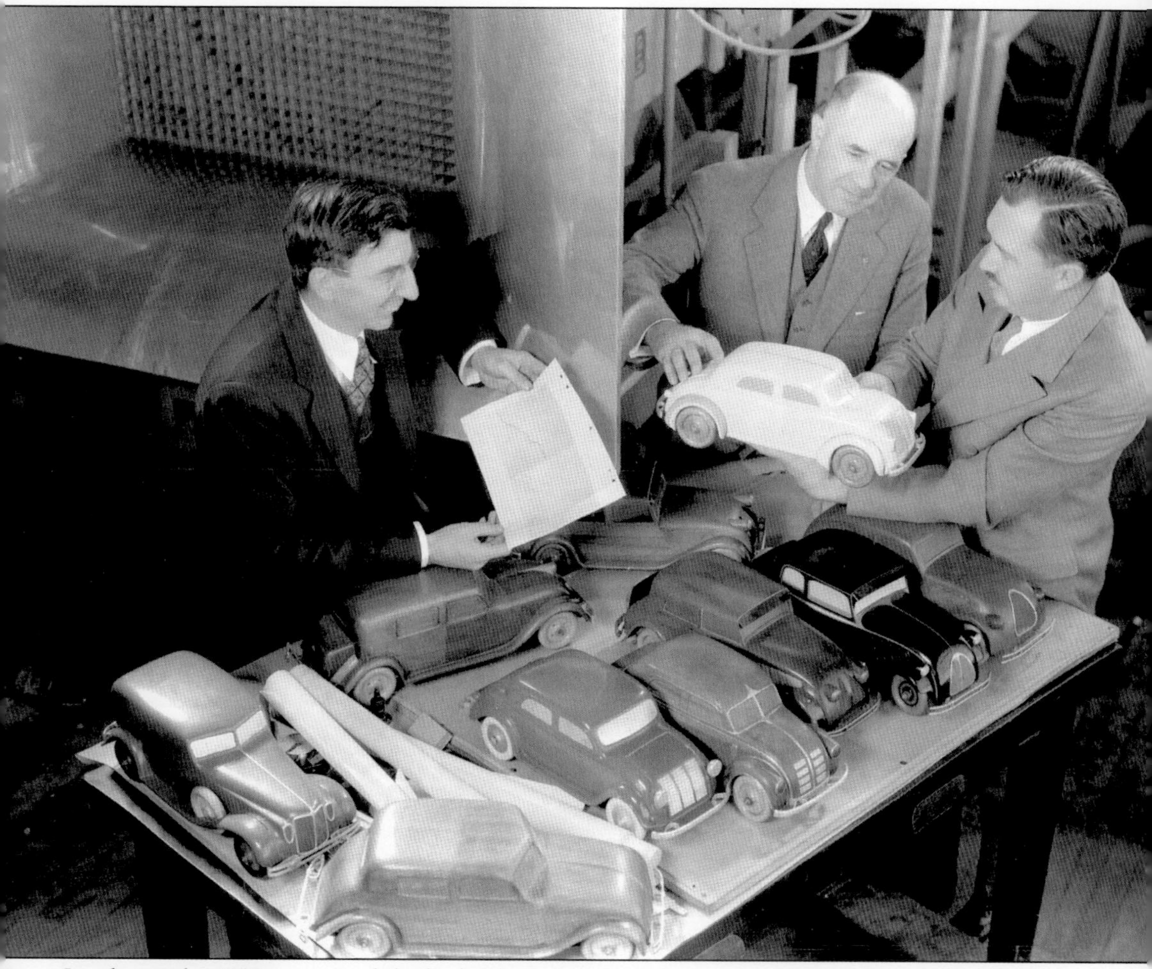

In the early 1930s, automobile body designs ceased to copy the boxy carriages of the horse-and-buggy age and gradually became more streamlined. To enable the most revolutionary of the new bodies, Chrysler engineers turned to miniature wind tunnels in their laboratories where they could test airflow over the new configurations. This photograph, showing scale models of proposed designs for 1934 De Sotos Airflows was issued in 1933 as a "teaser" for the forthcoming cars about which there had been much speculation in the press of the day. The De Soto and Chrysler Airflow models apparently were too advanced for their day and the cars were not sales successes. Conventional-bodied Airstream models were subsequently introduced and the Airflow phased out after 1937. Today Airflow models are much prized by classic car collectors for their distinctive, streamlined art deco design. (N.)

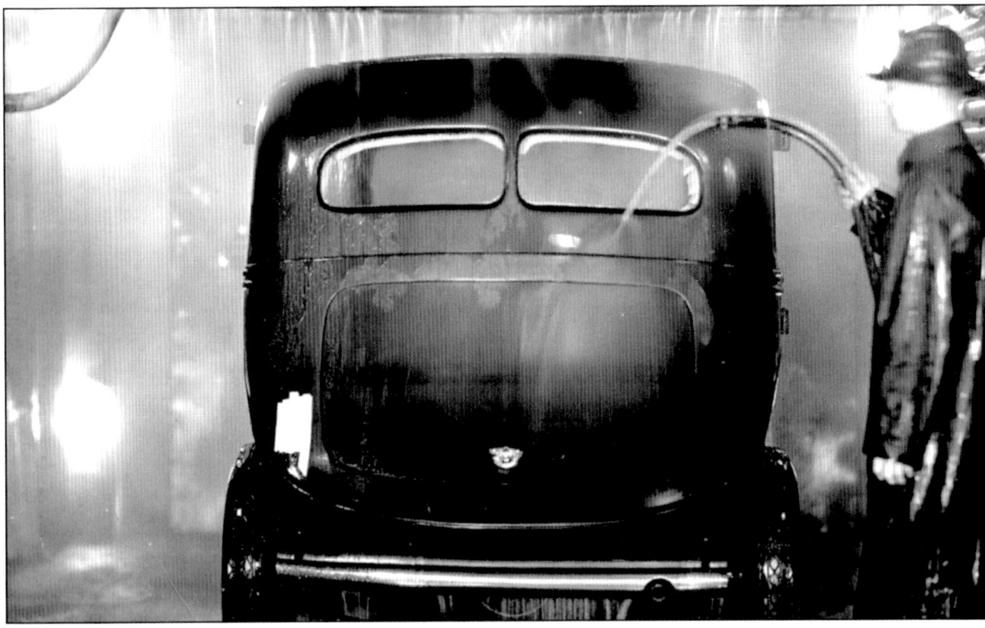

Here a Hudson body is soaked with water both from a hose handled by the man at the right and from overhead sprinklers. After 1926, the proportion of fully enclosed new cars produced in the United States steadily displaced open cars that were similar to most buggies of early ages. Closed cars, unlike open cars or convertibles, required absolute integrity from weather incursions, hence the tests of the De Soto in 1929 and this Hudson in 1935. (N.)

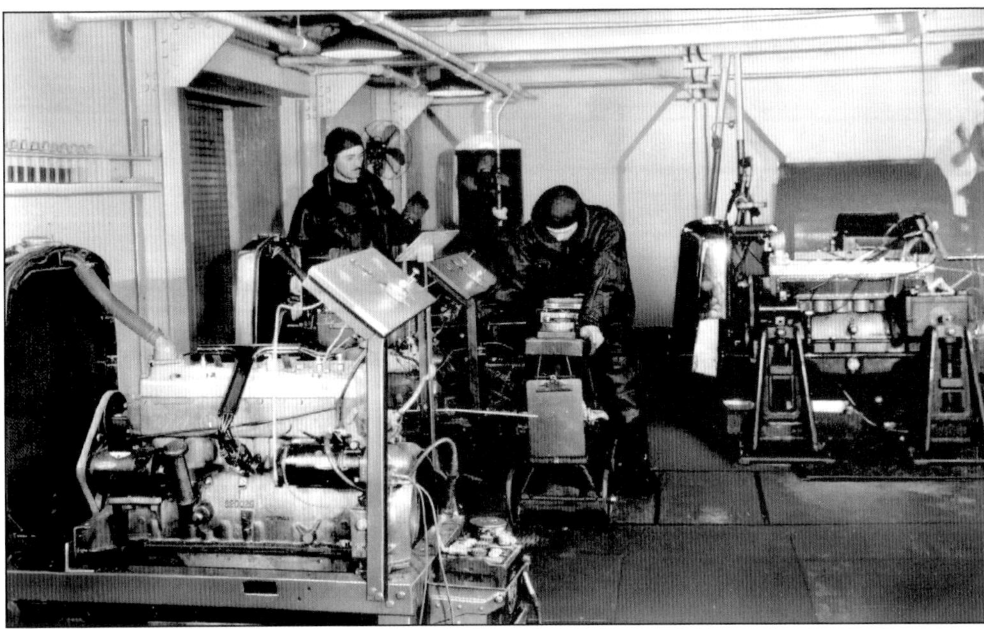

To provide occupant comfort as well as reliability, cold-weather testing became a requirement for new model development, including effectiveness of new, optional heaters and windshield defrosters. Laboratory cold rooms, as well as trips to winter testing stations in northern Michigan, Minnesota, and Canada, handled the task as shown in this view of subzero testing of Plymouth engines at Chrysler's Highland Park engineering laboratories. (N.)

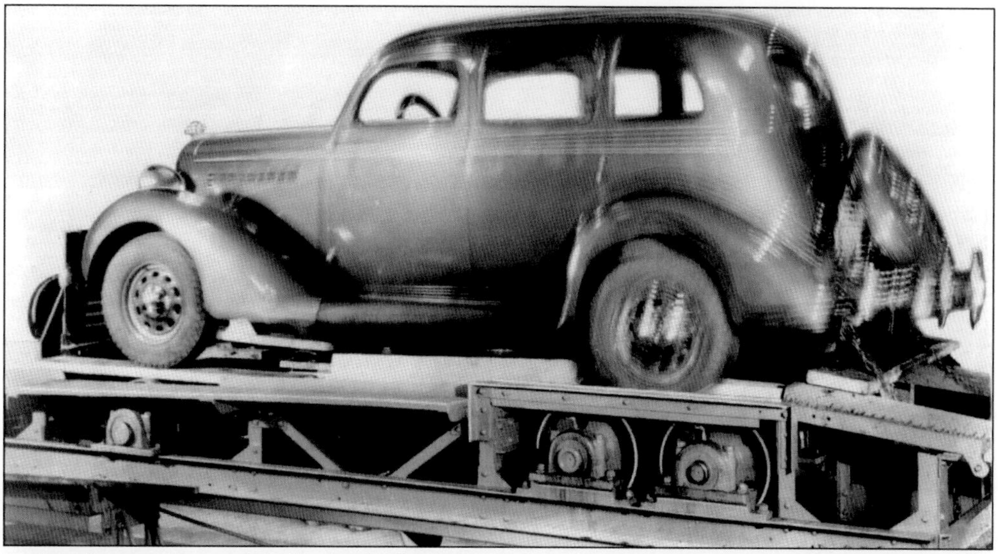

In this photograph, a 1935 Plymouth "drives" over four rollers studded with irregular cleats under its rear wheels, simulating the bouncy surface of a Belgian Block roadway. This test rig convinced Chrysler engineers that 24 hours of the test equaled thousands of miles of rough road driving. Later such laboratory tests became more sophisticated but essentially are still in use today. (N.)

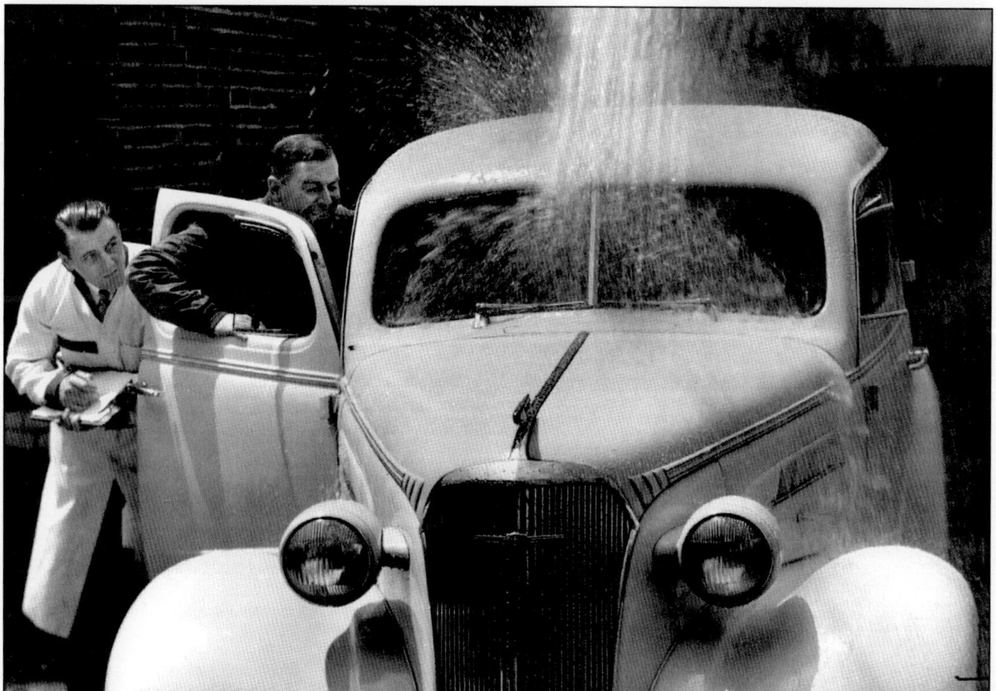

After introducing a two piece, slanted windshield for its 1935 Master Deluxe models, Chevrolet found that a better mounting system was required to keep water out and prevent glass cracking. Here preparing for 1937 model introduction, the new mountings were tested by blasting them with an overhead fire hose—meant to simulate the direction and force of a rain burst—while engineers observed. (N.)

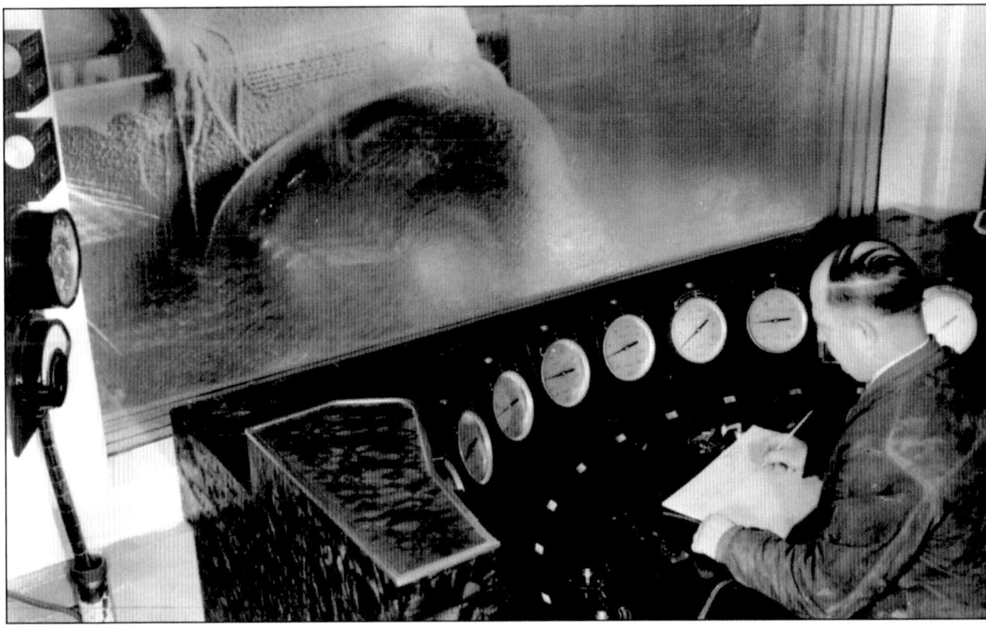

After transforming the Ford Airfield southwest of Detroit to its Dearborn Proving Ground in 1937, Ford Motor Company converted its former Tri-Motor airframe buildings and hangers into engineering garages and laboratories. Here a 1938 Ford V-8, covered with ice, undergoes a test in Ford's new weather tunnel lab while an operator outside at a control table monitors the procedure. (N.)

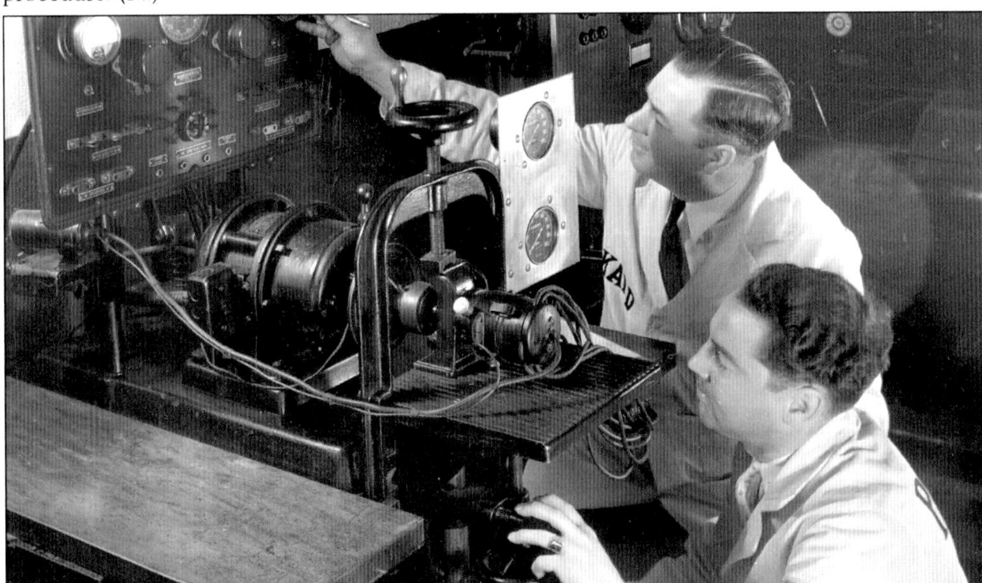

Packard Motor Company established its proving ground near Utica in 1927, equipping its engineering garages there with a variety of test laboratories. This shows two skilled technicians testing an electrical distributor for a six-cylinder Packard engine in the experimental garage. According to the caption on the photograph, the technician at the rear, Larry Gitschlag, was so valued that he was allowed to continue his experiments in a garage the company built at his Detroit home. (N.)

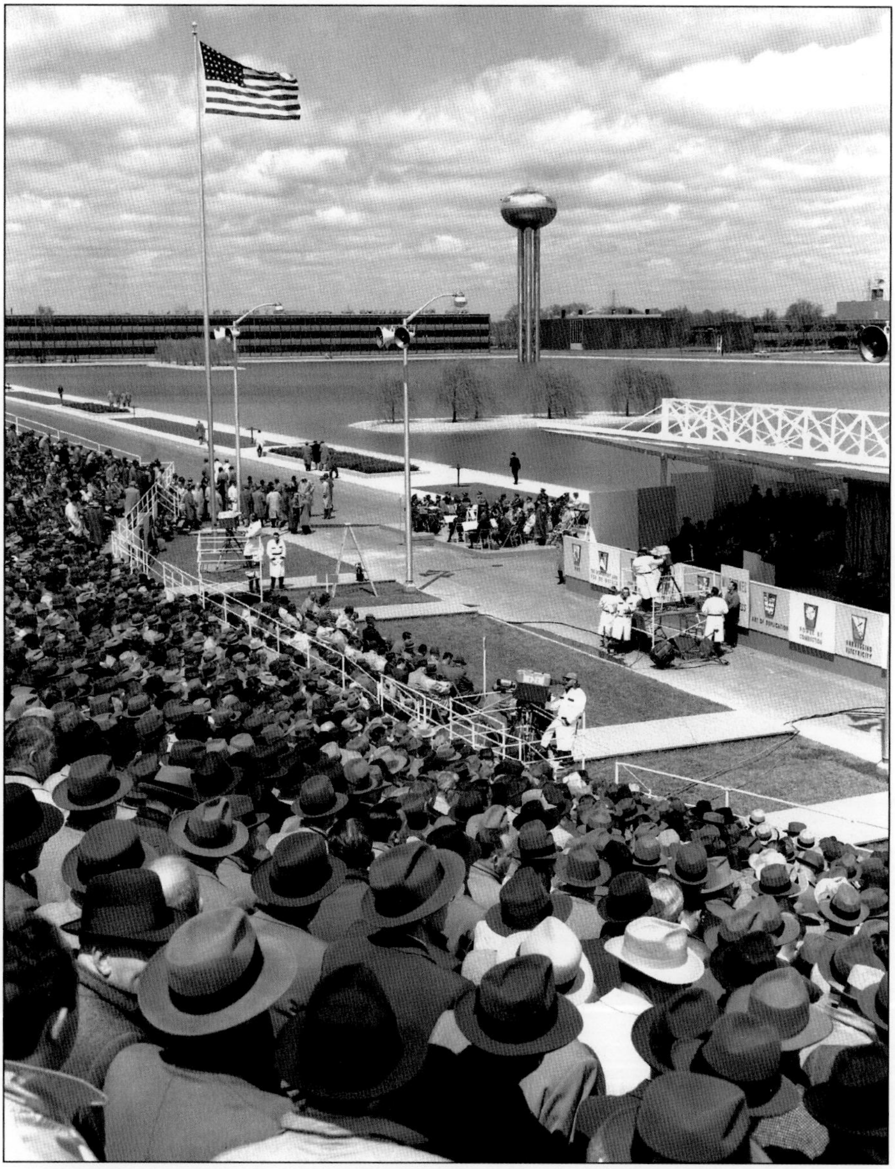

On May 16, 1956, General Motors (GM) formally opened its $100 million technical center in Warren, shown here. The technical center included the company's renowned styling studios, as well as numerous engineering offices and research laboratories. Product engineering laboratories and the extensive test tracks continued to be largely located at the Milford Proving Ground opened in 1924, located more than 30 miles west of Warren. Fundamentally, technical center labs were staff operated and indoors, whereas Milford supported the car divisions, such as Cadillac, Chevrolet, and Buick, and related more to ongoing road testing at the proving ground. Altogether, at its formal dedication, the technical center covered 330 acres with 11 miles of roads and more than a mile of tunnels between the center's 25 main buildings. At one time, the general offices of the Chevrolet division moved to the technical center from its historic location on Milwaukee Avenue behind the GM building on West Grand Boulevard in Detroit. After GM acquired the Renaissance Center complex on the Detroit waterfront, Chevrolet moved to offices there. (D.)

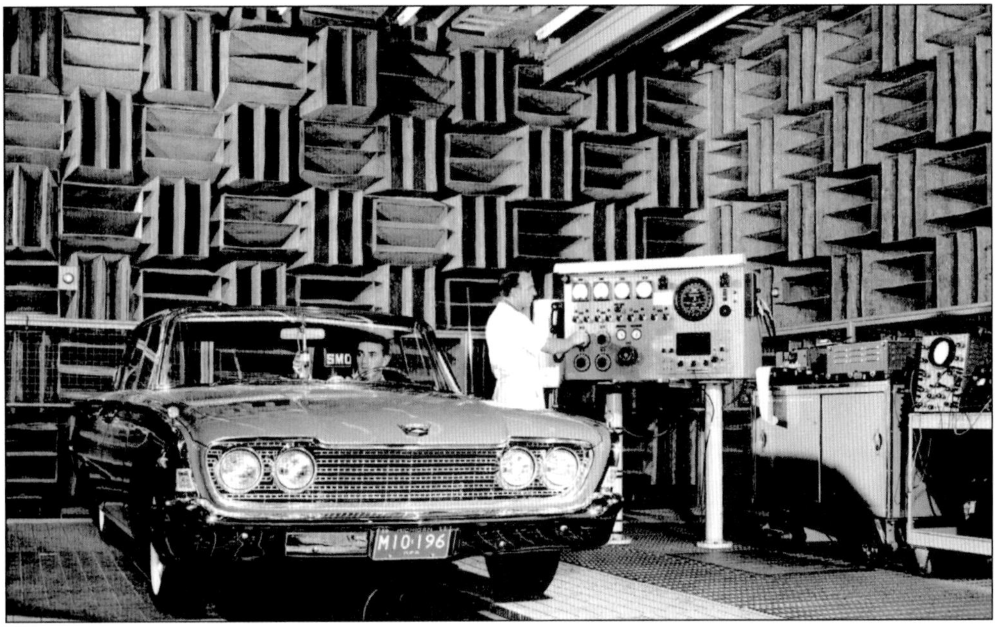

Among the many new facilities built after World War II at Ford's Dearborn Proving Ground was this soundproof anechoic chamber. In this laboratory, unwanted sounds and vibrations can be isolated with steps taken to modify them. Shown here is a 1960 Ford sedan under test. In such a controlled atmosphere, stationary sounds can be identified much more efficiently than when a car is driven over a road, even with the best instrumentation. (N.)

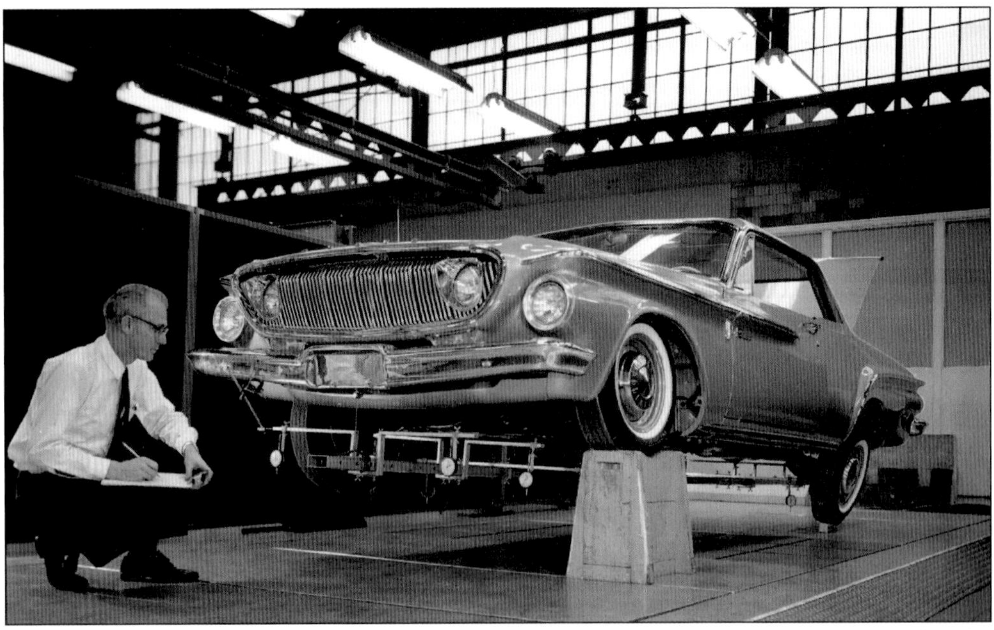

This 1962 Dodge is undergoing a twist, or static bending test, of its structure at a Chrysler engineering laboratory. The test determines the deflection of the body under various road conditions. This is one of hundreds of tests assuring structural strength and durability of cars under extreme operating conditions. On page 65 is an illustration of a GM car undergoing similar tests in 1931. (N.)

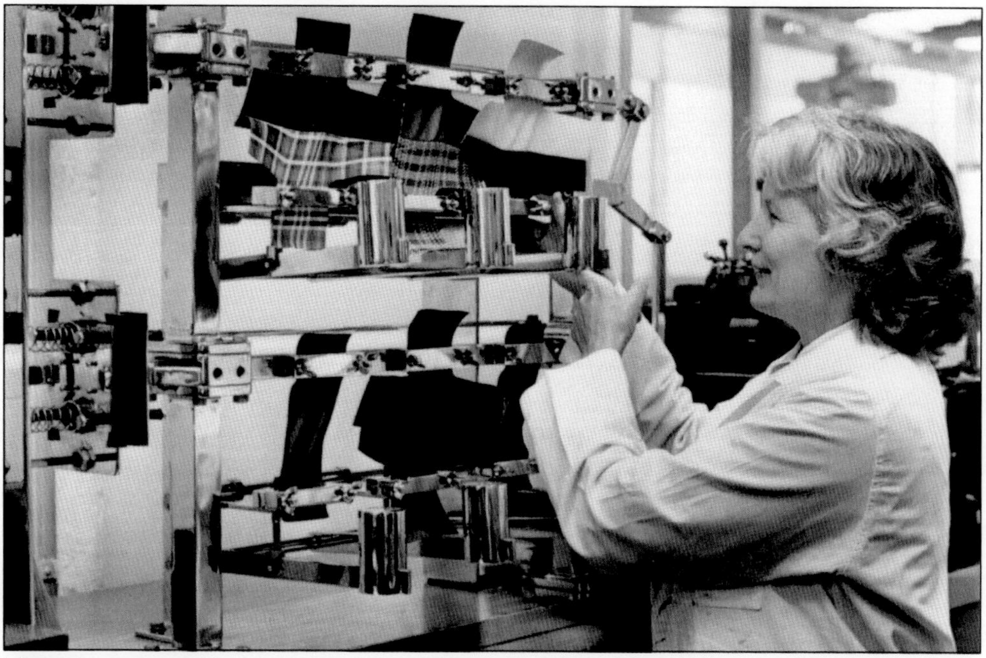

More than just steel structures get tested in automotive laboratories. In this photograph, a Chrysler technician is appraising the durability of upholstery fabrics by subjecting material samples to flexing and folding thousands of times per hour to screen them for release in new cars. (N.)

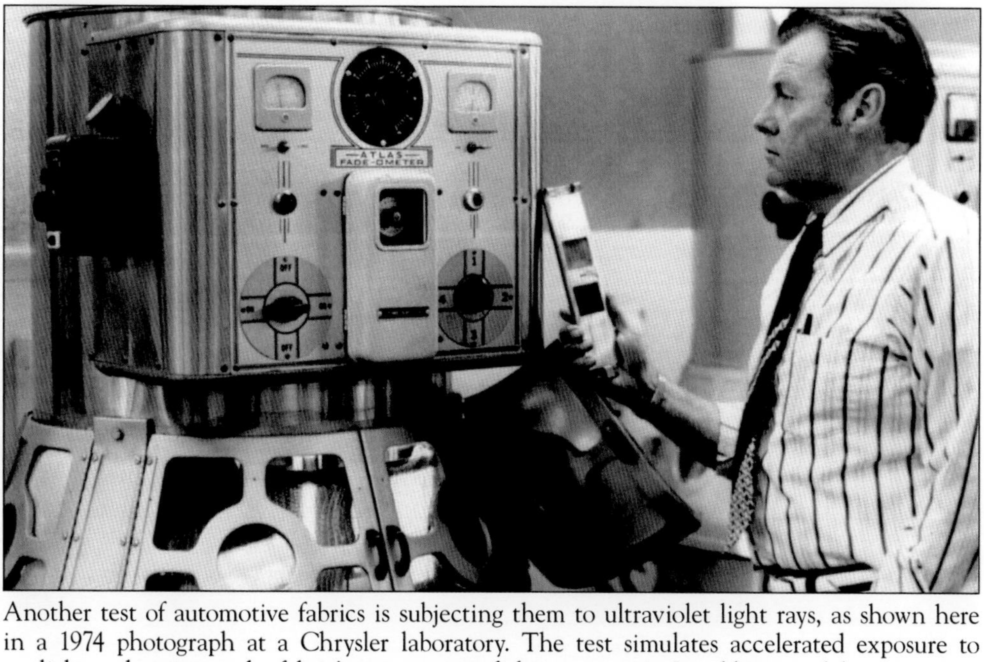

Another test of automotive fabrics is subjecting them to ultraviolet light rays, as shown here in a 1974 photograph at a Chrysler laboratory. The test simulates accelerated exposure to sunlight and measures the fabric's resistance to fading over time. In addition to laboratory tests in Detroit-area engineering facilities, automakers have maintained field stations in southern Florida and southwestern deserts to test fabrics, paints, and plastics in extreme sunlight and humid conditions. (N.)

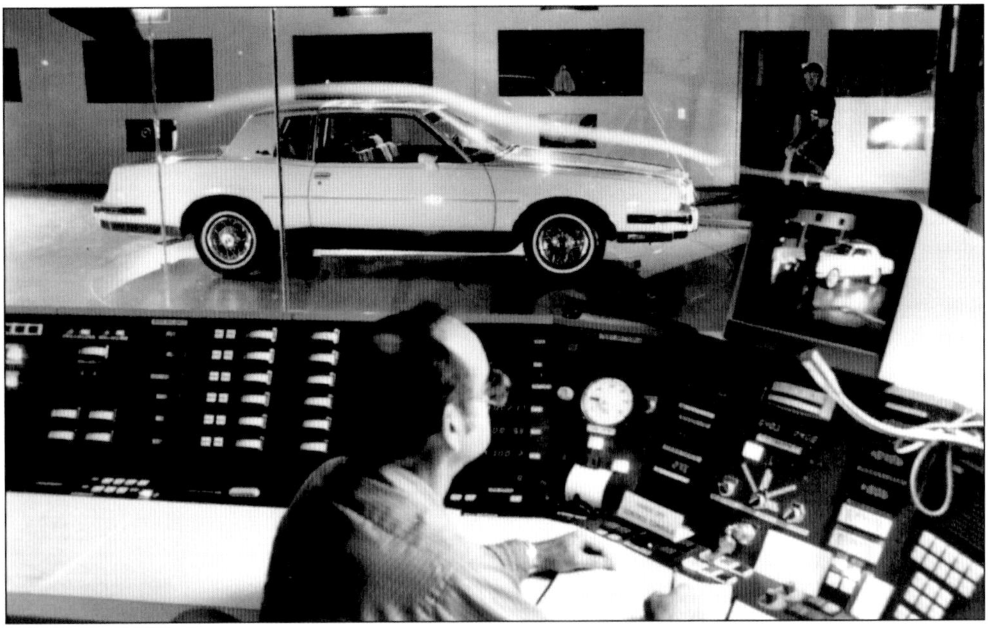

Automakers still may use small models of future cars to test aerodynamic body designs, as was the case for 1934 Chrysler and De Soto Airflow models shown on page 23. After World War II, they built full-scale wind tunnels to test prototypes or regular production cars for their streamlining qualities, as seen in this photograph of a 1981 Pontiac Grand Prix coupe at a GM wind tunnel laboratory. (N.)

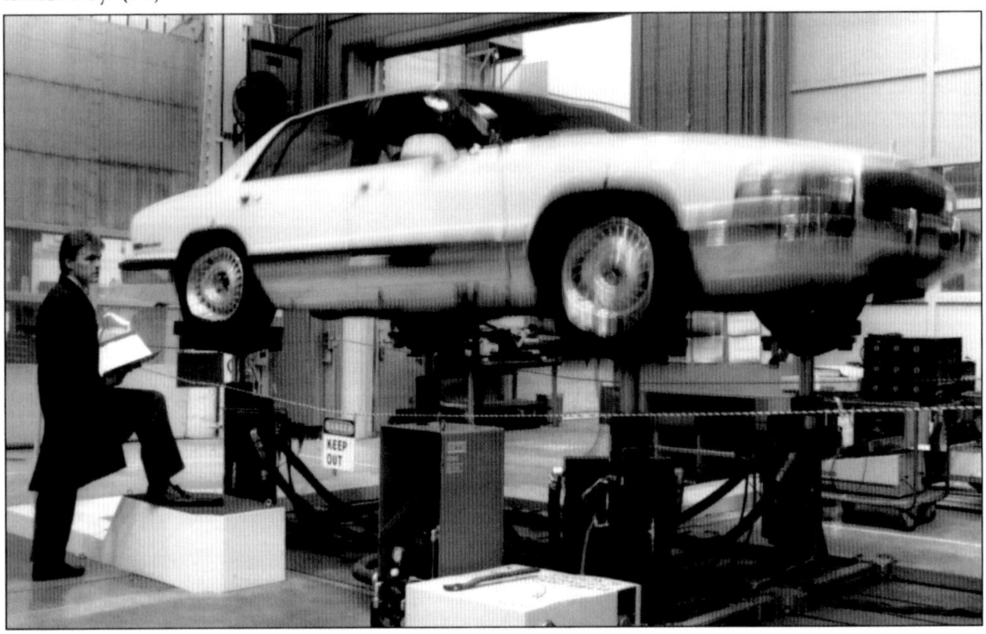

Although this test of a 1991 Buick appears similar to that of the 1935 Plymouth on page 25, GM moved the large road simulator to Detroit's Cobo Hall for the 1991 North American International Auto Show. It demonstrated the tortures a new model is subjected to during development, including computer-driven pistoning of a car's suspension system to duplicate 128 miles of rough roads in which 10 years use can be simulated in six days. (N.)

Four

First Test Track

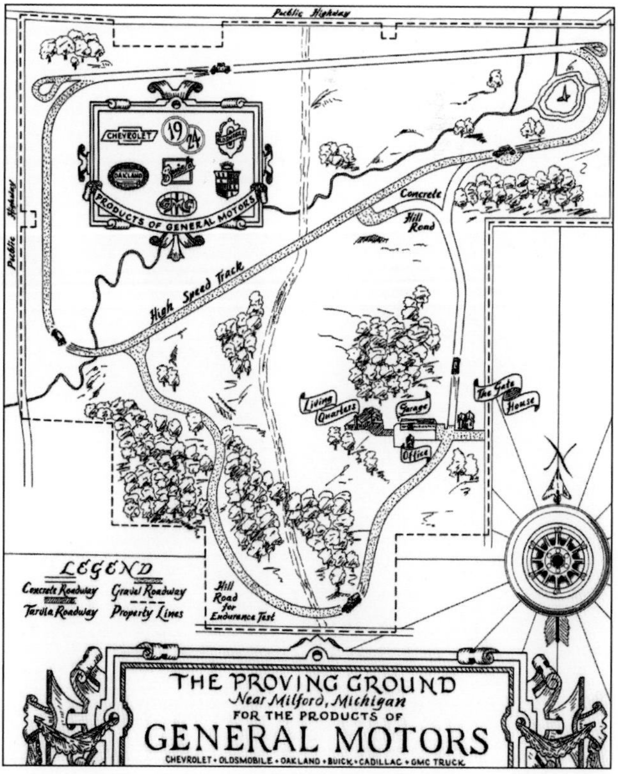

After the fiasco with the copper-cooled Chevrolet (described in the introduction), GM quickly moved in 1924 to establish the world's first automotive proving ground near Milford. This artistic rendering shows the features of the initial 1,300 acre farmland-and-woods tract, including hills and level ground, on which GM built miles of concrete, tarred gravel, gravel, brick, sand, and dirt roads. The Milford track was conveniently 40 to 50 miles from GM's engineering offices in Detroit, Flint, Lansing, and Pontiac. By the 21st century, GM had built 132 miles of roadways on what had expanded to 4,000 acres, with 107 specialized buildings and 4,800 employees. (G.)

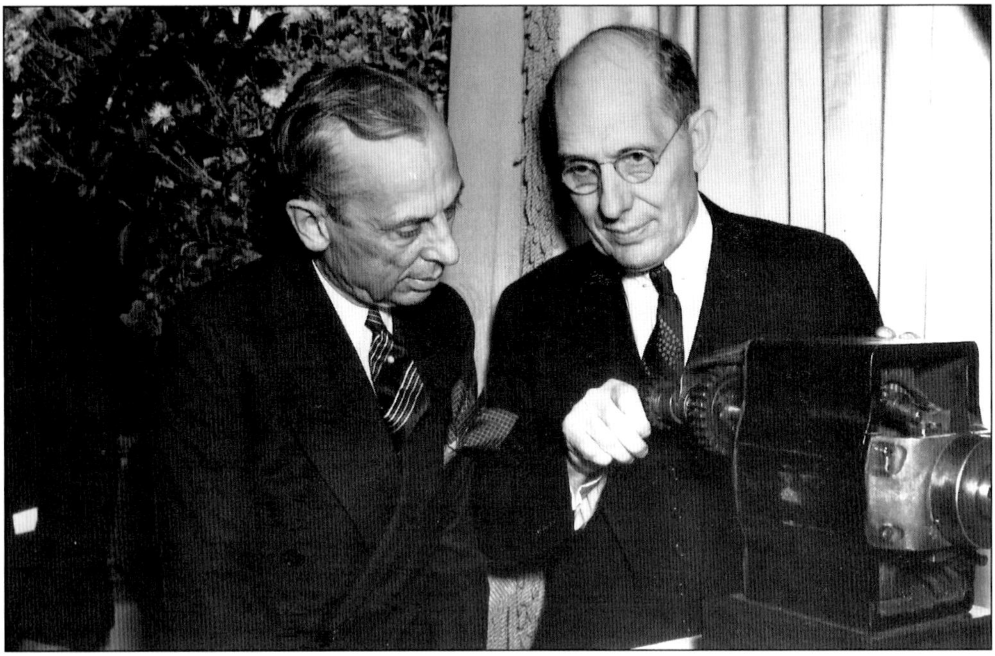

Shown here in a 1942 photograph are the two principal creators of the GM Milford Proving Ground, GM board chairman Alfred P. Sloan Jr. (left) and Charles F. Kettering, vice president in charge of research. The two foresighted executives established a test-track system eventually emulated by most of the world's automakers. (D.)

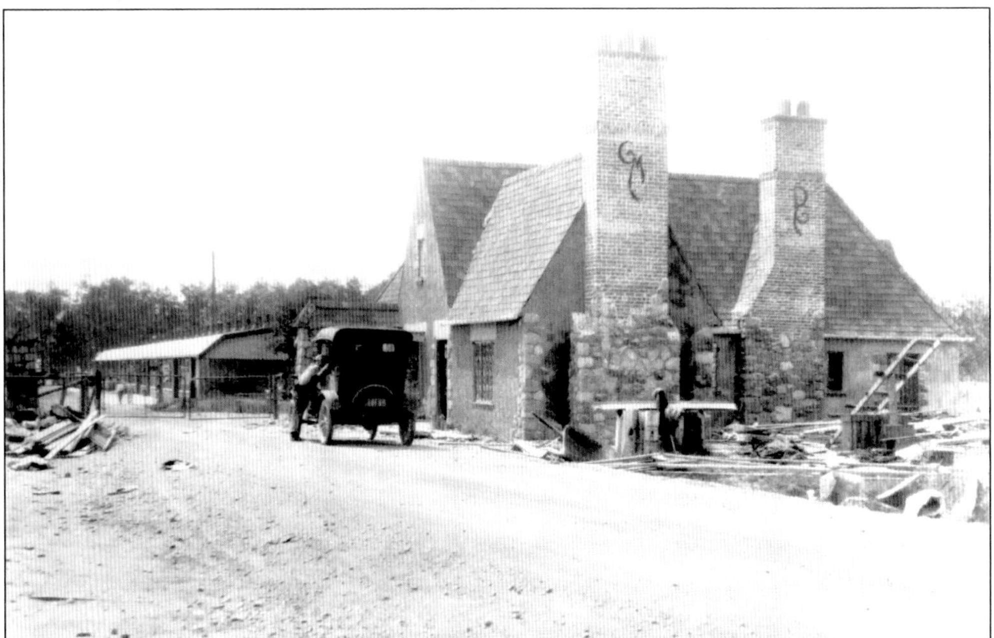

Among the first buildings erected at the Milford facility was this handsomely architected gatehouse, shown in 1924 with construction materials still scattered about. Behind the gatehouse, a hangarlike garage building is situated. At this point, the entrance is without either gate or landscaping. (G.)

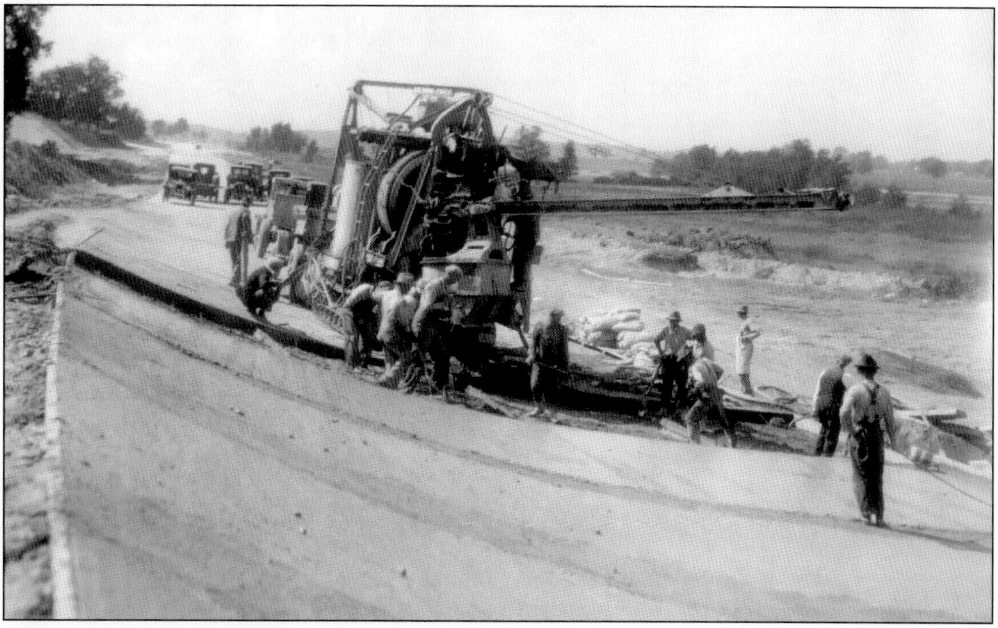

When GM set out to build its test track at Milford, there was no place to turn for a pattern. The U.S. Army had established its Aberdeen Proving Ground in Maryland during World War I, but it was initially used just to test munitions not vehicles. Nor was much known about building high-speed roads. This shows equipment laying concrete at one of GM's proving grounds high-speed turns in 1926. (G.)

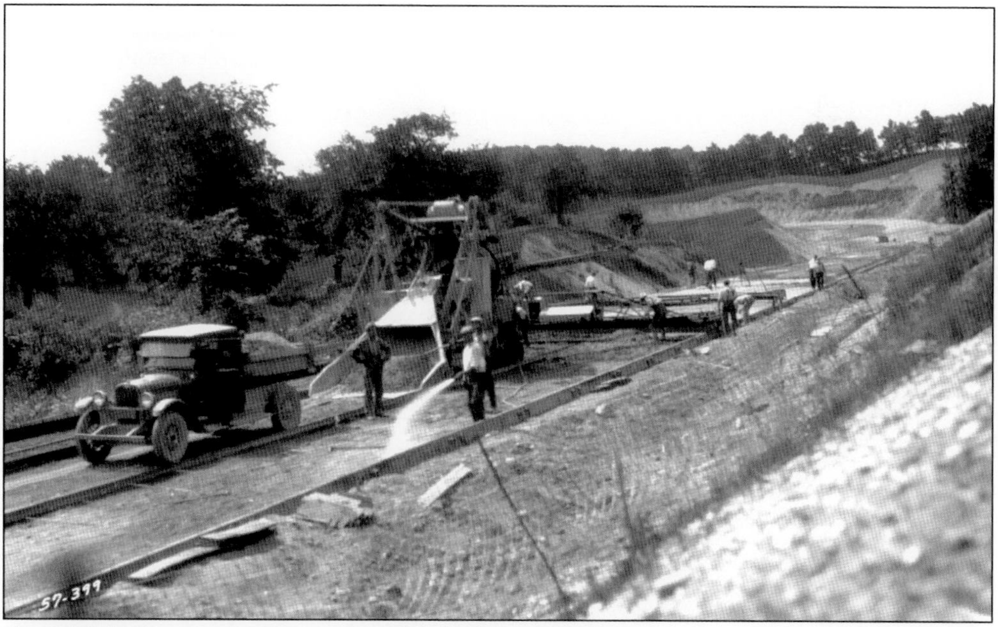

The U.S. highway system was not established until 1925, a year after GM starting building its proving ground. The engineering science of road building, although well developed in ancient times, only recently had been rediscovered. For instance, the first mile of concrete highway in America had been constructed in Detroit only in 1909. Here a crew at Milford is preparing the 11 percent hill road for paving. (G.)

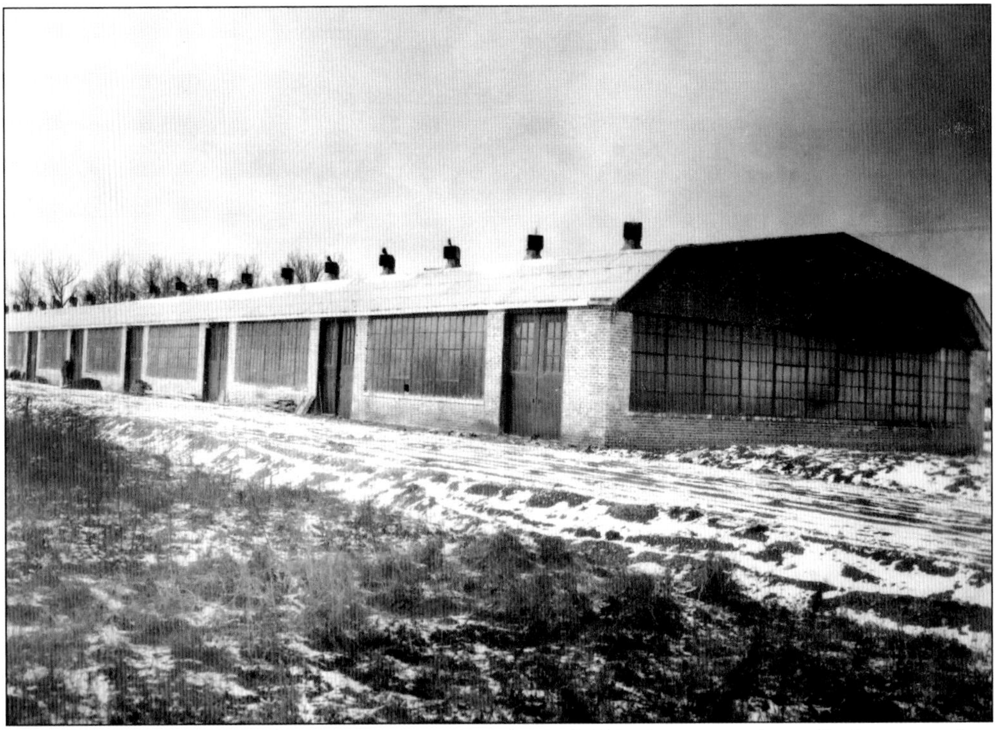

Building construction at the GM proving ground near Milford continued rapidly during its first year. The above photograph, taken in November 27, 1924, shows a just-completed garage building where the pavement has not yet been finished. The 1925 photograph below was probably taken late in the year when snow was already on the ground. It shows the same or a similar garage as shown above—there were several in a row—very busy with cars and trucks moving about. One of the reasons for the rush was the development of two new GM cars, the Pontiac for 1926 and the LaSalle for 1927. (G.)

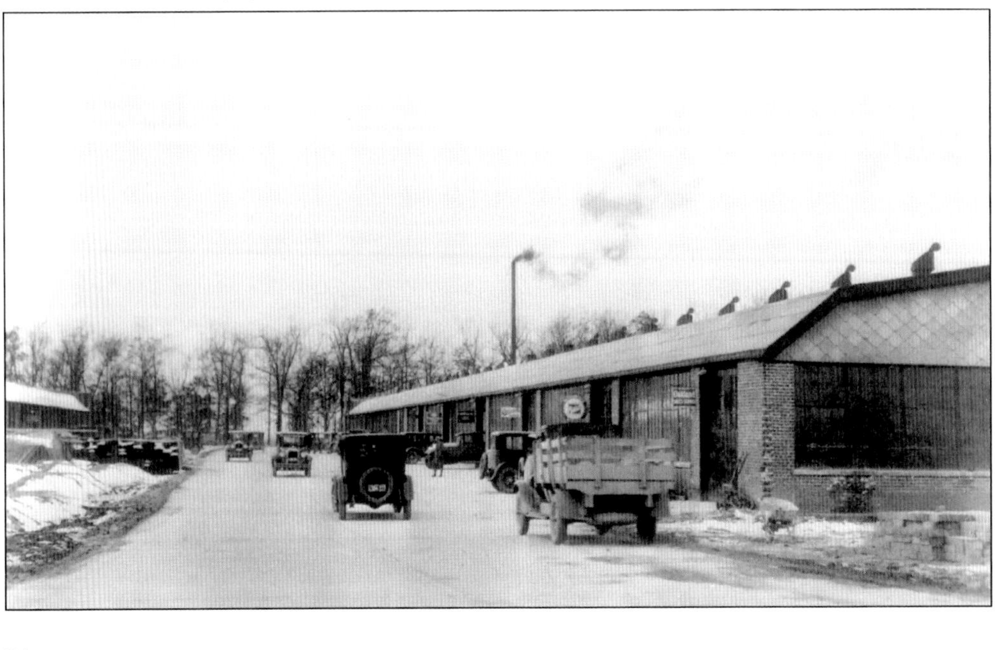

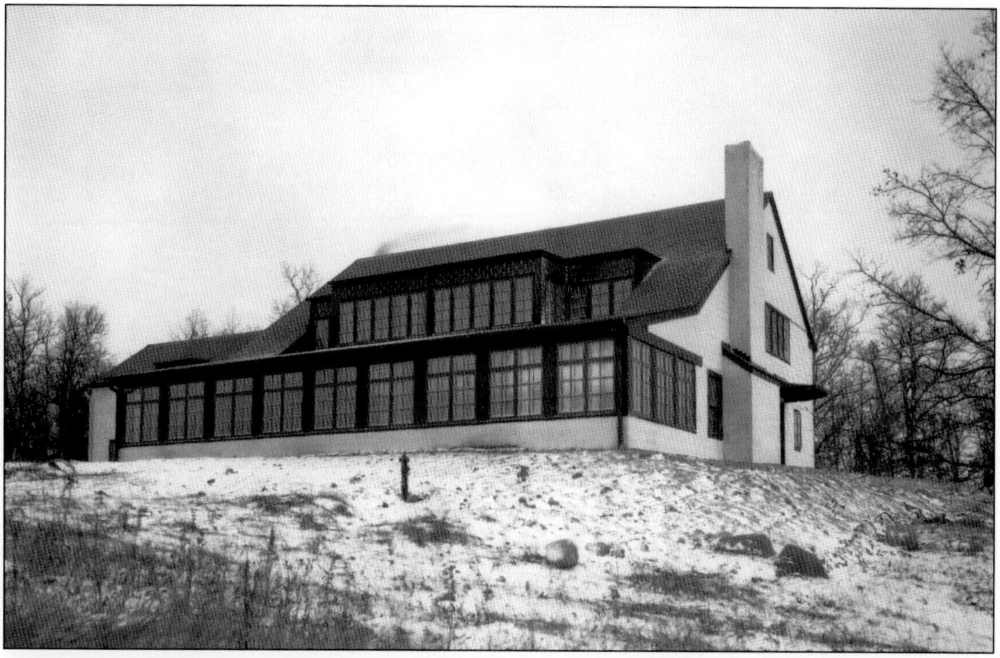

Because the Milford test track was so far out in the country, some 40 miles from GM headquarters in Detroit and a similar distance from various divisional engineering offices, the company had to build a lodge, called the Club House, for its employees to have convenient overnight lodging and meals. This photograph of the brand new Club House was taken on October 18, 1924. (G.)

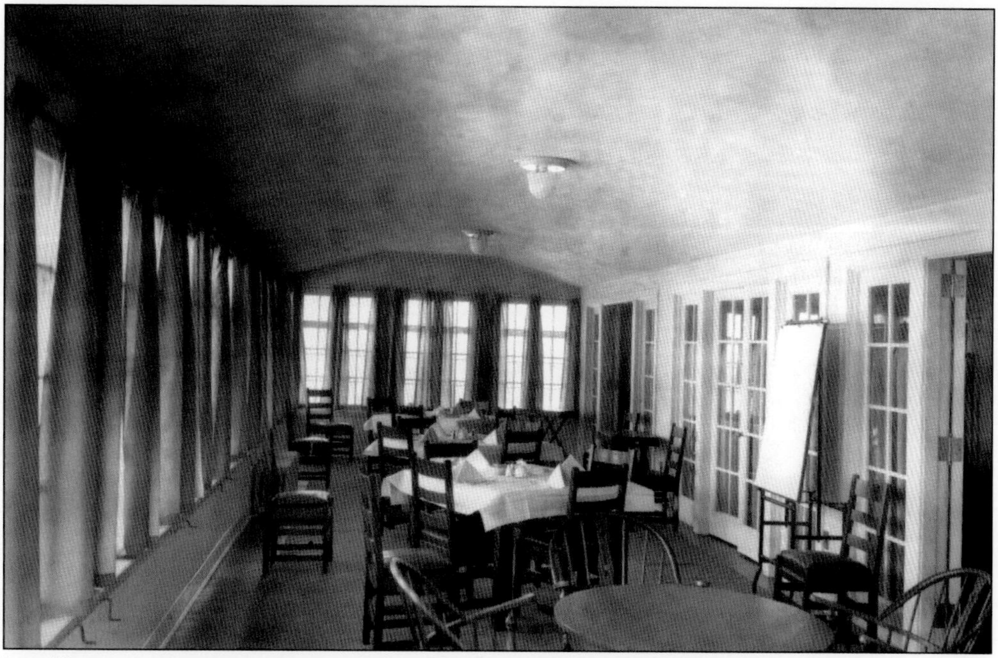

In addition to sleeping quarters and recreational facilities, the Club House provided a nicely furnished dining room, shown here, for employees to have their meals. The building was situated atop a hill to the west of the gatehouse and garage buildings. In the 1924 map (see page 31) it was labeled "Living Quarters." (G.)

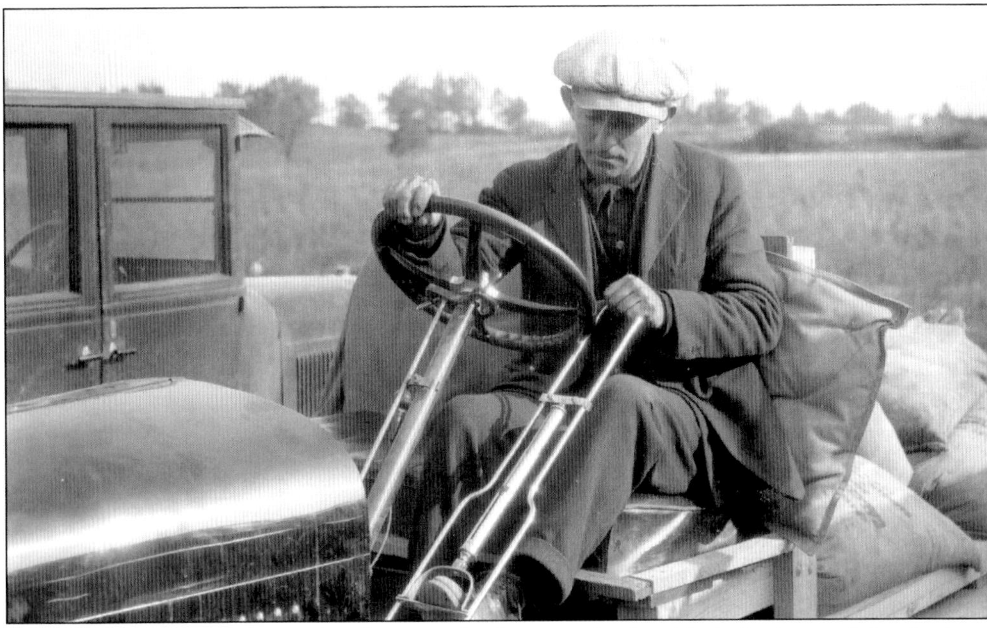

At Milford, GM engineers and technicians had to cope both with designing and developing a proving ground and the technology of road building and figuring out new ways of testing key vehicle components in consistent, repeatable ways. This photograph shows a technician working in an early cabless Chevrolet truck with a device to measure clutch pedal effort, very important in the pre-automatic transmission days. The gadget was called a fish scale. (N.)

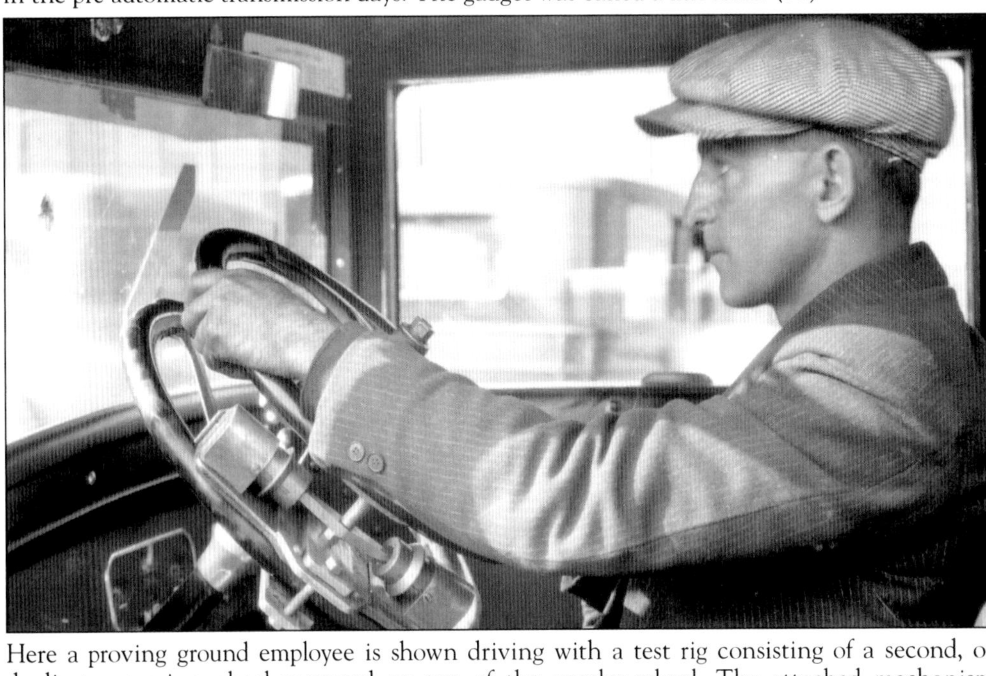

Here a proving ground employee is shown driving with a test rig consisting of a second, or duplicate, steering wheel mounted on top of the regular wheel. The attached mechanism measures the steering effort in various maneuvers, particularly parking. Power-assisted steering did not appear on production cars until 1951 and was subsequently widely offered in mass production by GM. (N.)

As mounted on the bare chassis of the truck shown here, GM's apparatus in 1924 for measuring fuel consumption consisted of a five-gallon gasoline can, two burettes, a bicycle pump, piping and tubing, and a piece of twine tied to a front headlamp. With modern electronics, many of today's cars and trucks have accurate readouts of both instant and average fuel mileage right in their instrument clusters. (N.)

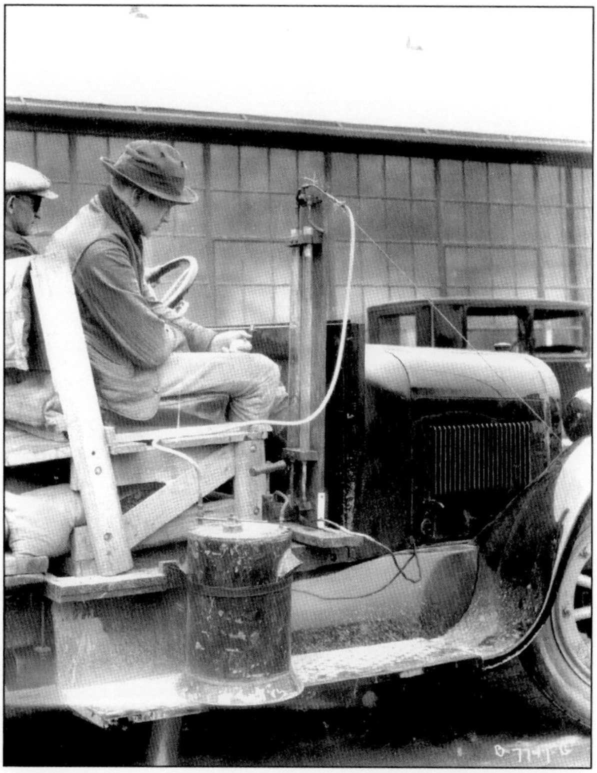

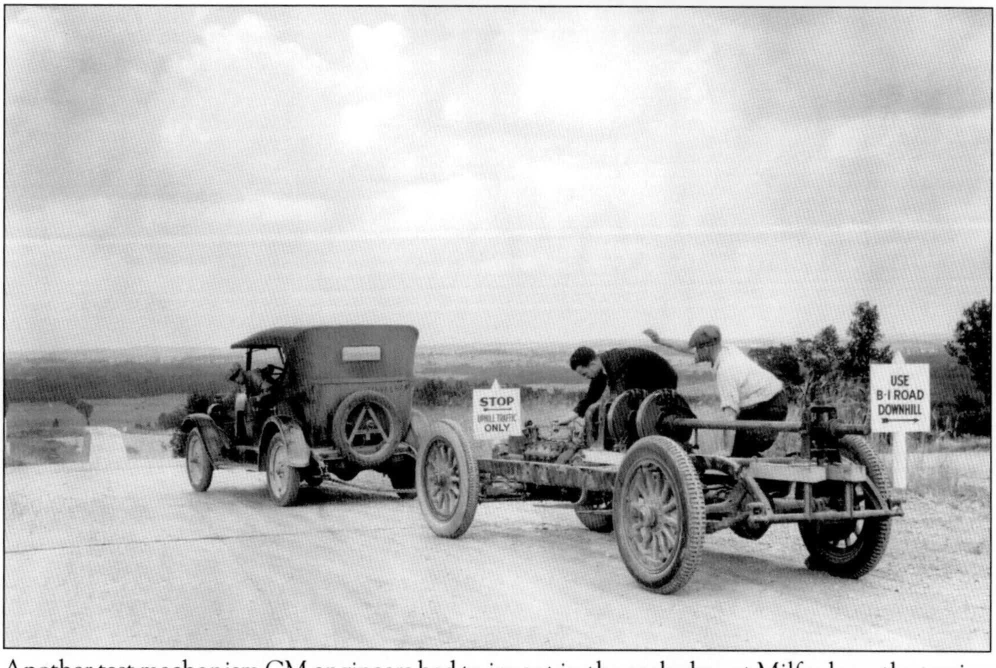

Another test mechanism GM engineers had to invent in the early days at Milford was the towing dynamometer shown here. A 1926 Chevrolet touring car pulls the bodyless chassis behind it that is weighted with large barbells. Instruments measure the touring car's power and torque under various load conditions such as hill climbing. (N.)

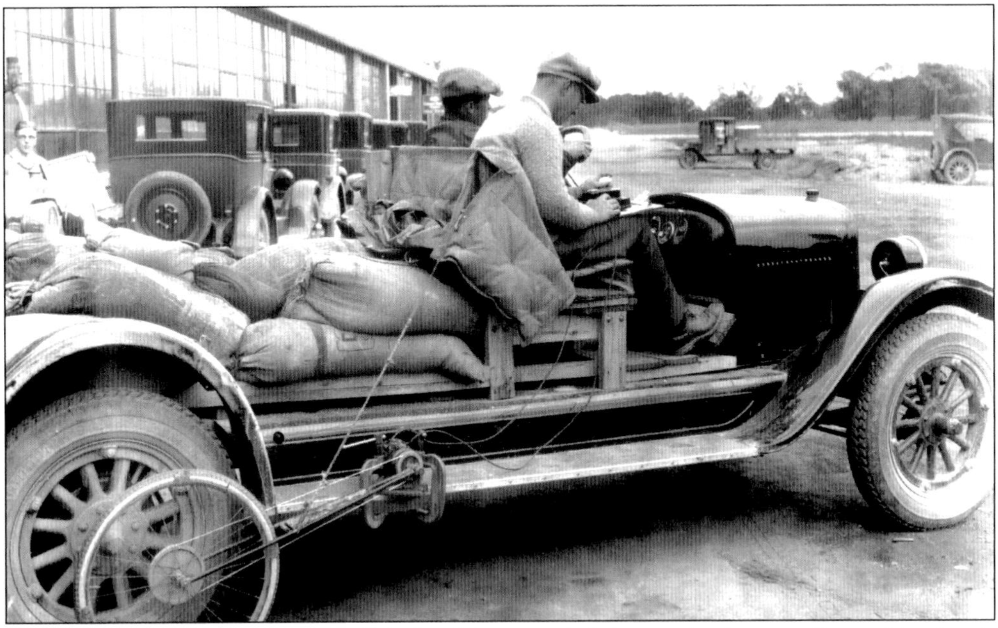

A mid-1920s GM brochure stated, "Much of the recorded data at the Proving Ground is of such a nature as to call for measuring and indicating instruments never before required. The General Motors Research Laboratory is proving indispensable in making available in rugged form for road test work most of the delicate apparatus familiar to the scientific laboratory." This shows an electric "fifth wheel" speedometer mounted alongside the rear wheel. (G.)

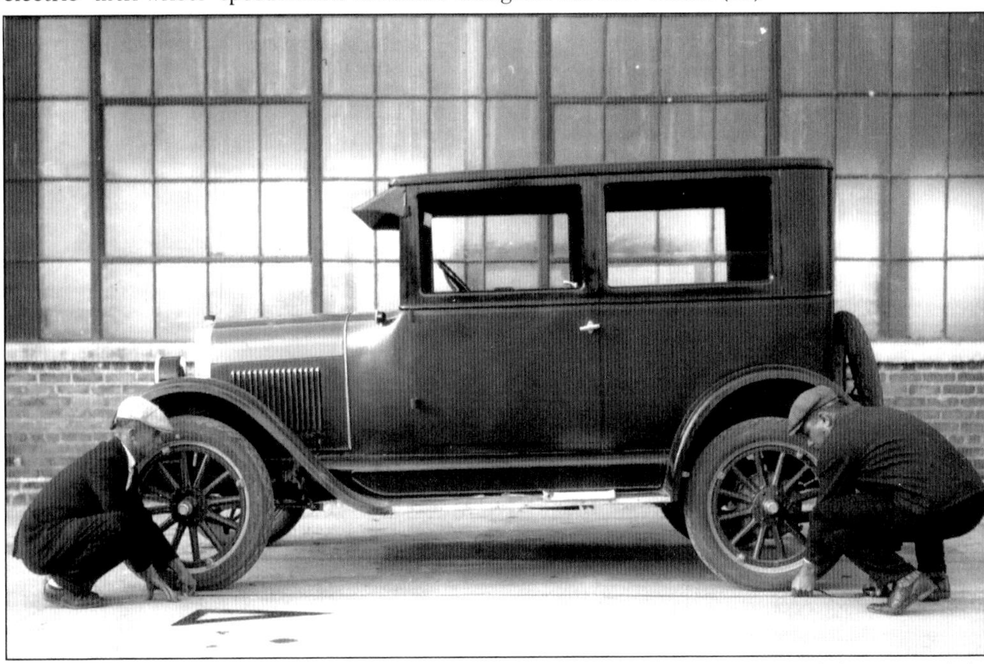

It is hardly high-tech, but this is the way engineers at the GM proving ground determined the basic measurements of various models of GM and competitive cars: they used tape measures and triangles and took dimension measurements. Here the exact wheelbase of this 1926 Chevrolet Superior Coach is being determined. (N.)

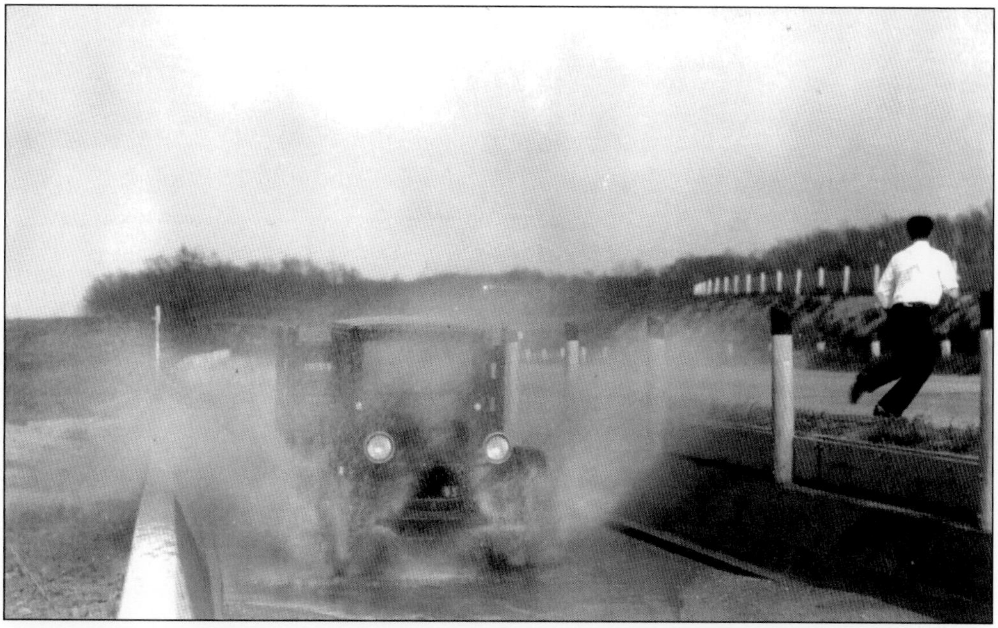

Among a number of the features at a test track that could not be duplicated on public roads and only with difficulty in engineering laboratories is the bathtub, at it was called at Milford. Here a prototype 1928 Chevrolet truck was driven through the water pit while an onlooker can be seen at right dashing to avoid the splash. All automotive test tracks came to feature these baths, always popular among photographers, as later pages will show. (N.)

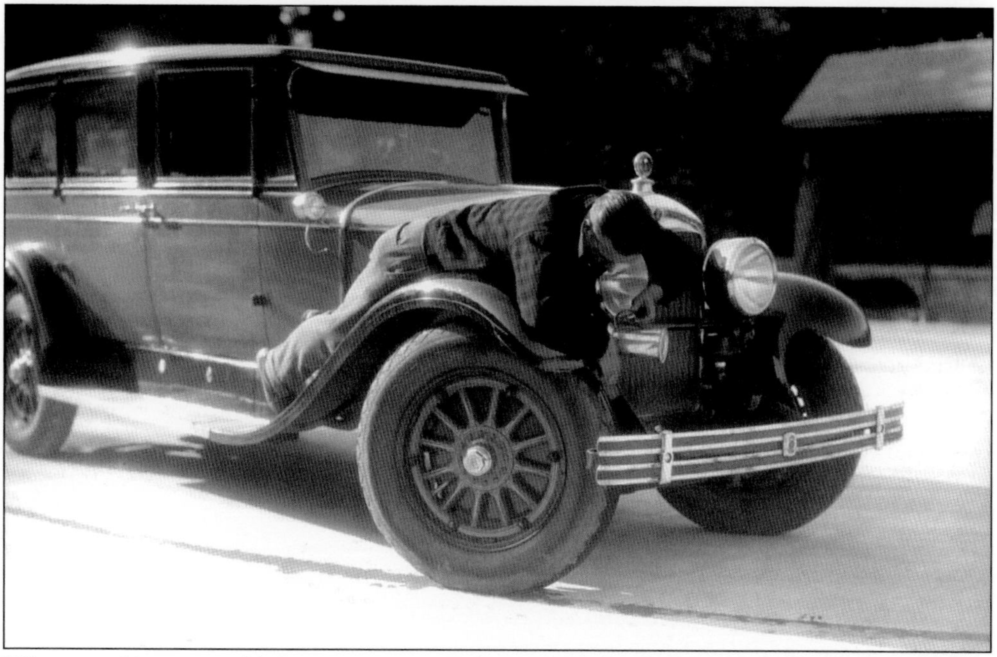

What possible test could this engineer or technician at the GM proving ground be making as he hangs over the front fender of this 1926 Cadillac? According to the information with the photograph, the employee was testing the turning radius of the car by dripping oil or water from the front to help determine the circumference of the turn. (G.)

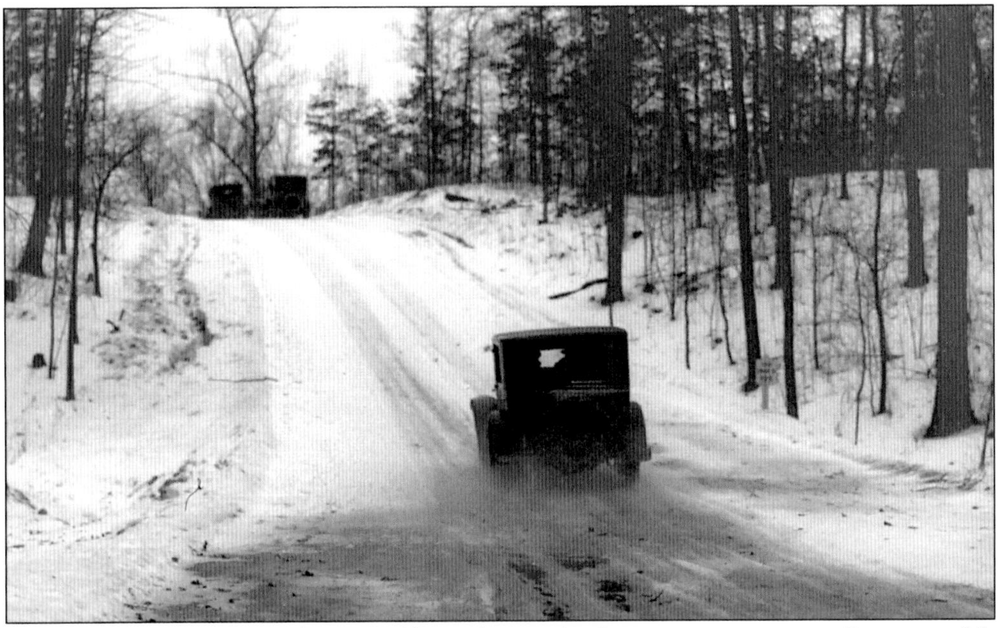

While laboratory tests provide repeatable results in a fixed environment, eventually new models had to hit the road to prove their designs. The enclosed grounds of GM's Milford test track provided a more controlled and safer environment than public roads, one where vehicles could be operated continuously all seasons of the year. This winter view shows a 1926 Cadillac V-8 on the endurance road. (G.)

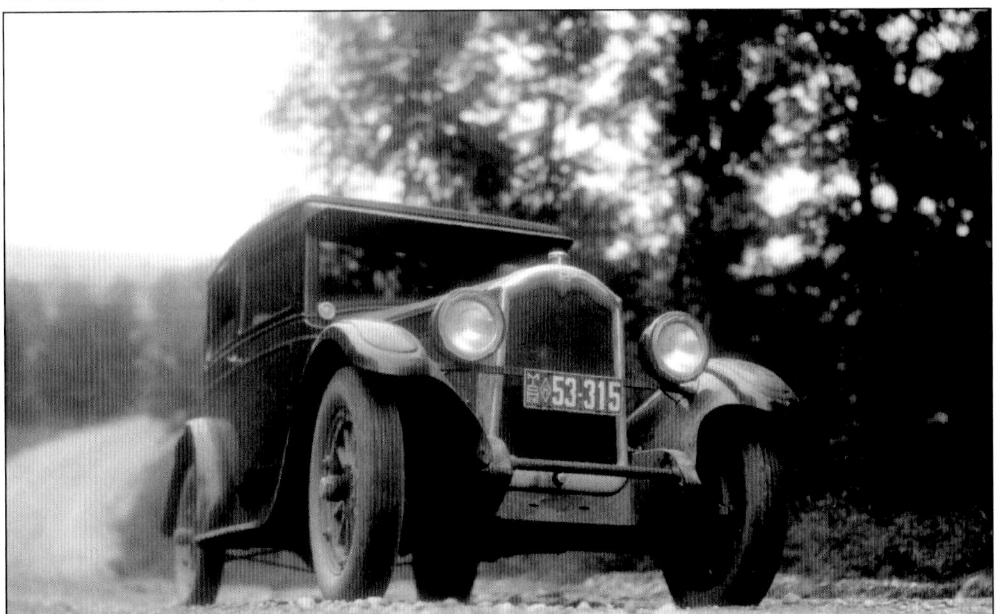

This view shows a 1926 Buick coach (two-door sedan) on the same graveled Milford durability road in a season when the surrounding trees were leafed out. It also illustrates the fact that many automobile models of this era were produced without bumpers, which were an extra-cost option. The base Buick was priced at $1,195 with a 207-cubic inch overhead valve six-cylinder engine producing 60 horsepower. (G.)

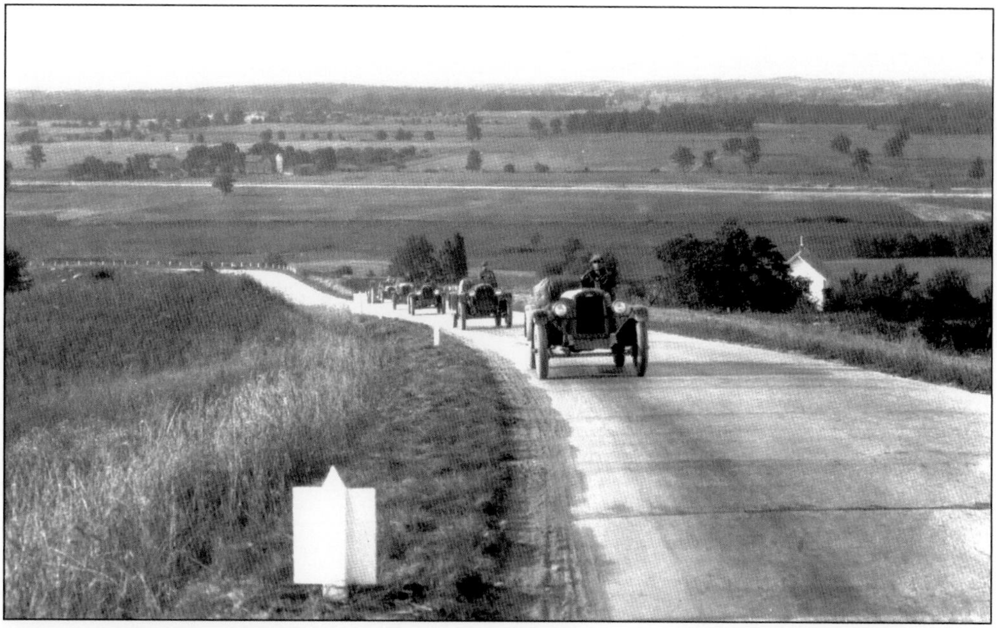

Here a 1925 Chevrolet Cowl Chassis truck leads a string of other test vehicles up a concrete-paved section of the hill course in the Milford Proving Ground. Driving such a vehicle without a cab limited testing to fair weather. At the time, it was customary for light trucks to be sold without cabs, which were later added by the owners according to their needs—panel, stake, pickup, or platform, for instance. (G.)

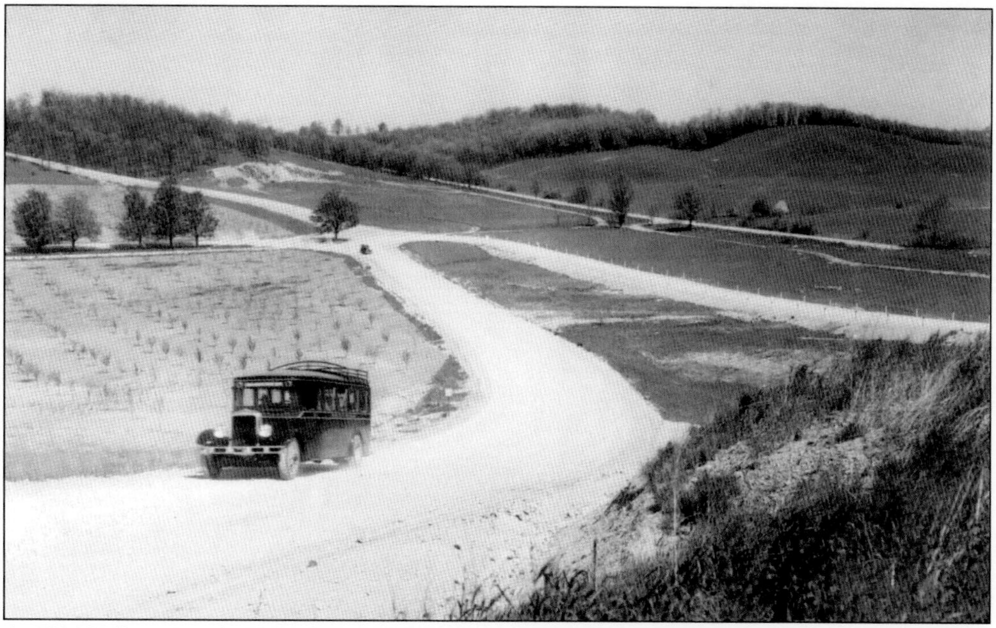

A 1926 Yellow Coach Manufacturing Company bus is shown racking up miles over a dirt or gravel test track road, a familiar type of road surface at the time. GM acquired a majority interest in Yellow, a Chicago company, in 1925, completing its ownership in 1943 when it was folded into the renamed General Motors Truck and Coach Division. Newly planted trees can be seen in the field beyond the bus. (G.)

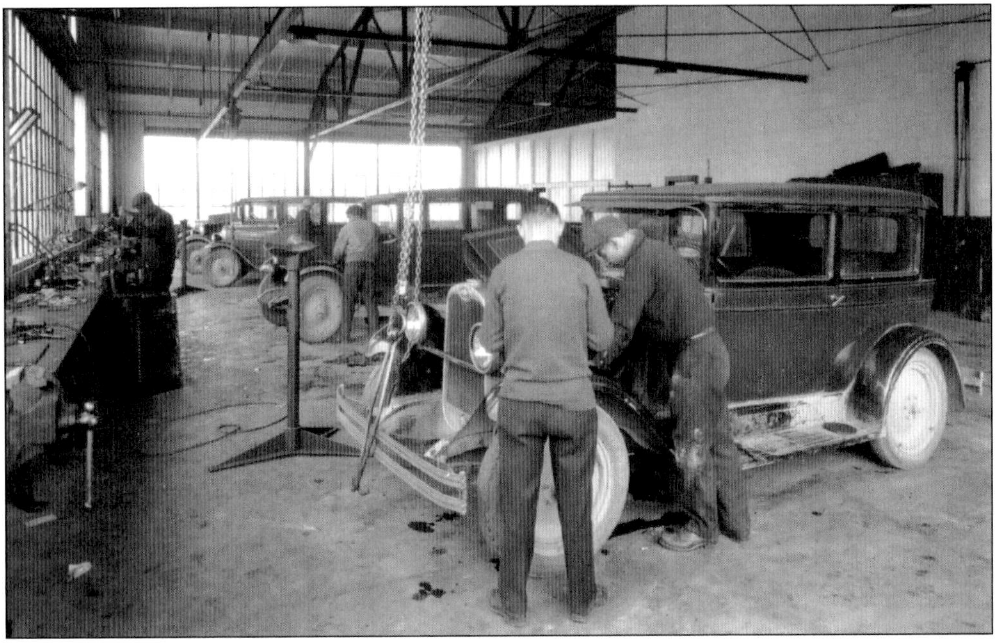

In a proving ground engineering garage, a pair of mechanics tends to a 1927 Chevrolet Series AB coach under test. Other test vehicles can be seen in the background. Cars of the time required much more routine maintenance than those of today; for example, chassis lubrication and oil changes were needed every 1,000 miles or less. In addition, test cars suffered failures, and engineers and mechanics had to determine the causes and fixes. (G.)

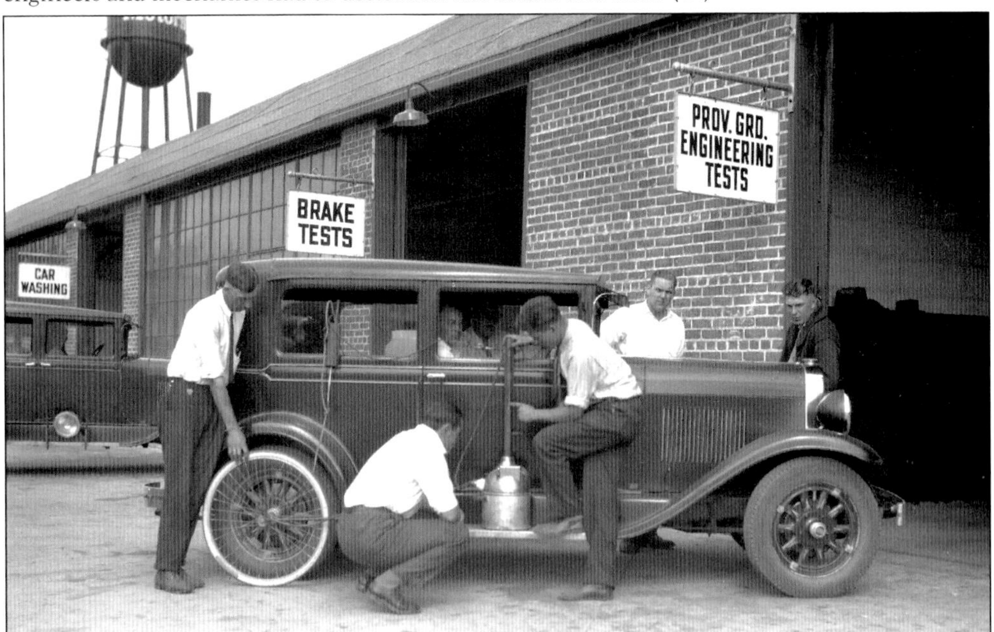

A team of engineers is shown setting up a 1929 Oldsmobile for a fuel economy test. The man at left is adjusting the fifth wheel for accurately measuring distance and speed, while the others work on the external test gasoline tank and connections. The 1929 model featured a more powerful 61-horsepower engine, up from 55 the year before. (G.)

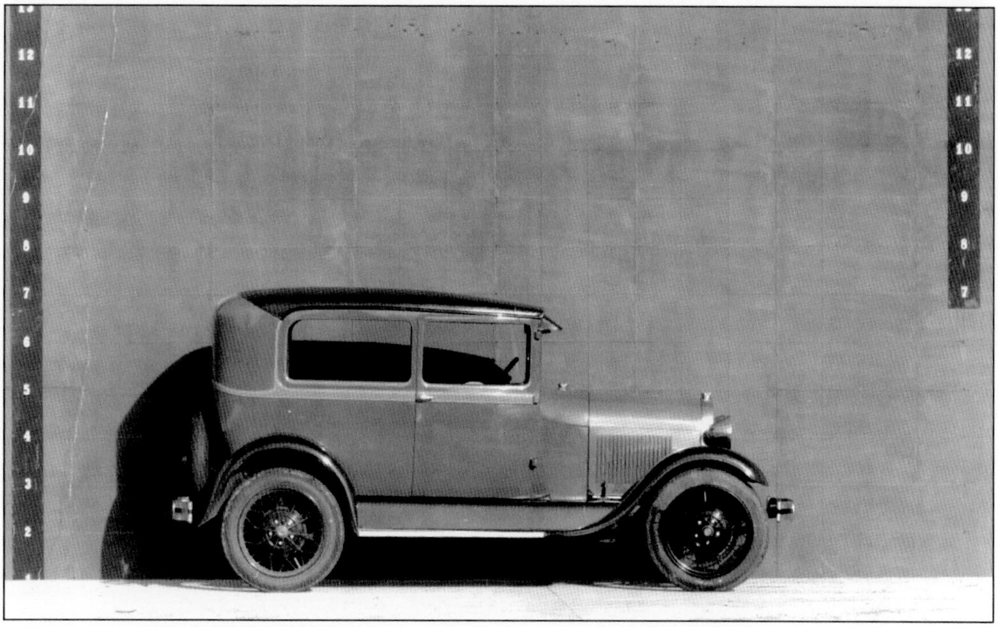

It was customary for automakers to examine the products of their competitors closely. Here a 1927 Ford Model A was posed at a dimensional setup within GM's Milford Proving Ground for a "reference photo." Typically the cars would be photographed side, front, and rear and their dimensions measured before undergoing endurance tests to see how they stood up and how any new features performed. (G.)

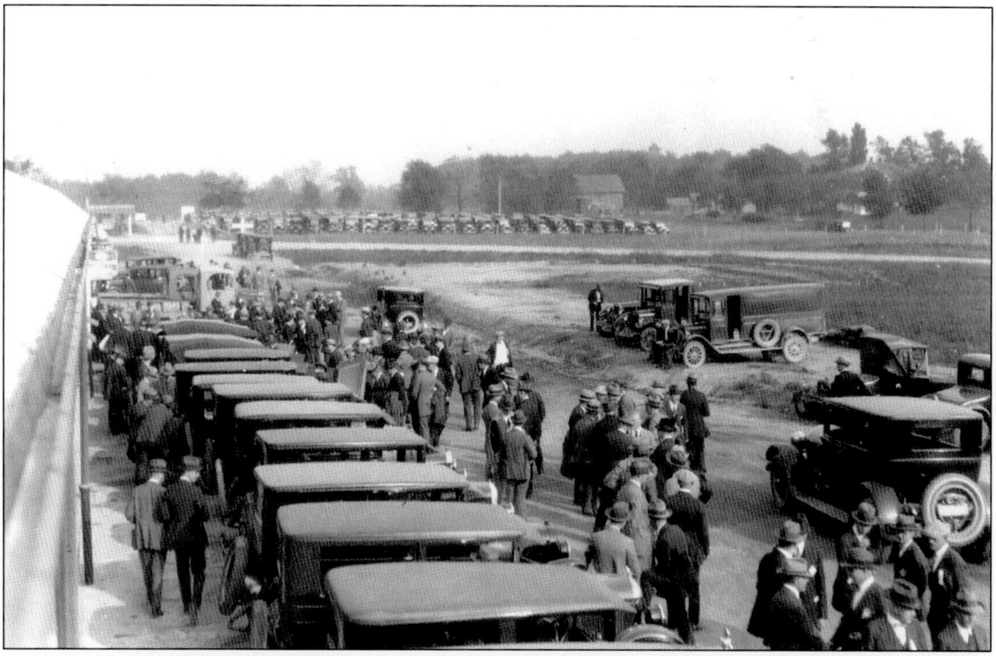

A proving ground also provided the manufacturer with a secure space to hold programs for company and dealer personnel to inspect and drive new models, hold press events, and take advertising photographs, unfettered by public curiosity. This shows a 1925 gathering of GM executives and dealer groups to compare GM and competitive vehicles. (N.)

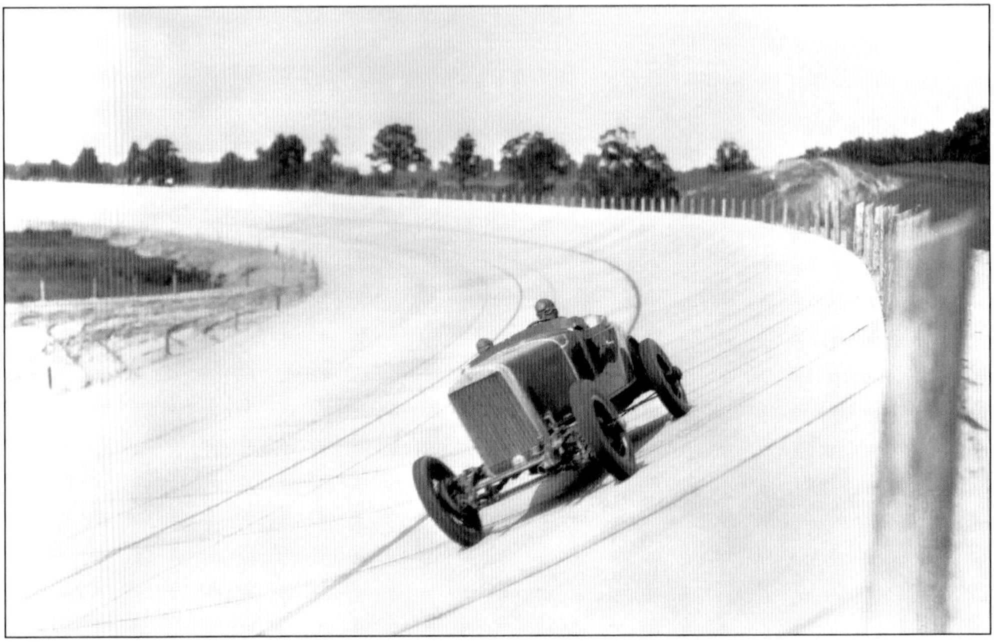

For introduction of the LaSalle by Cadillac in 1927, GM engineers stripped a roadster of fenders and headlamps and ran it around Milford's high-speed track (above) in a speed and endurance demonstration. Just as at a racetrack, a team of experts (below) clocked the speed of the prototype LaSalle pace car as it circled the test track inside the proving ground. The sign being held up told the driver what speed he attained on the lap just completed. For LaSalle, it was a successful promotion even though the car failed to complete the demonstration due to an oil system problem. The car ran 952 miles at an average speed of more than 95 miles per hour, just two shy of the average speed at the Indy 500. This was a very credible performance for a production car in 1927. (G.)

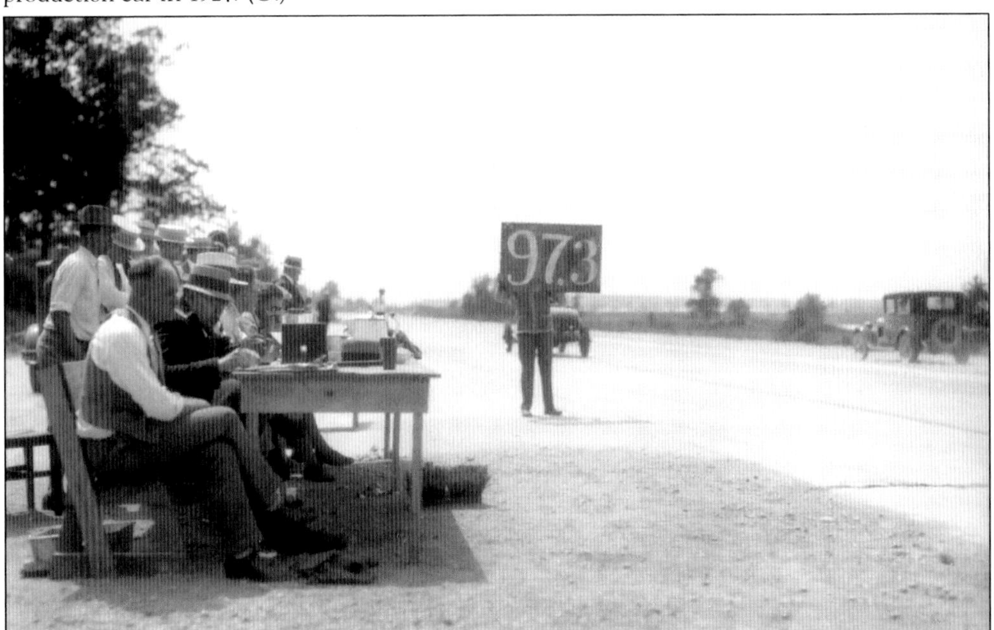

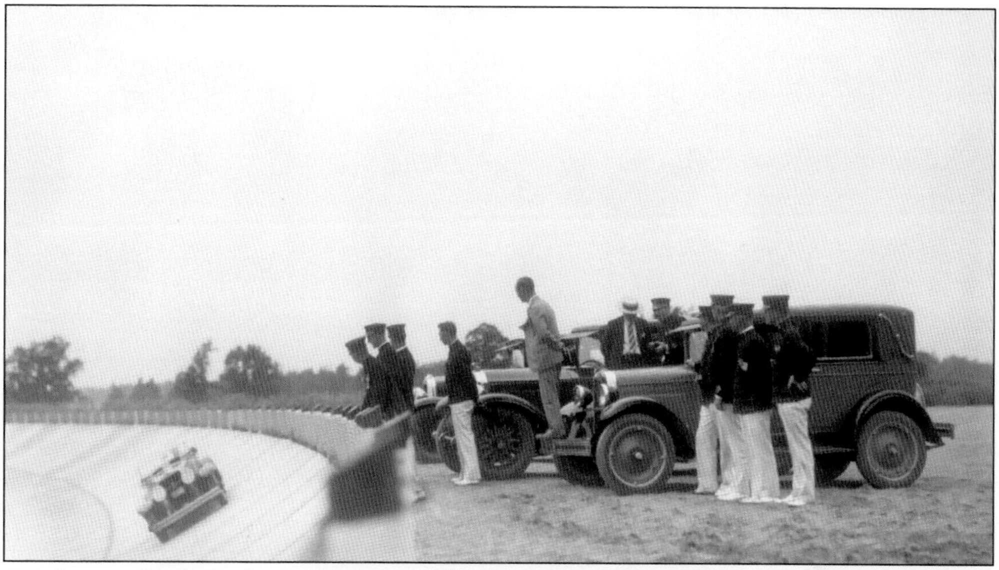

Another use for the high-speed track at Milford was demonstrations for special groups of invited guests. Here members of the Knights Templar Masonic order observe a 1928 Cadillac Model 341 roadster circle the track. For safety reasons, today outside guests are not permitted to stand so close to the track. (G.)

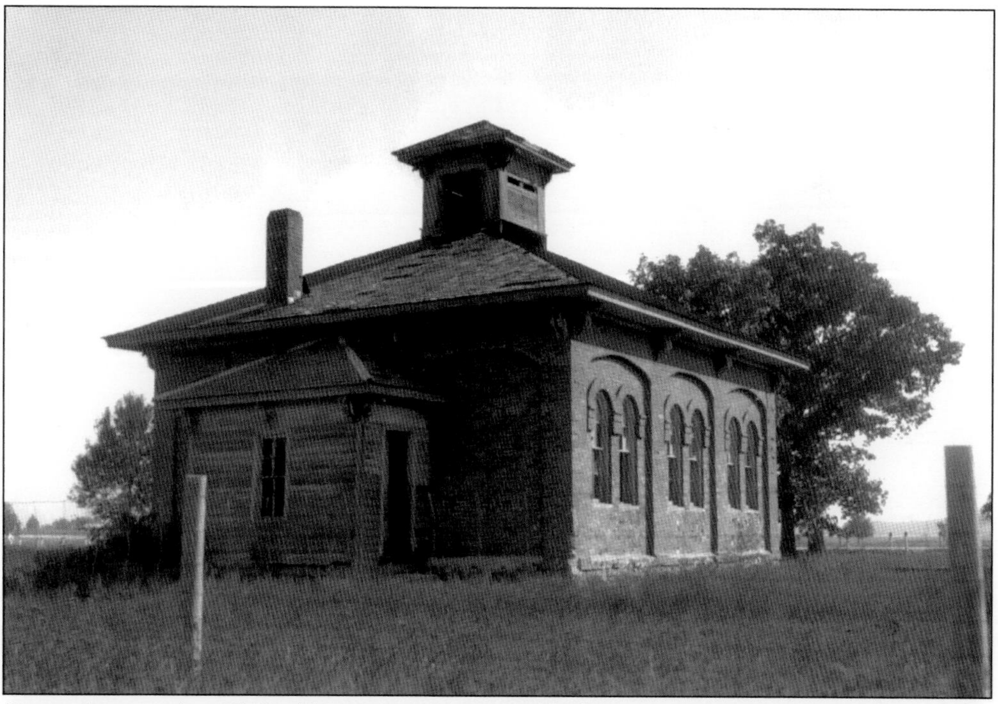

Curiously even after GM had been occupying its Milford Proving Ground for several years, some of the original community buildings still stood. This shows a sturdy rural schoolhouse, intact in 1928, maintained but unused by GM. Farm buildings and rural residences, however, had been removed as the test track roads were constructed. (G.)

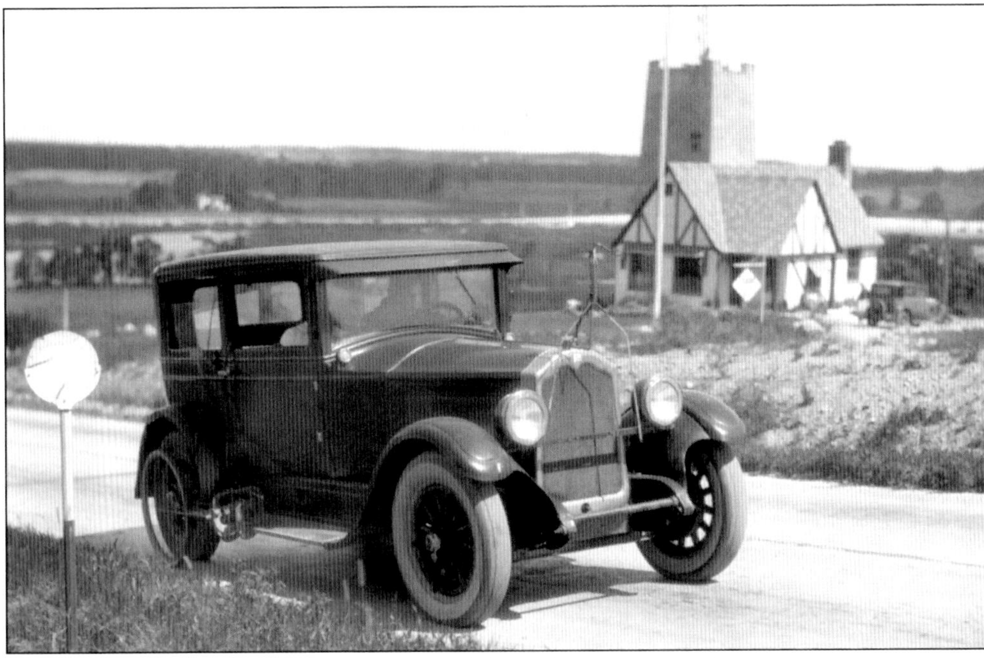

Here a 1926 Buick is shown ascending a hill with the test track's weather station in the background. Precision measurement of temperatures, humidity, and winds were important for exact duplication of test conditions or adjustments. The proving ground was constructed with both east–west and north–south straightaways to ensure proper comparison of test runs. (G.)

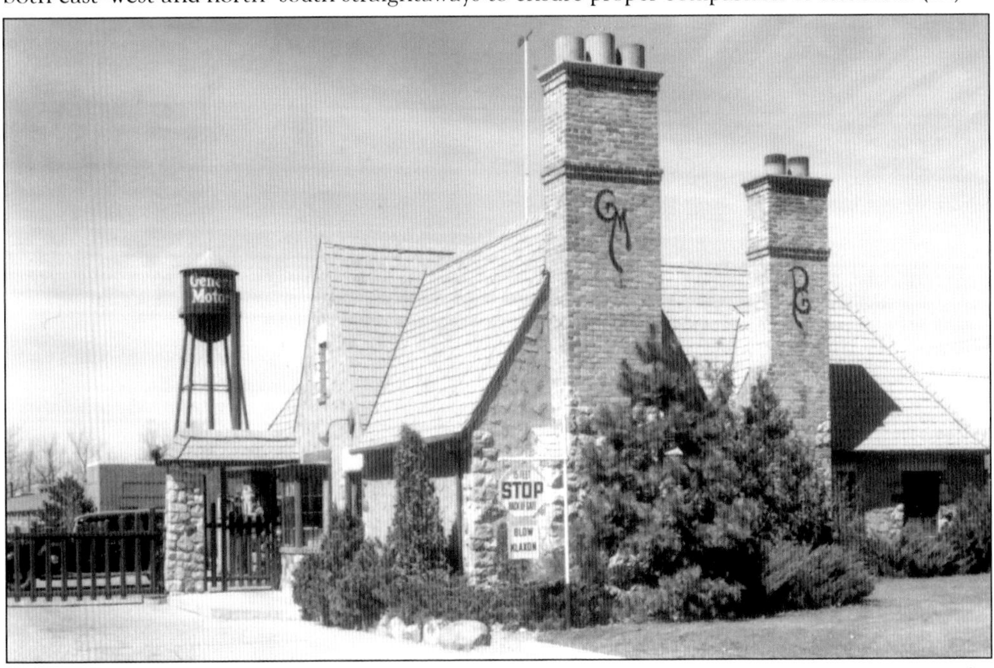

Numerous improvements to the proving ground gatehouse and the buildings behind it can be seen in this 1928 photograph. Both landscaping and a formal gate have been added to the gatehouse, and a water tower has been erected in the background. In addition, offices had been added to the fronts of the several garage buildings, largely unseen here. (G.)

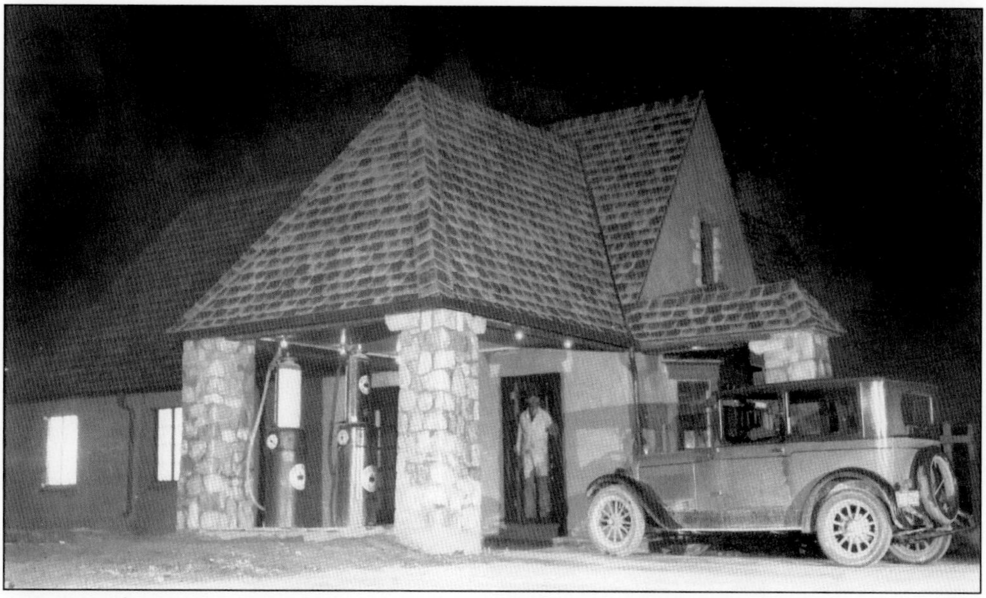

Immediately behind the gatehouse at the entrance to GM's Milford Proving Ground was the facility's fashionable gasoline station, shown here in a nighttime photograph with a 1926 Pontiac getting ready for a refill. The gasoline pumps were identified by the brand logos of the supplier, and in total, it looked just like a commercial gasoline station in an upscale neighborhood. (G.)

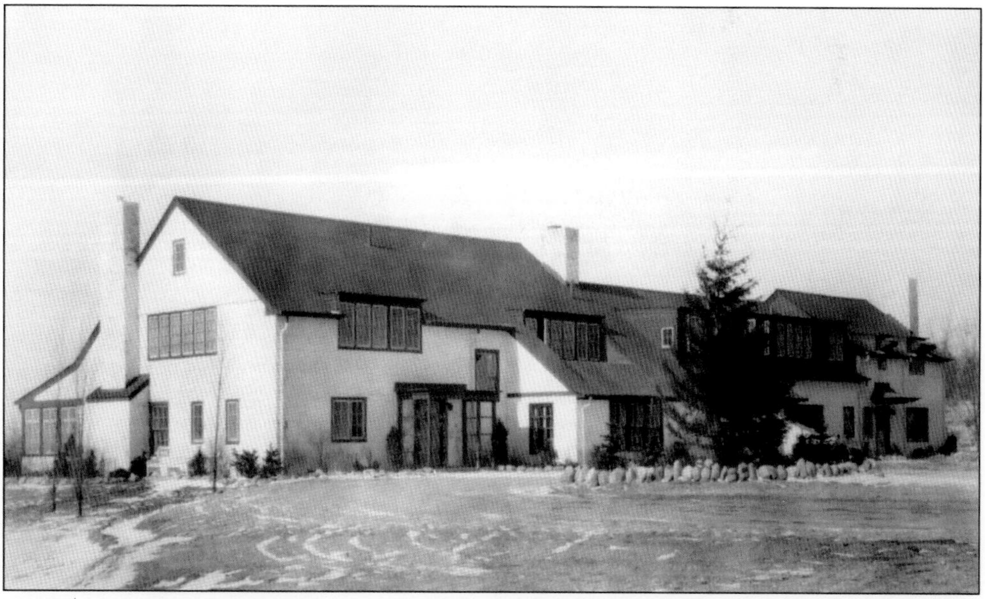

By the time this photograph was taken in April 1928, the original proving ground Club House had more than doubled in size to accommodate the growing number of employees and provide additional facilities. This view shows the front of the building, opposite from the earlier photograph of the rear (see page 35). (G.)

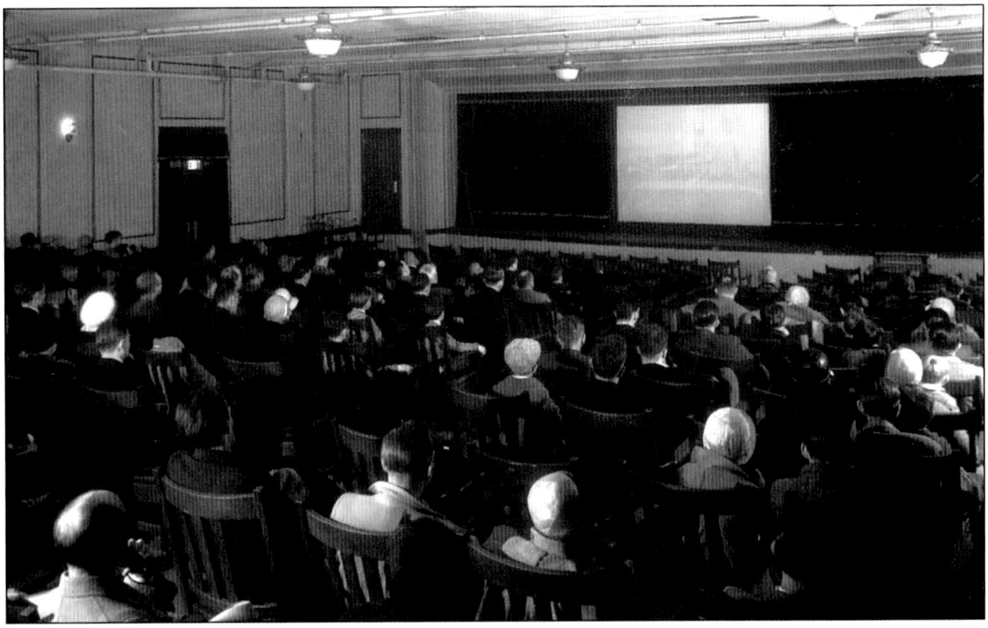

Among new facilities in the expanded Club House at Milford was this large auditorium for holding company as well as industry meetings, such as for the Society of Automotive Engineers. GM was proud to show off its facility, which dwarfed anything else in the industry at a time when the corporation was just rising to the industry's number one position. The auditorium also provided an entertainment venue for employees. (G.)

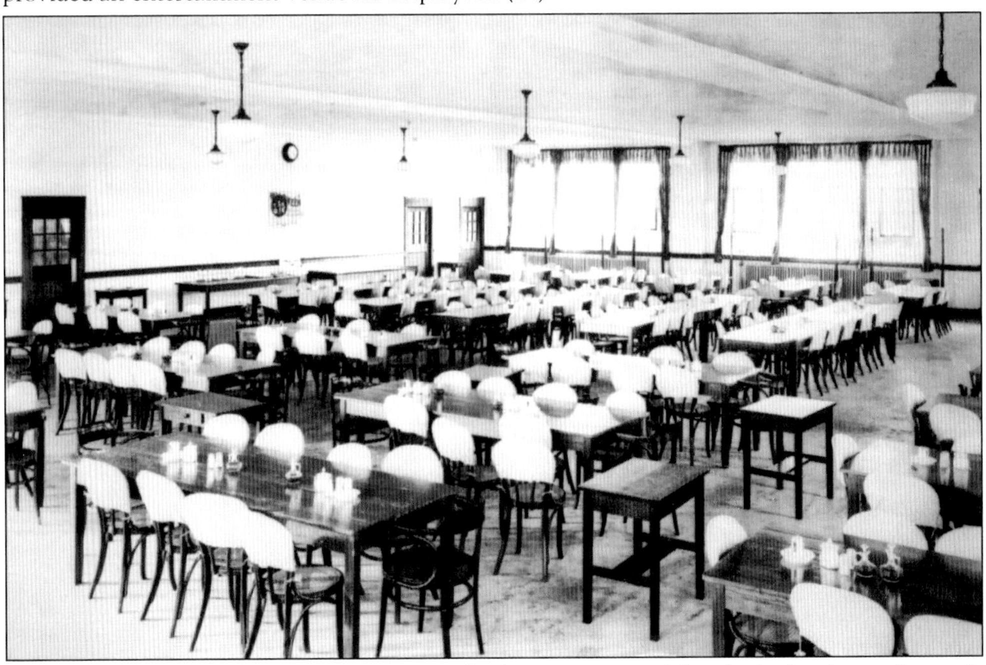

The growing number of employees requiring food services around the clock also dictated a much larger dining room, shown here, and kitchen at the proving ground Club House. Compare this to the small dining room at the building in 1924 (page 35). Guests at industry meetings, press events, or other promotions could be accommodated here as well. (G.)

Five

Packard Motor Car Proving Ground

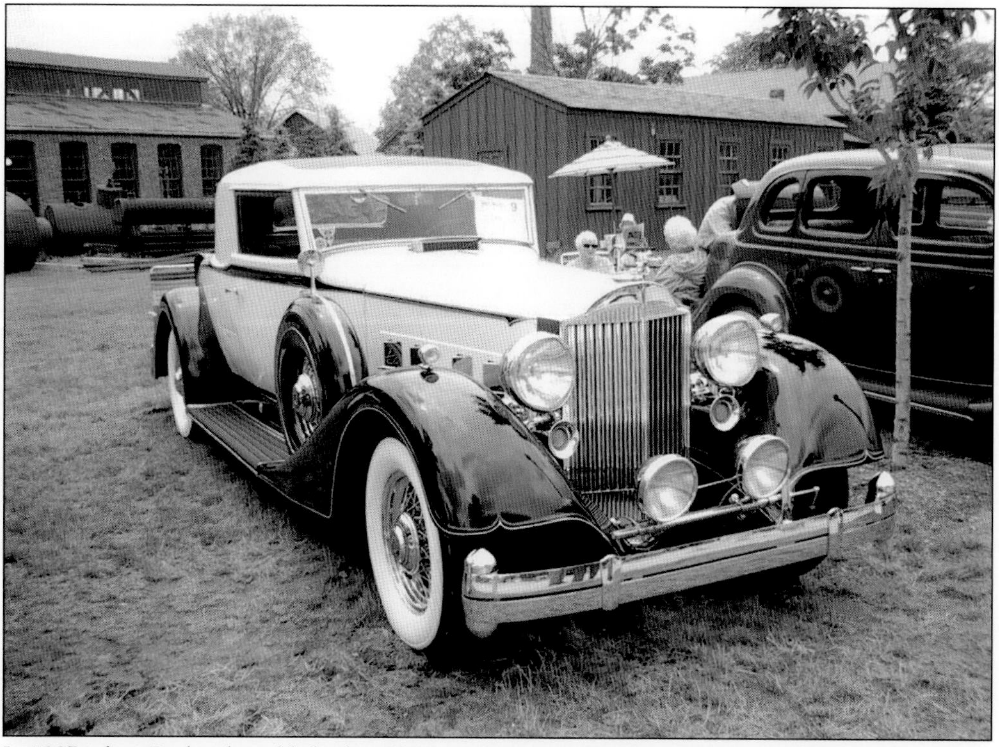

In 1927, when Packard established its 500-acre proving ground near Utica, some 20 miles north of its Detroit factory and headquarters, the company was the undisputed king of luxury carmakers, selling 32,500 Packards to Cadillac's 19,400. This shows a 1934 Packard convertible at a recent classic car show. (D.)

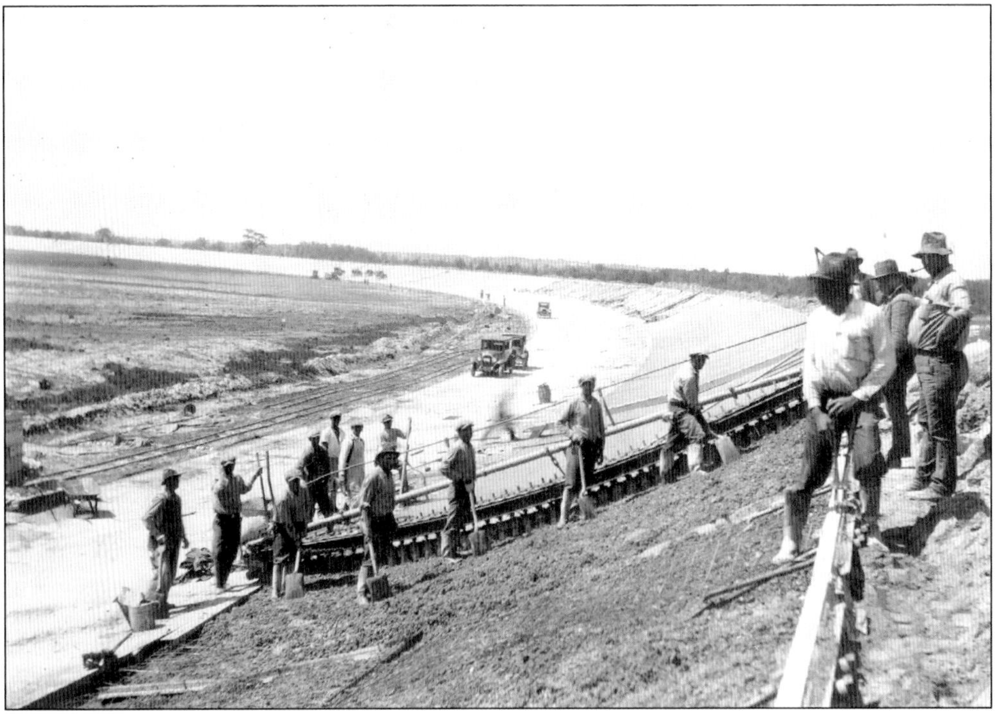

After learning of the GM proving ground northwest of Detroit, Packard lost no time acquiring land and starting to build its own test track. This shows road-building equipment laying concrete for the slanted surface of turns on the high-speed oval, a difficult task not duplicated on even the newest of public roads. (N.)

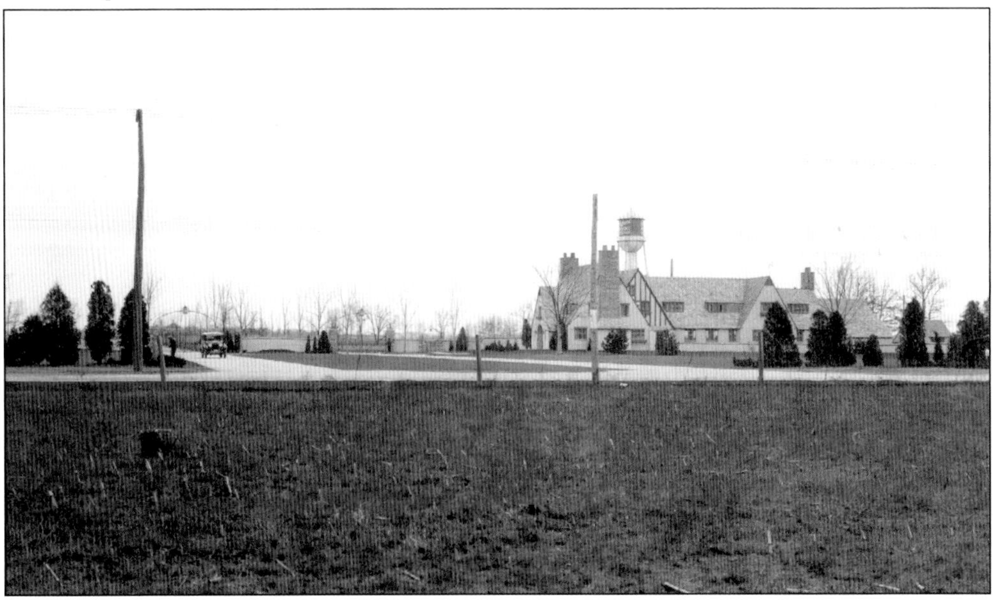

Packard commissioned famed Detroit industrial architect Albert Kahn's firm to design its proving ground buildings and utilities, with the entrance lodge, shown here, even larger and more imposing than the gatehouse at GM's facility. Kahn had gained experience in such assignments building army and navy airfields for World War I. This view was taken before landscaping. (N.)

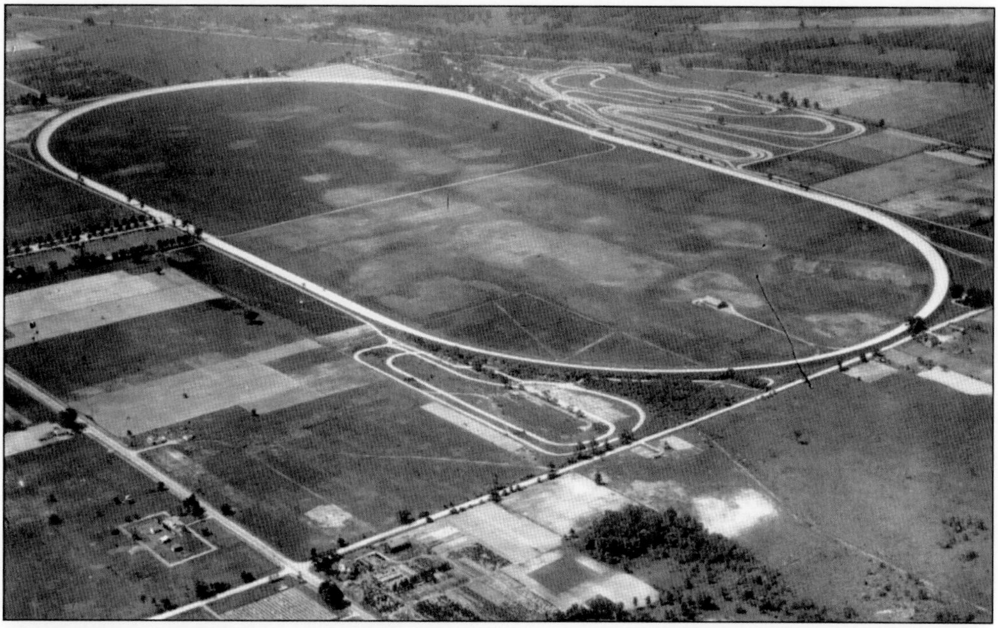

This southwest aerial view of the Packard test track in the 1930s shows many twisty test roads, as well as the high-speed oval. The garage and lodge were just out of the photograph to the left. The community of Utica is about two miles to the south. Because southeast Michigan is generally flat, automakers had to seek rolling countryside some distance from Detroit, either to the north (Packard and Ford) or to the west (GM and Chrysler). (N.)

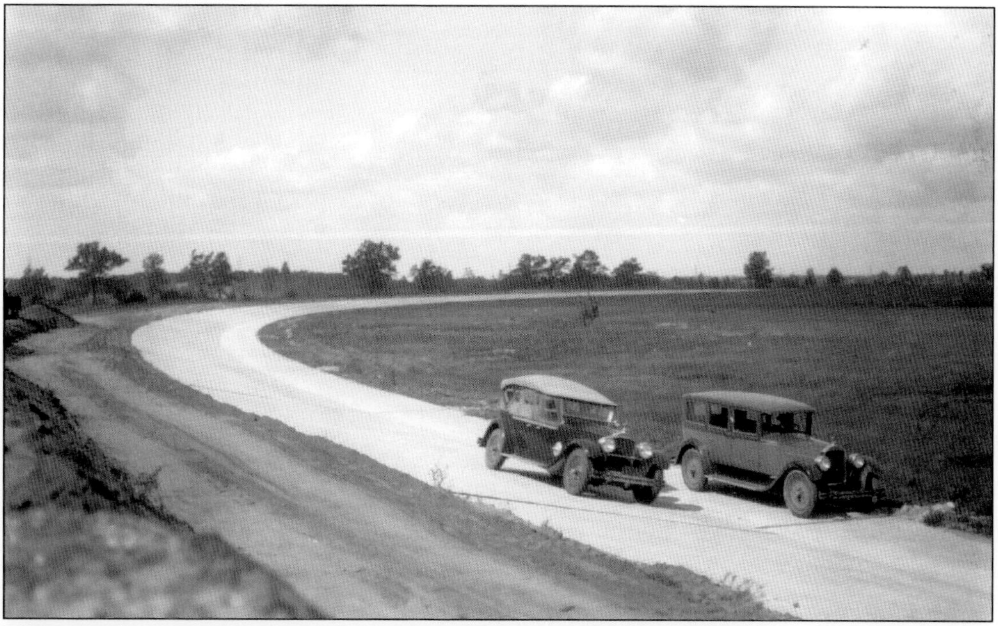

This view shows a c.1927 Packard touring car passing a different model sedan on the 2.5-mile test track oval at Utica before the high-speed roadway was completed. Packards of the time, under the direction of engineering vice president Col. Jesse Vincent, were renowned for such advances as four-wheel brakes, hypoid rear axles (permitting lower driveshafts and bodies), and Twin Six V-12 engines. (N.)

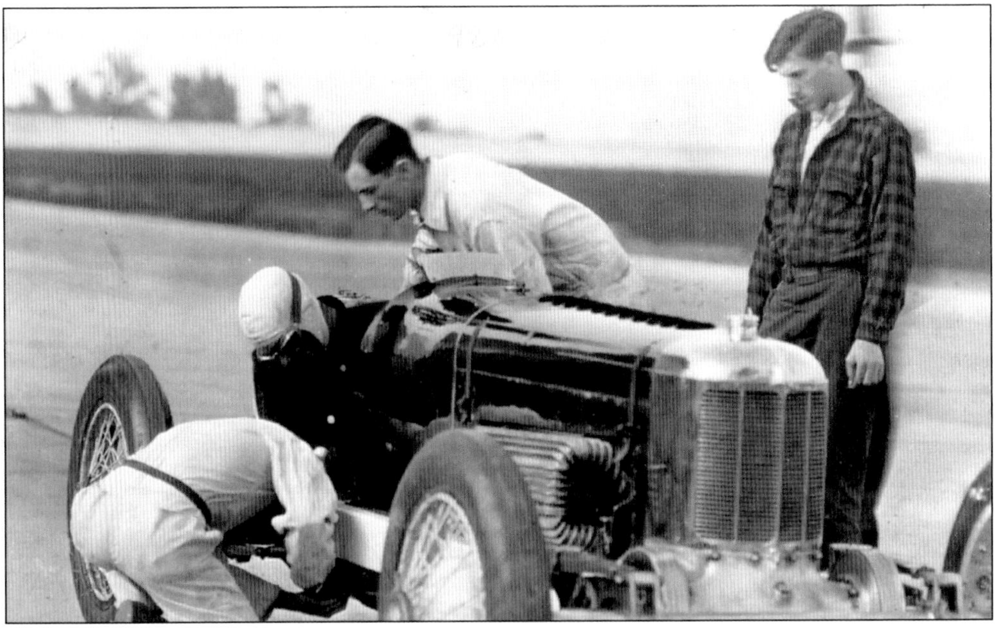

Col. Jesse Vincent, commissioned in World War I through his involvement in the Liberty aircraft engine joint-industry project, piloted his own airplane and became a speedboat-, automobile-, and airplane-racing enthusiast. In 1928, he directed a speed run with the Miller Special race car shown here, which achieved a 148.7 mile per hour lap record over the test track's oval, making Utica the world's fastest speedway. (N.)

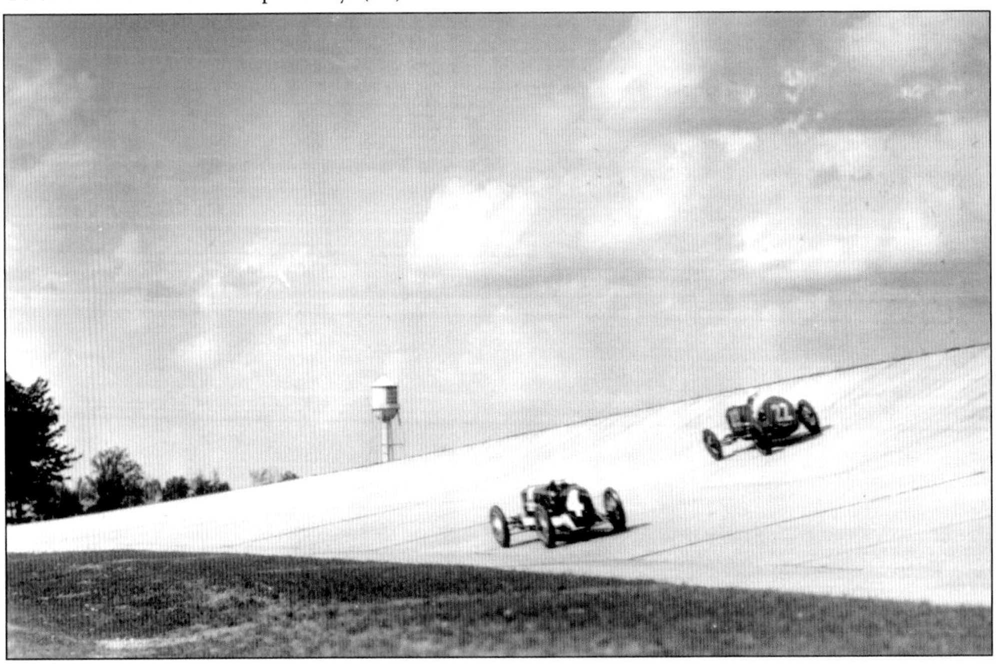

This photograph shows two speedsters on a graded curve of the Packard Proving Ground, traveling at more than 140 miles per hour. Car No. 4, at left, reached the fastest lap on June 14, 1928. The record had little to do with Packard cars but promoted Packard's test track as being superior (faster) to rival GM's track. (N.)

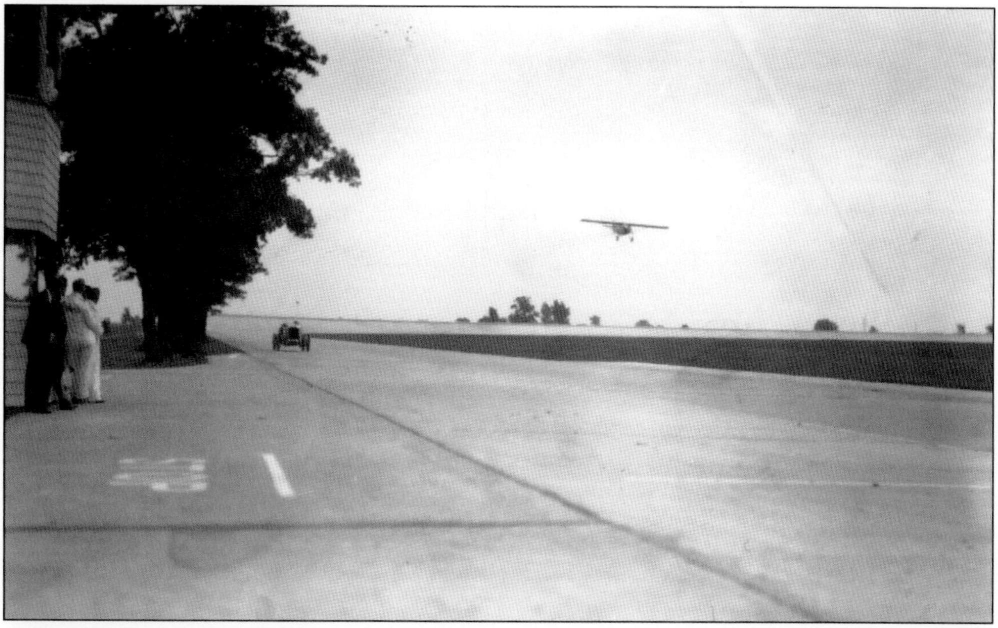

Packard's engineering chief Vincent also pushed development of a V-12 diesel aircraft engine by the automobile company. The dream for a reliable, fuel-efficient diesel aircraft engine ultimately failed commercially because diesel engines were too heavy for aircraft and took too long to heat up. Here an aircraft powered by the experimental engine races a speeding car down one leg of the Utica oval track. (N.)

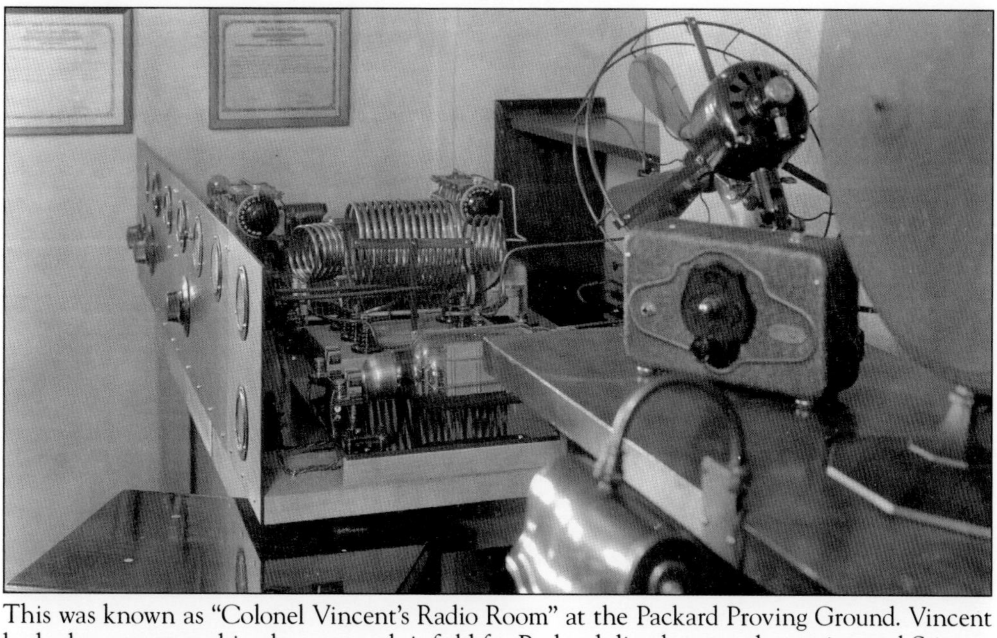

This was known as "Colonel Vincent's Radio Room" at the Packard Proving Ground. Vincent had a hangar erected in the test track infield for Packard diesel-powered experimental Stinson and Waco aircraft, his own airplane, and visiting airplanes that could land either on the north–south pavements or the infield. Aerial navigation and radio communications were still in their infancy in the 1920s, but inventor Vincent, who held more than 400 patents himself, pushed development of aircraft as well as motorcars. (N.)

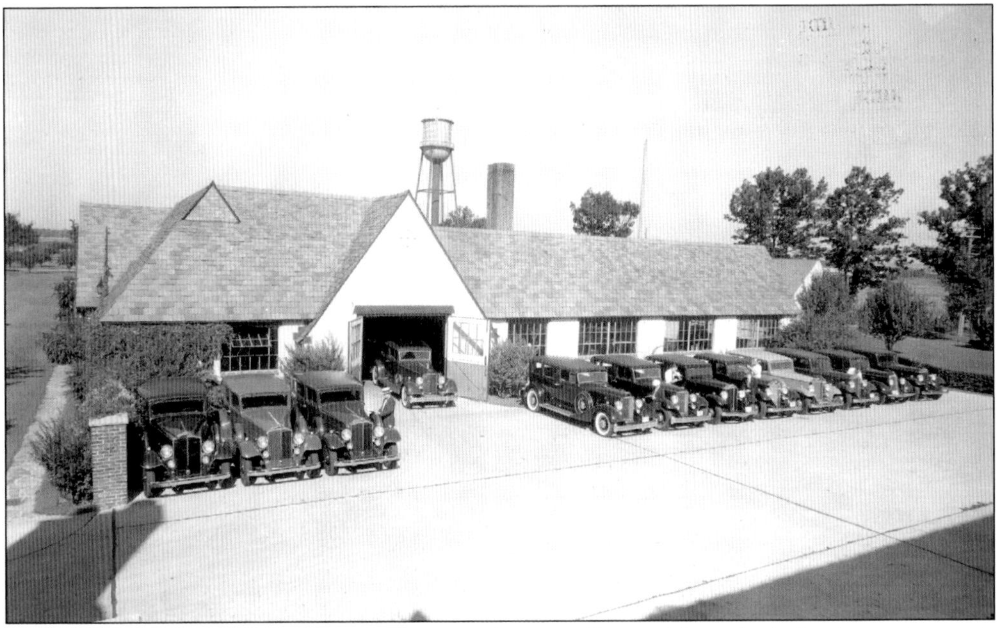

The Packard Proving Ground garage was as architecturally notable as the lodge (opposite page). By intent, both were designed to match the upper aspirations of Packard buyers. In addition to bays for working on test cars, the garage contained laboratories for testing engines, chassis, electrical, fuels, and lubricants. Parked in front of the garage in this photograph is an array of 1932 and 1933 production and 1934 prototype Packards. (N.)

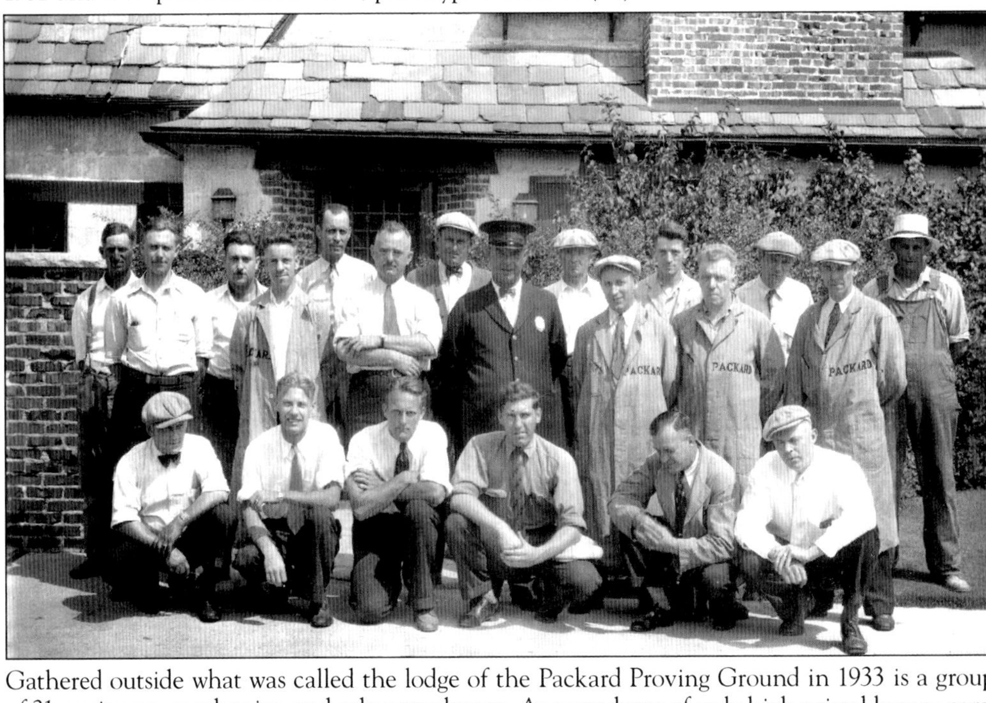

Gathered outside what was called the lodge of the Packard Proving Ground in 1933 is a group of 21 engineers, mechanics, and other employees. As a producer of only high-priced luxury cars, Packard suffered terribly in the Depression, with sales dropping to 6,552 in 1934. The solution was the introduction of a lower-priced Series Eight for 1935 and a Series Six for 1937. (N.)

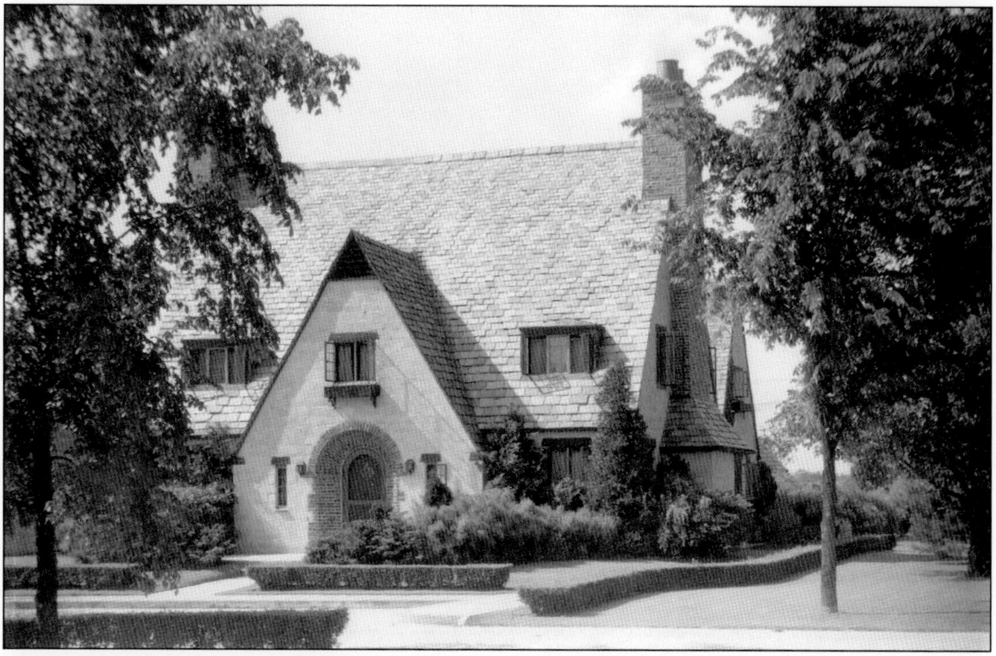

The Packard Proving Ground lodge is shown here in a 1932 photograph after foliage has had time to fill out in the five years since the structure was erected. Inside the lodge were quarters for the manager, his family, and guests, with nine bedrooms and four baths, plus a dormitory for drivers and an eight-car garage. (N.)

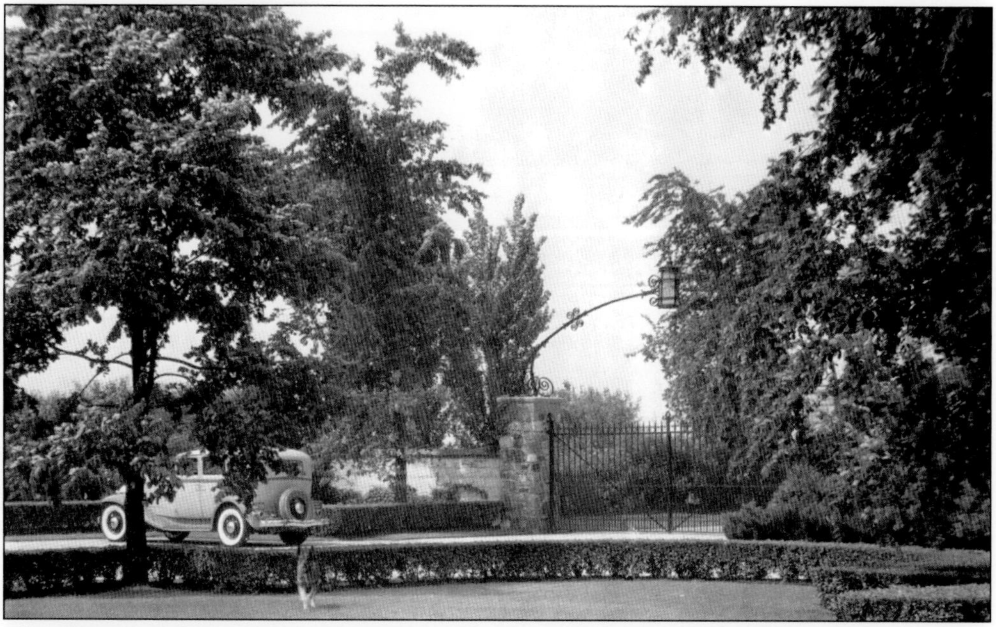

The elegant gardens at the iron-gated entrance to the Packard Proving Ground near Utica are illustrated in this photograph, which shows a 1932 Packard sedan parked at the side. The ornamentally landscaped entrance was designed to impress visitors and boost morale of employees. Today classic car collectors prize Packards, especially the upper series of the 1930s—the Eights, Super Eights, and Twelves. (N.)

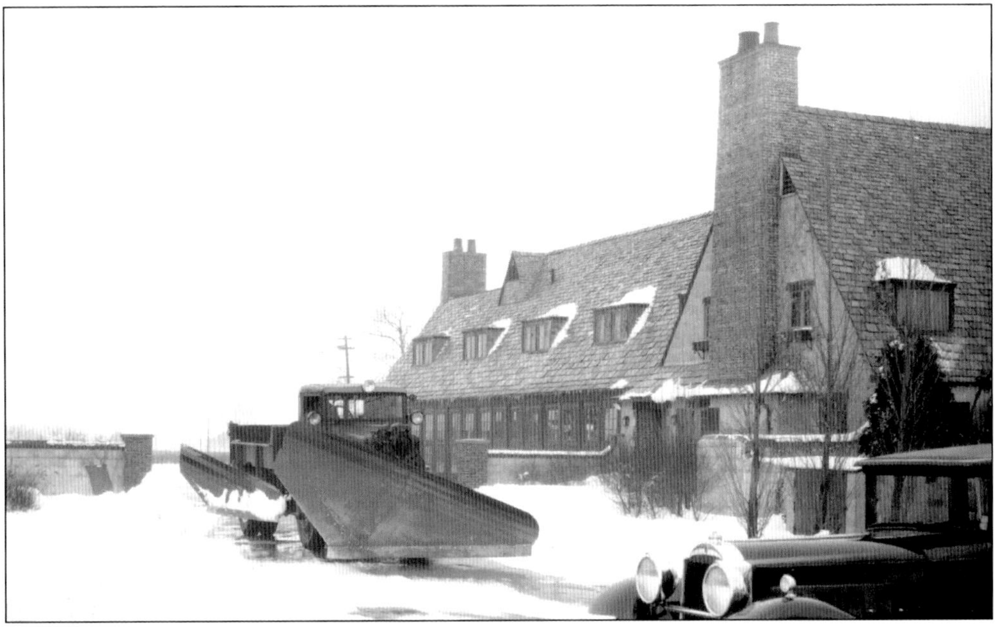

This view from March 1931 shows a stately 1931 Packard while a snowplow clears the roadways for test-driving, which continued year-round. Automotive historians believe Packard's move to medium-priced cars with the 110- and 120-Series models introduced in the mid-1930s ultimately damaged the marque's reputation as a luxury brand, and the Packard nameplate finally lost sales leadership to Cadillac in 1950. (N.)

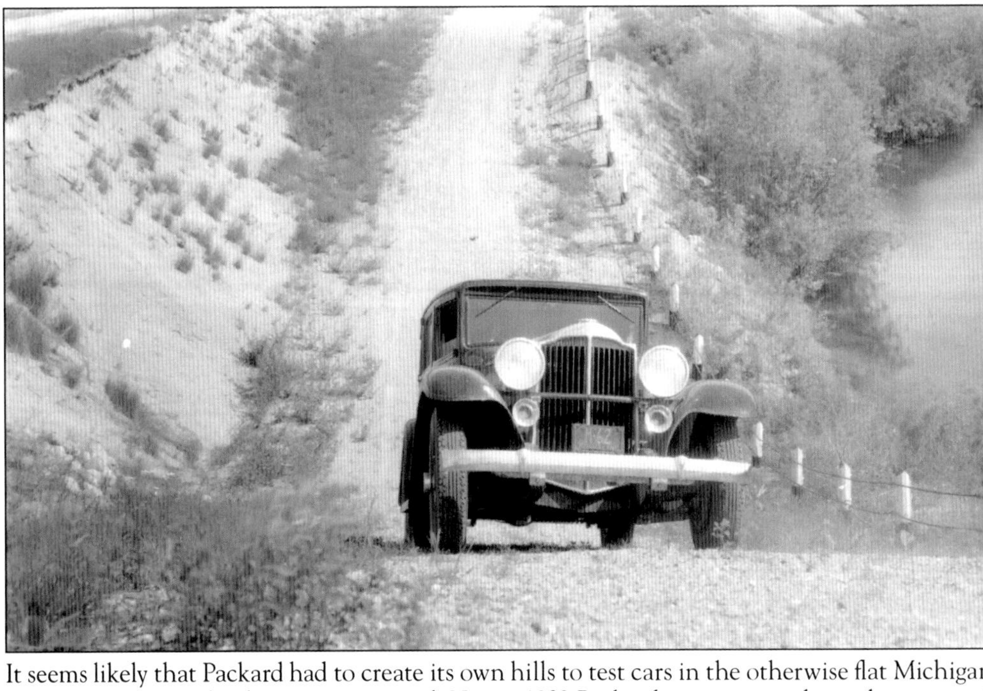

It seems likely that Packard had to create its own hills to test cars in the otherwise flat Michigan farmland it bought for the proving ground. Here a 1932 Packard prototype is shown being tested over a gravel road that ran up and down alongside the high-speed oval to the left. Packard was the only stand-alone luxury carmaker to survive the Depression. (N.)

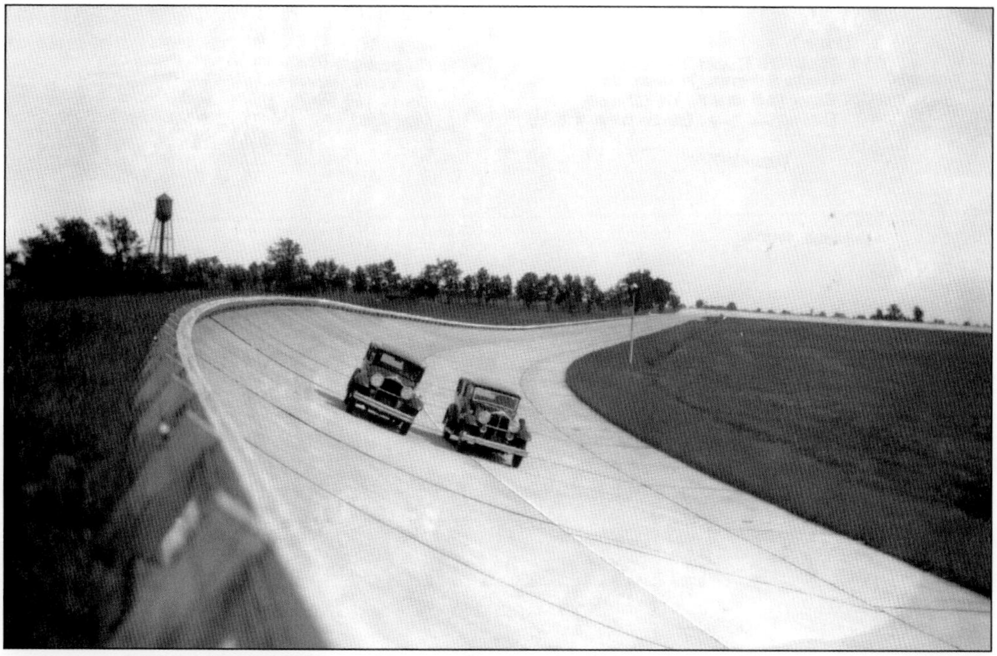

In this mid-1931 photograph, a 1931 production Packard and a 1932 prototype are seen rounding the curve at the northeast corner of the high-speed oval track. The speedway now was approximately four lanes wide, up from only two shown in a 1927 photograph taken at the same or a similar location when the track was still under construction (see page 51). (N.)

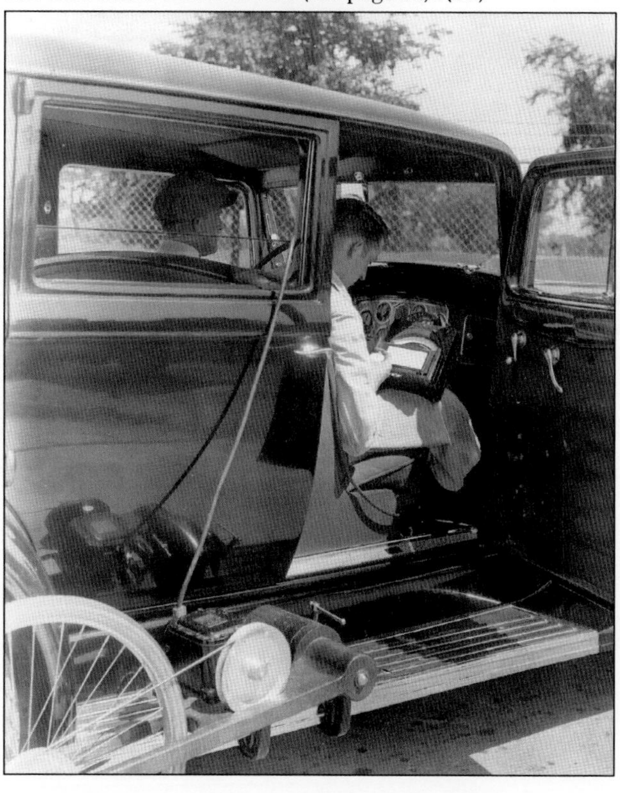

Here a fifth wheel apparatus for accurately measuring speed and distance is shown attached to the right rear wheel of a 1934 Packard prototype under test at the company's proving ground. An engineer checks out the recording instrumentation, while the driver prepares to follow instructions. Industry competitors readily shared information on new test equipment at meetings of the Society of Automotive Engineers. (N.)

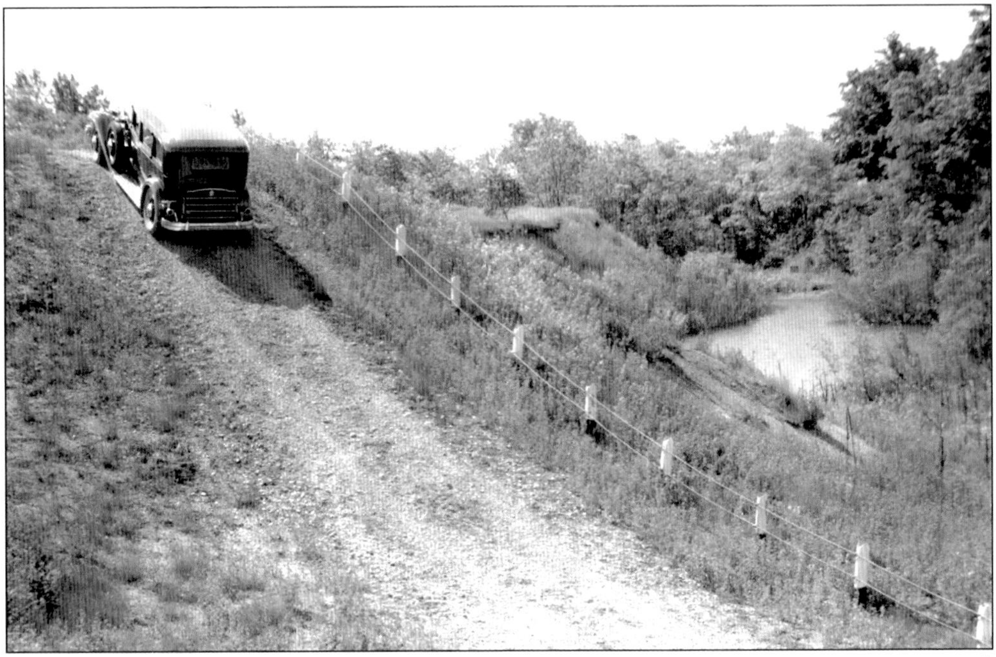

This hill, probably man-made in the otherwise flat former farmland at Packard's proving ground, was known as the roller coaster because of its rapid rise on one side and descent on the other. In the 1930s, Packard typically put its prototypes and selected production models pulled from the factory line through 25,000-mile durability tests over all types of roads at the test track. (N.)

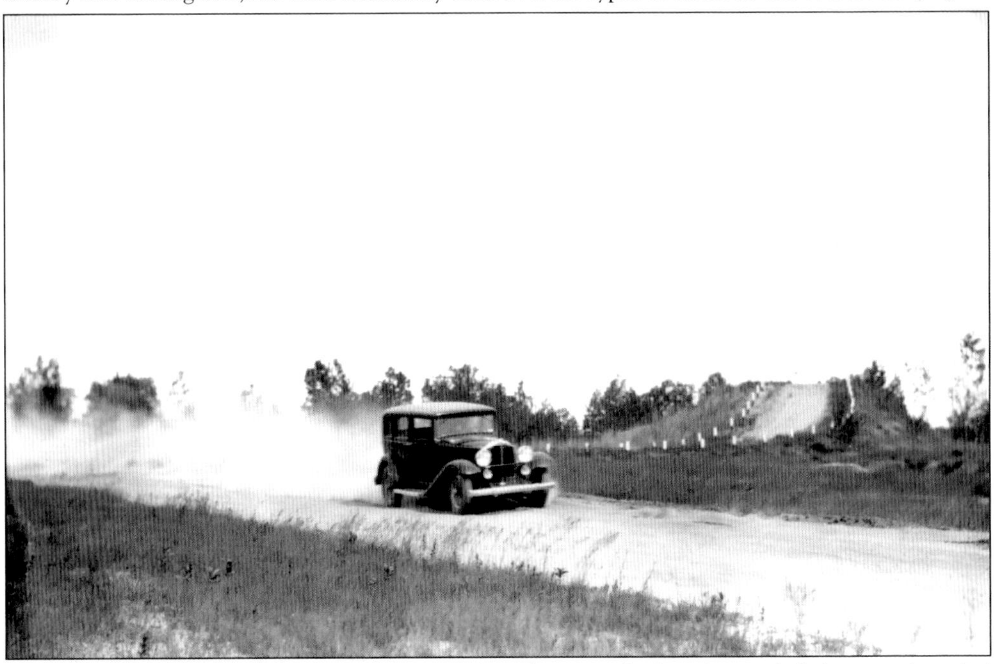

Here the 1932 Packard prototype shown in other photographs has descended the gravel-roaded hill. Packard had to compress its testing into the relatively small 500-acre area, much smaller than the GM proving ground's original 1,300 acres. But Packard was concerned with only one car line, while GM had to test eight brands plus trucks. (N.)

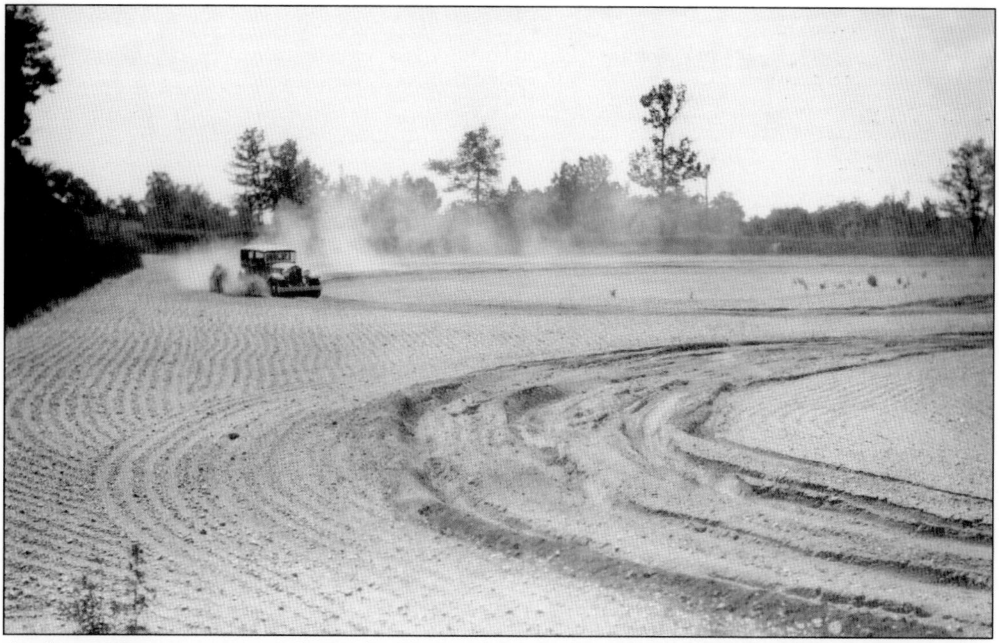

At the southwest corner of the Packard proving ground property, near the hill described on the opposite page, the company installed what a 1935 brochure described as a "Sahara-like" giant sand trap. Here cars were tested for handling, braking, traction, and body sealing, as seen in this photograph of a prototype 1932 model Packard. (N.)

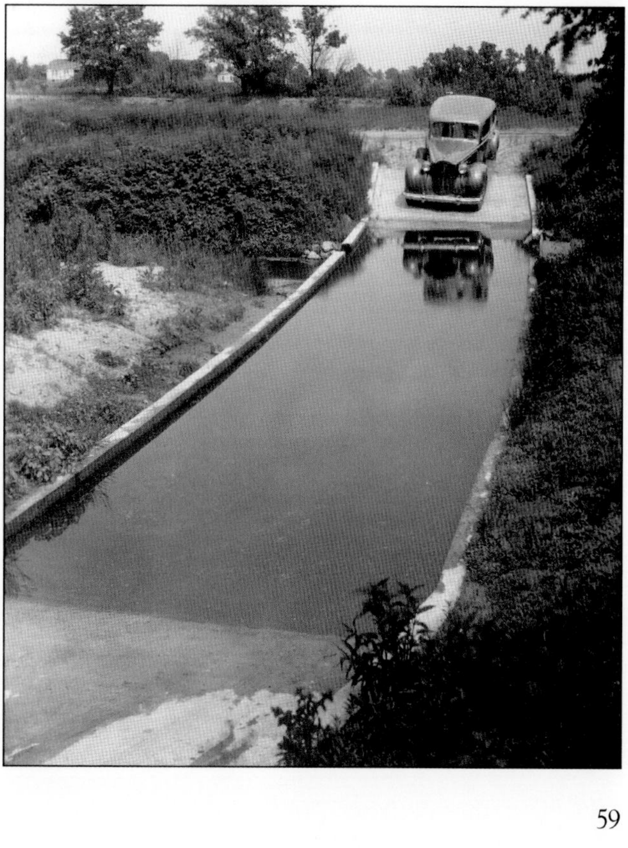

Packard's water test pit was located at the opposite side of the high-speed oval from the sand trap at the northeast corner of the test track. In this photograph, a 1938 Packard prototype is preparing to "take its bath," which tested for wet brake fade, body integrity, and ability to keep the engine running after water has been splashed over it. (N.)

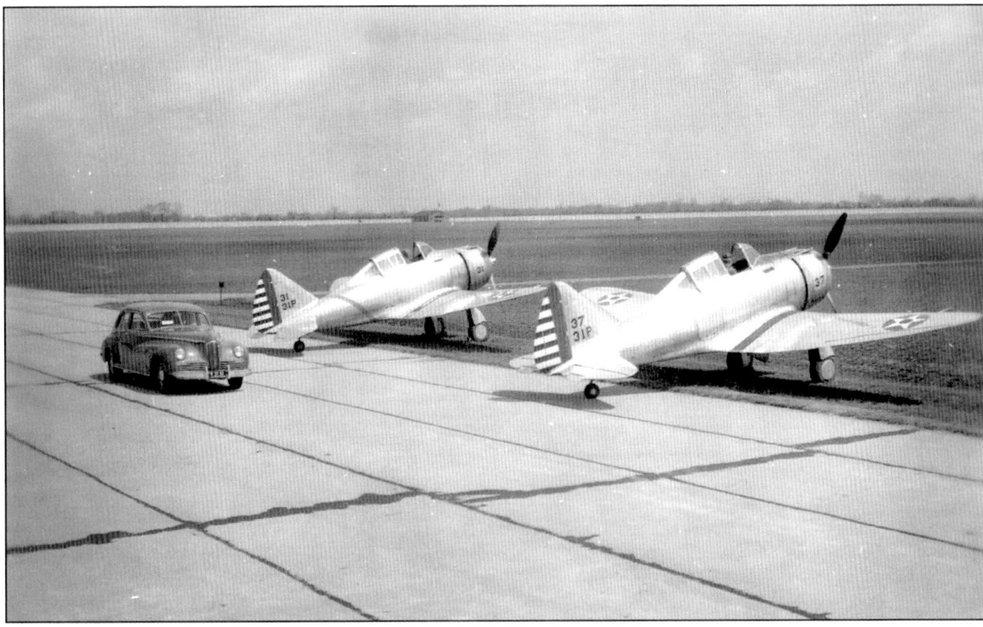

World War II brought big changes to the automobile industry, which virtually overnight became the "Arsenal of Democracy." The industry's test tracks, only three in number in 1942, were pressed into service testing military vehicles. This shows a 1941 Packard Clipper on the high-speed track with two Republic P-41/43 fighter planes from nearby U.S. Army Air Corps's Selfridge Field. There was no explanation for the circumstances of the photograph. (N.)

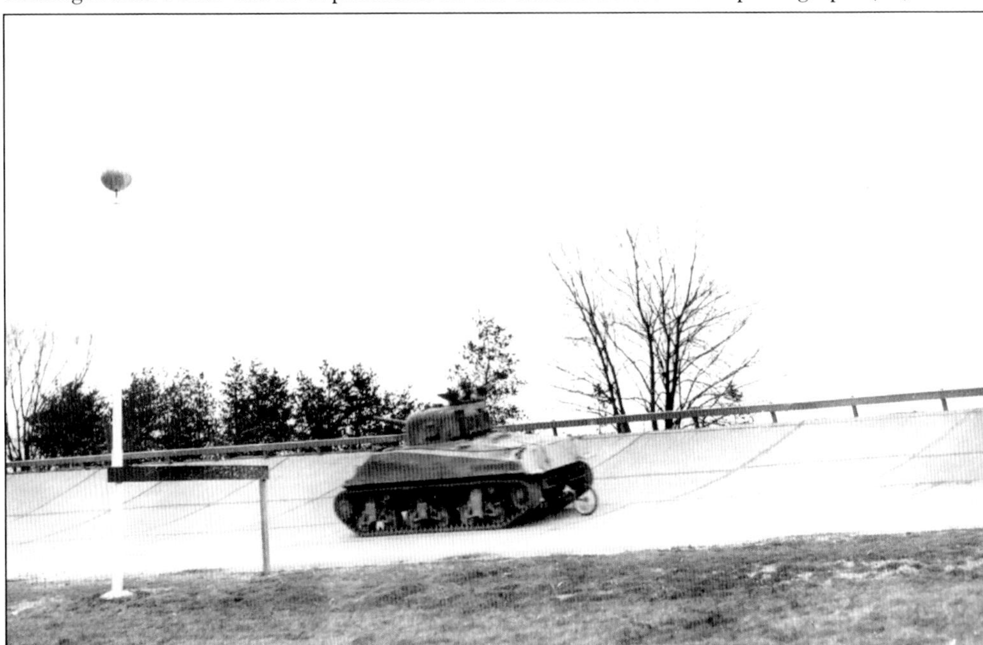

During the war, Chrysler Corporation, lacking its own test track, rented the Packard Proving Ground to test the Sherman M4 medium tanks it was building at the Detroit Arsenal tank plant in the southwest part of the same county. Here an M4 is shown circling the high-speed oval with a fifth wheel on the rear to record speed and fuel economy. (N.)

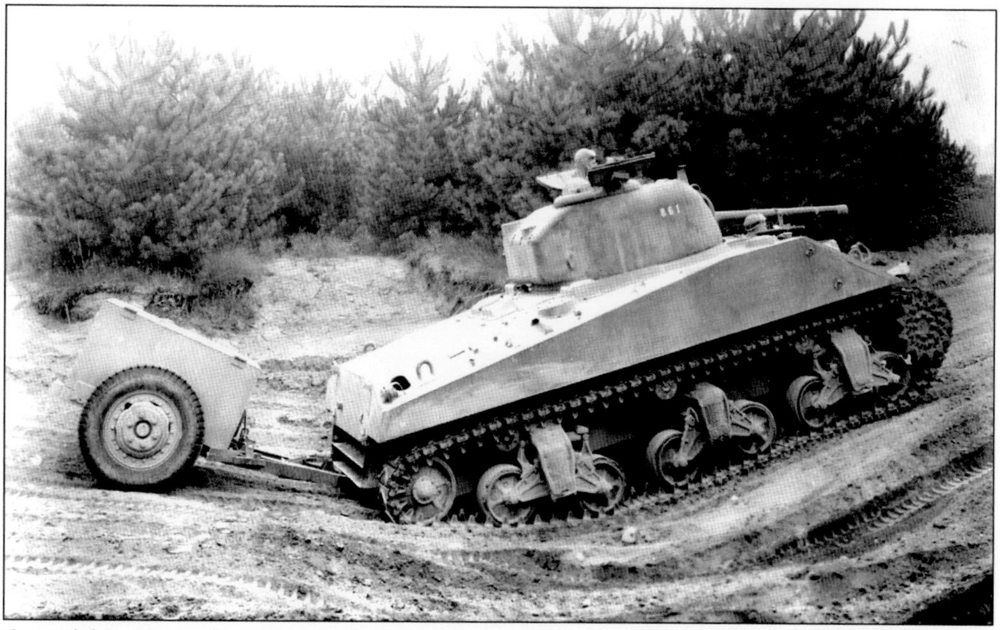

One of the tests performed with the M4 tanks at the Packard Proving Ground was evaluation of auxiliary equipment, such as this trailer. The hitch appears to be rubbing against the back of the tank as it climbs a hill. Chrysler erected its own garage at the Utica facility for its tank-testing work. Packard's war production was largely devoted to Merlin aircraft engines and Packard engines for PT boats. (N.)

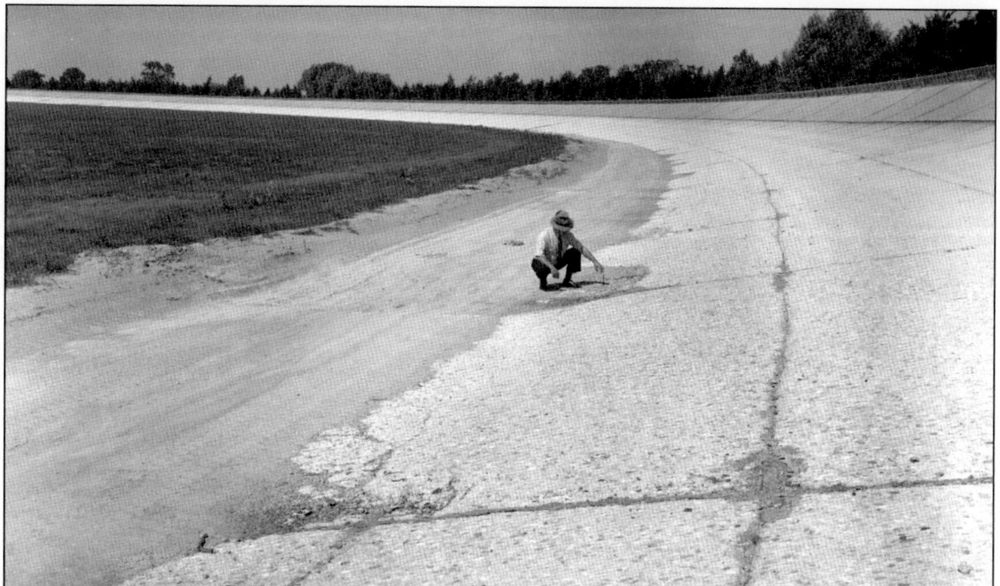

At the end of World War II, Packard found that the concrete surface of its treasured high-speed oval had been severely pockmarked by testing of the 30 ton, steel-tracked tanks. Here a technician is shown examining the damage. On the other hand, Packard learned that America's two five-star generals, Dwight D. Eisenhower and Douglas McArthur, had preferred Packards as their chauffeur-driven limousines. (N.)

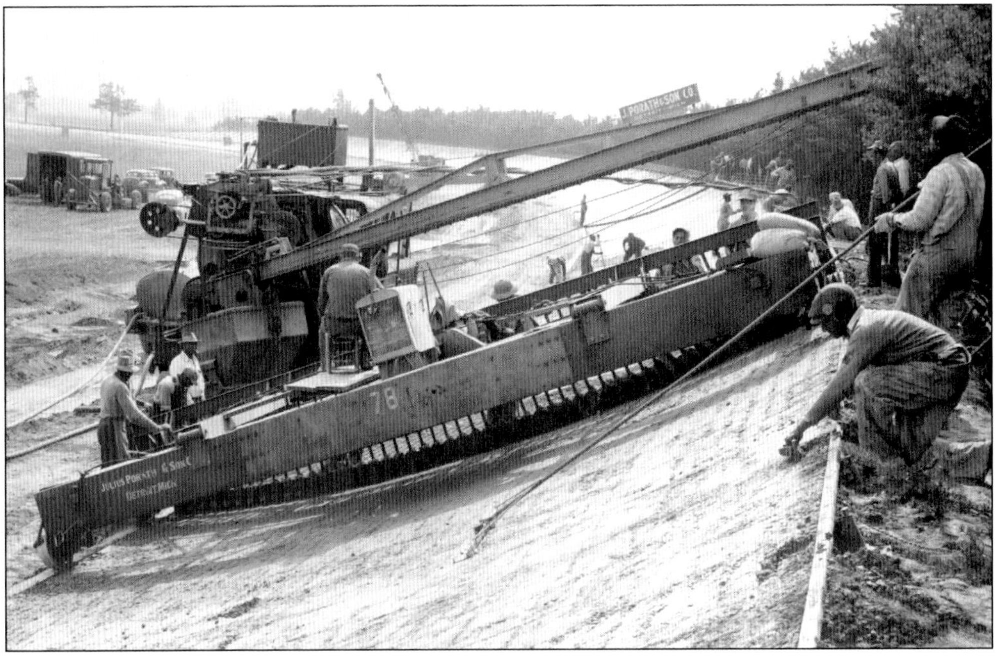

Before it could put the high-speed track back in service in 1946, Packard had to resurface the concrete oval, akin to building it some 20 years before. The difference was the smaller number of men required to perform the work, presumably because they had greater knowledge in road building and better equipment. Compare this photograph to that on page 50. (N.)

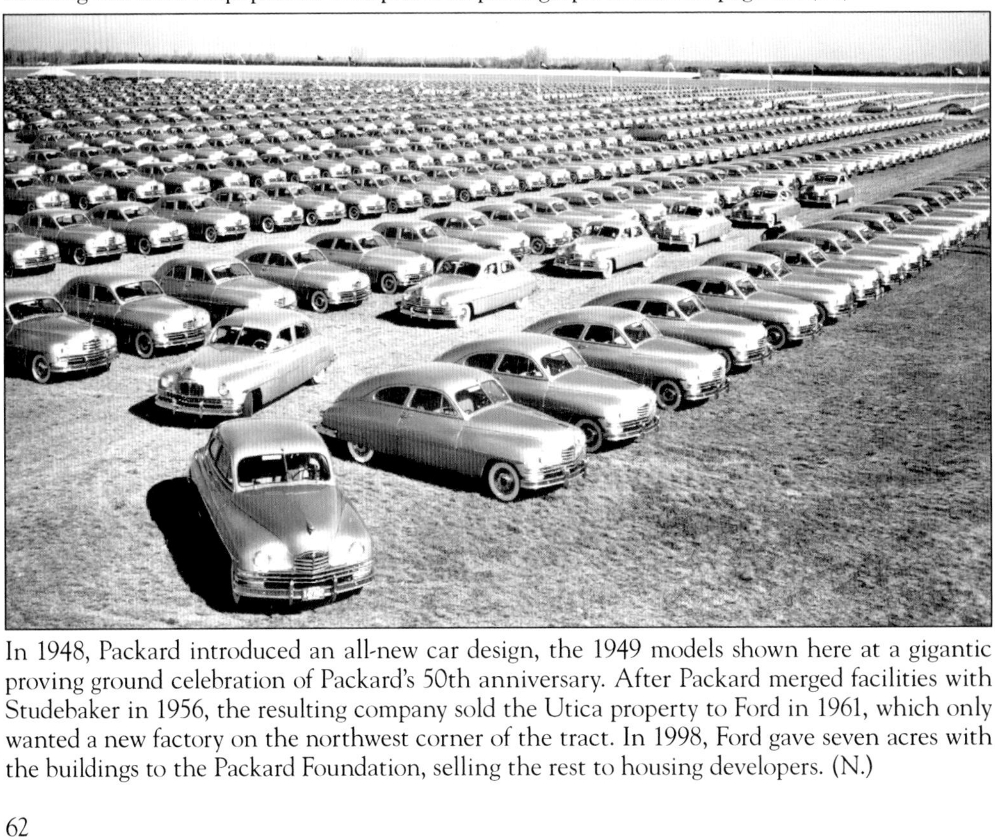

In 1948, Packard introduced an all-new car design, the 1949 models shown here at a gigantic proving ground celebration of Packard's 50th anniversary. After Packard merged facilities with Studebaker in 1956, the resulting company sold the Utica property to Ford in 1961, which only wanted a new factory on the northwest corner of the tract. In 1998, Ford gave seven acres with the buildings to the Packard Foundation, selling the rest to housing developers. (N.)

Six

General Motors from 1930 to 2009

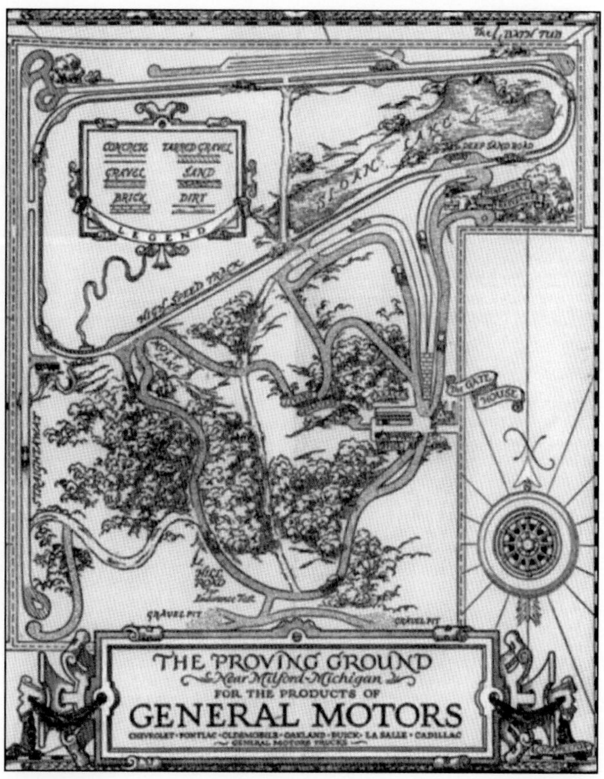

This map of GM's proving ground, dated June 1, 1928, shows many changes in less than four years from that shown on page 31. Through land acquisitions, GM has squared off the property to the southwest and along the west and northern edges and put in many additional test roads and other facilities. Unlike the Packard Proving Ground, GM's high-speed track is kidney-shaped rather than oval like a racetrack. (G.)

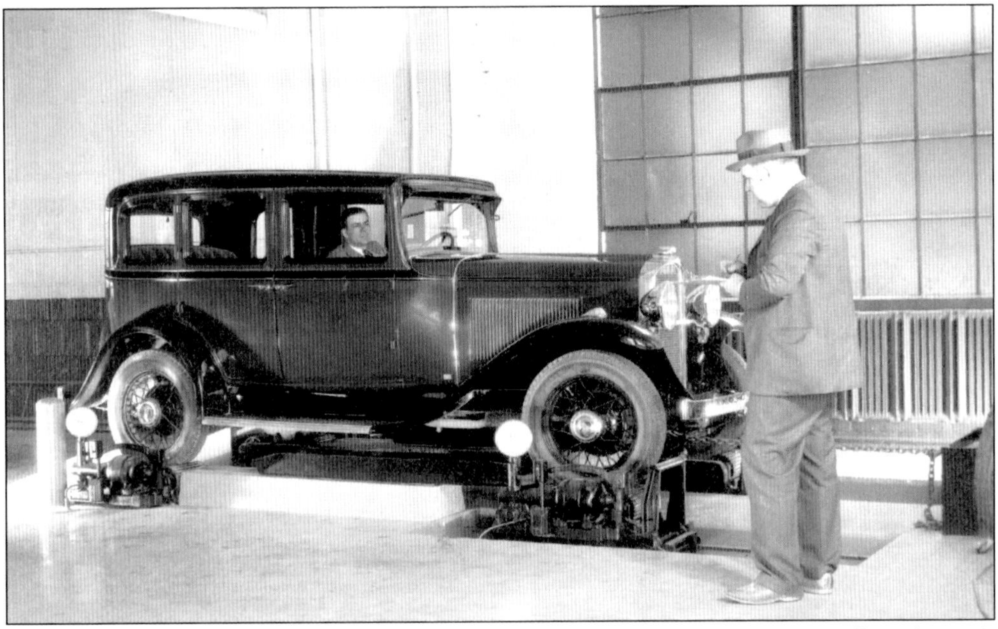

The chassis roll dynamometer was a major development in test equipment. It allowed a car's wheels to turn under power or be turned by the rolls beneath the wheels without the vehicle having to be driven over roads, allowing engineers to monitor closely what was going on in an observable and repeatable manner. The car shown here on a brake dynamometer test is a 1931 Pontiac. (G.)

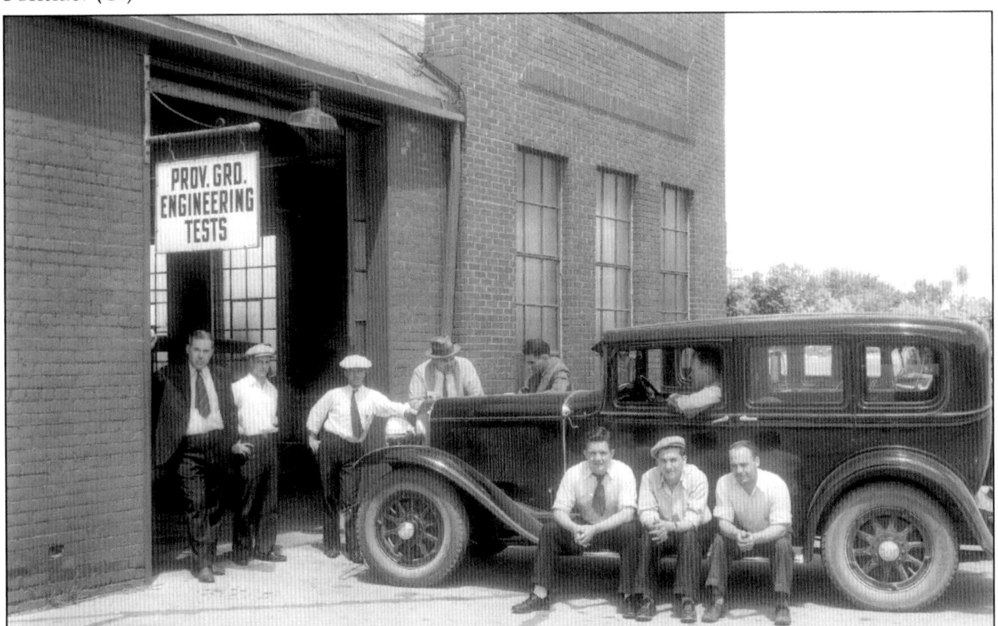

Outside one of the garages at GM's proving ground, a group of engineers pose during a break from their test routines with a 1931 Buick. GM established Flint's General Motors Institute (now Kettering University) in 1919 to train young men through co-op programs in the new profession of automotive engineering, awarding its first degrees in 1923. (G.)

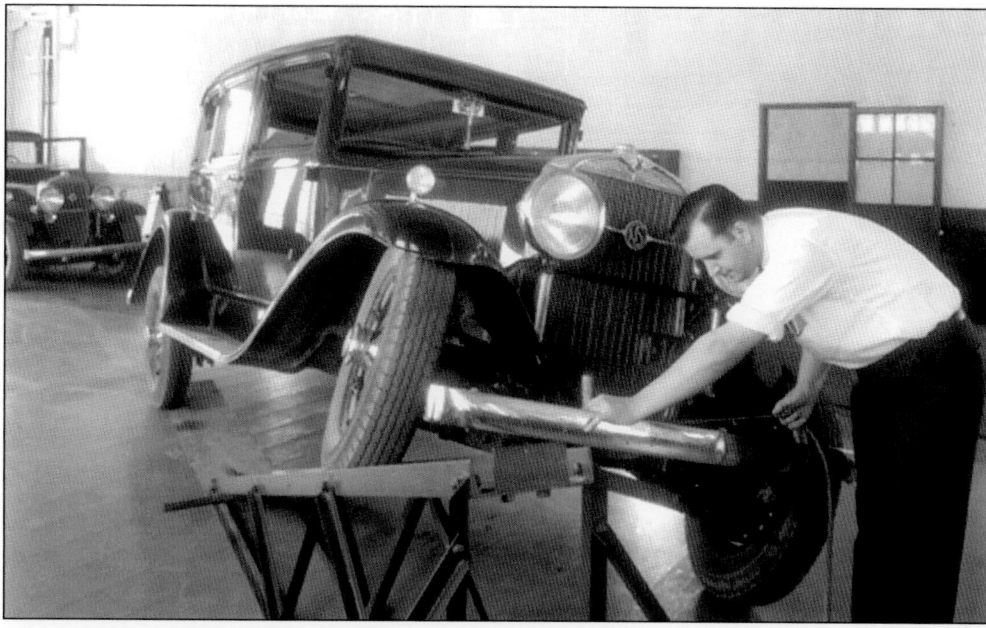

Here a 1931 La Salle is shown undergoing a static bending test in one of the garages at the proving ground. This was a routine test in automotive development, used for many subsequent decades to measure the strength and flexibility of a vehicle's body and frame structure (see page 28). Today computer modeling performs such tests. (G.)

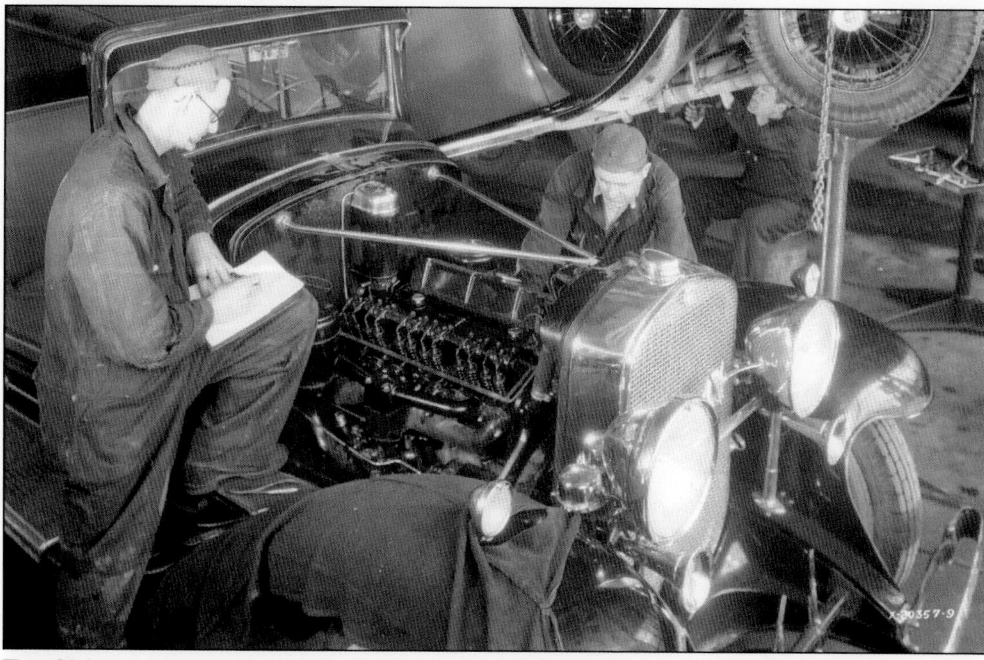

Two GM proving ground mechanics are shown working on the new V-12 engine of a 1931 Cadillac. The V-12 engine models fitted between the regular V-8 and the massive V-16 introduced in 1930. At $3,795 for a standard sedan, Cadillac V-12s with 140-inch wheelbases sold for roughly $1,000 more than the 134-inch-wheelbase V-8s but generally $2,000 less than the 148-inch-wheelbase V-16s. The V-12 was discontinued after the 1936 model year. (G.)

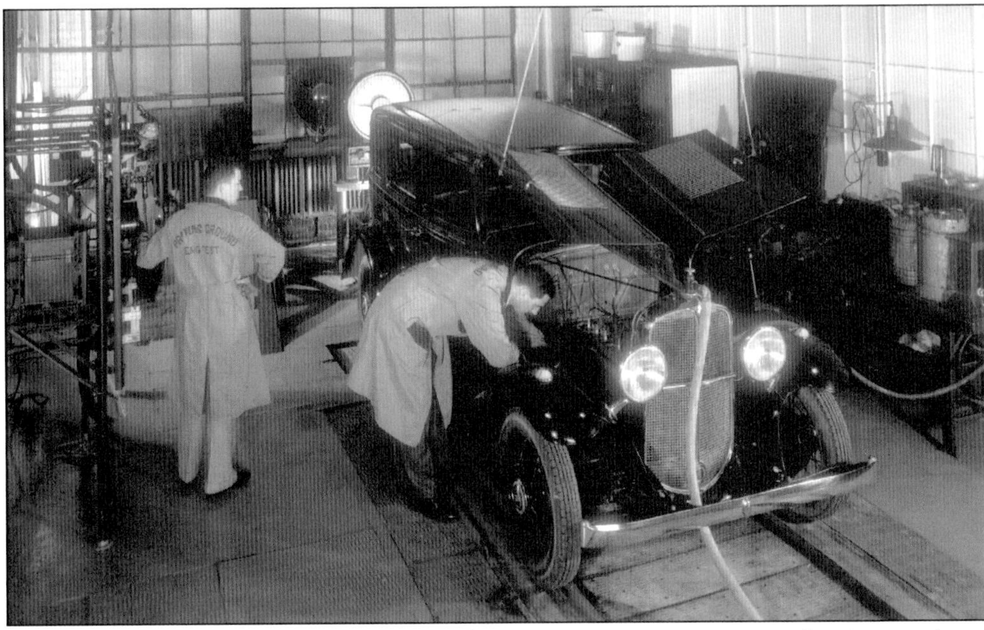

Elsewhere in the expansive proving ground engineering garages, two mechanics are shown monitoring a test of a 1931 Pontiac Fine Six Custom Sedan. The caption information with the photograph merely stated it was "in the shop," with no indication of the type of test the car was undergoing. Note the scales at the rear and the hose from the floor at the front of the car to the engine compartment. (G.)

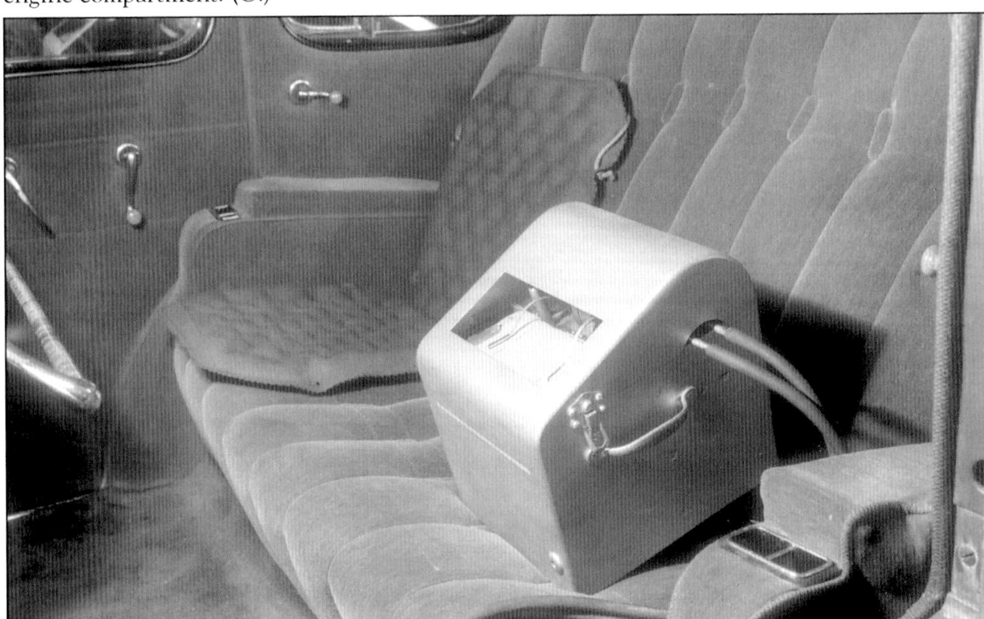

Test instrumentation has advanced considerably in appearance and presumably function from the earliest days at the proving ground, as can be seen in this mid-1930s photograph. Still it seems strange for instrumentation to be sitting unattached in the back seat of what is described as a "1936 Fisher Body 4-door sedan." The padded auxiliary cushion apparently was there for the comfort of the technician monitoring the measuring instrument. (G.)

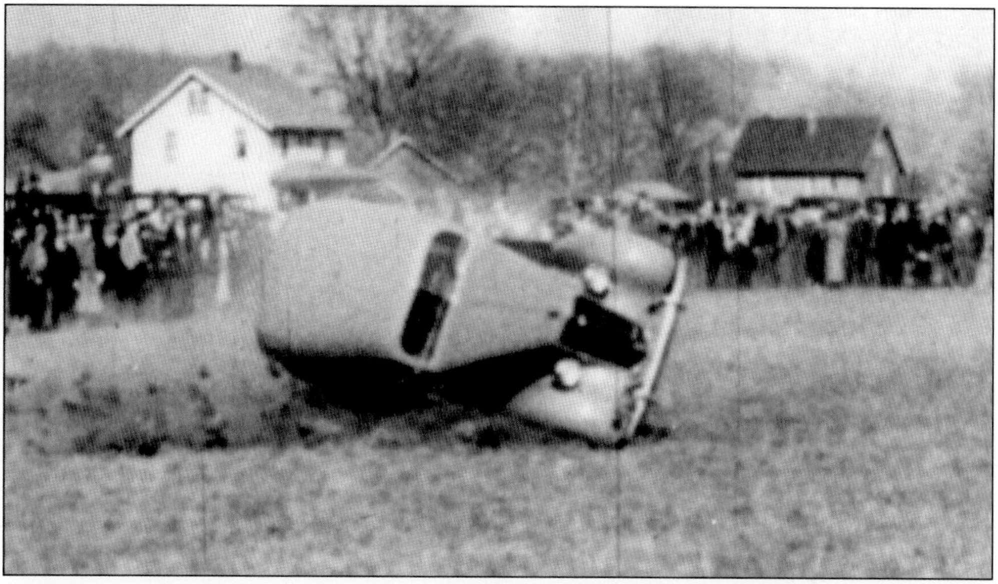

Automotive safety testing had its beginnings in the mid-1930s. In this photograph, possibly extracted from a motion picture film, a 1936 Chevrolet Master Deluxe sedan is induced into a rollover sequence in a staged demonstration before dozens of onlookers. The photograph had no explanation with it as to the circumstances of the test or the location. (N.)

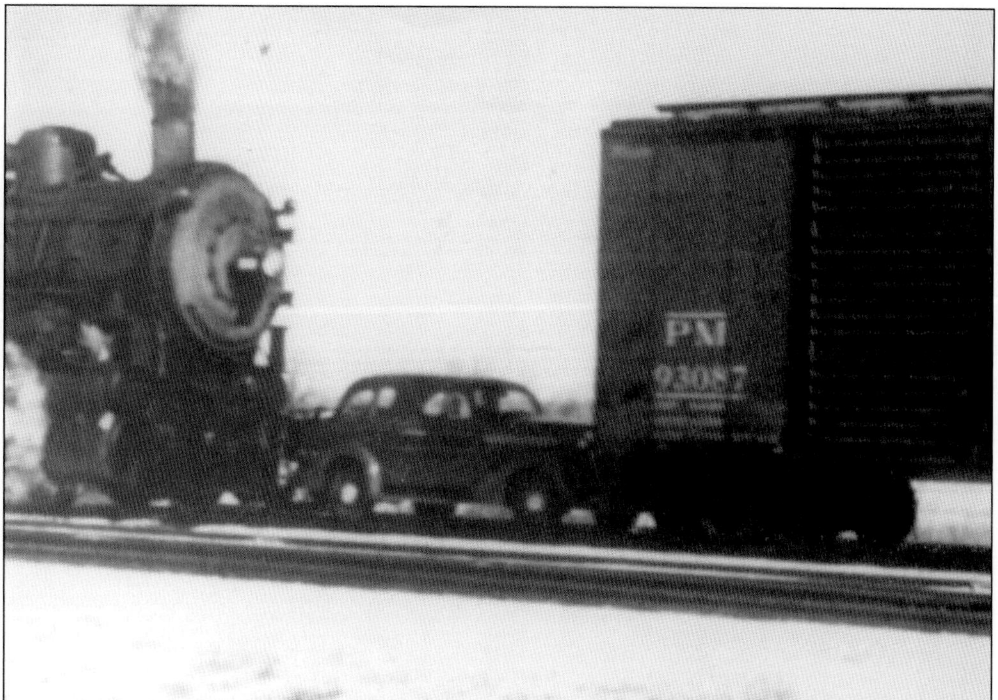

It is unclear what this photograph of a 1938 Chevrolet being squeezed between a Pere Marquette Railroad steam locomotive and a boxcar is supposed to be showing. The photograph in the National Automotive History Collection at the Detroit Public Library had no explanation as to whether this was a test or a demonstration nor of what. (N.)

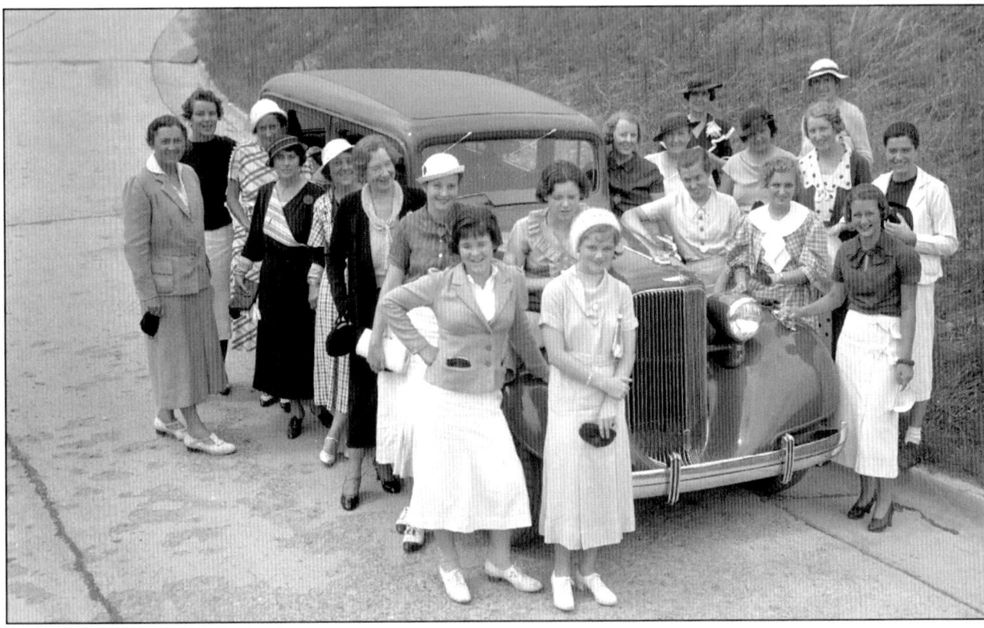

Automakers used their proving grounds for other purposes than purely product development, as seen in this photograph of comely young women posing with a 1934 Pontiac. The information with the image stated it was a "publicity shot of women and junior golfers in blindfold test." Presumably they had been induced to take a Pontiac comparison ride, hopefully judging it might be a more luxurious car than typical for its market niche. (G.)

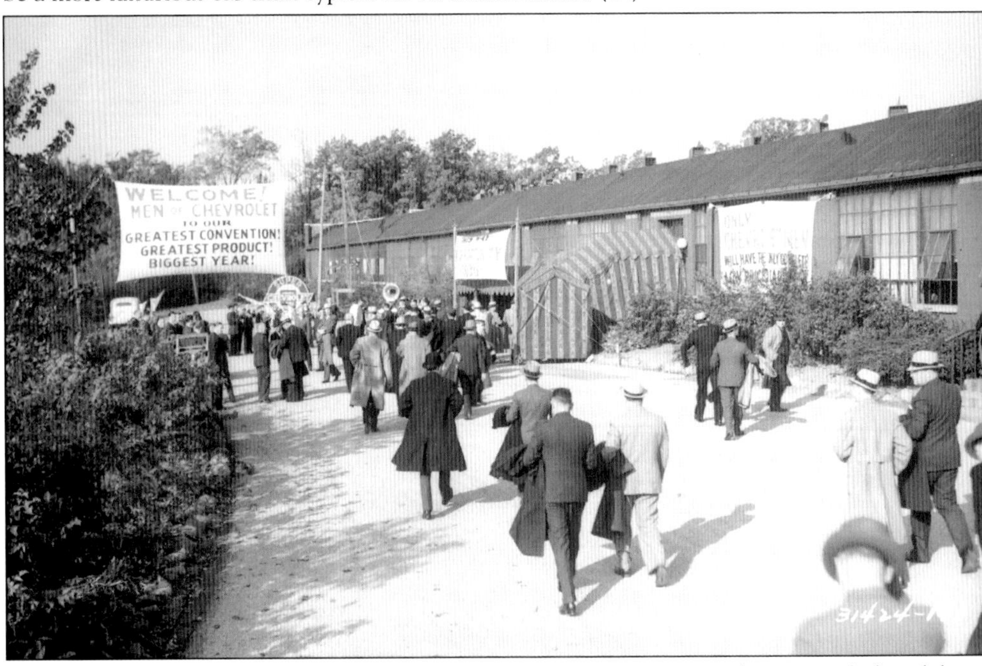

In this view, "Men of Chevrolet" are shown arriving at a proving ground garage to help celebrate at a "Greatest Convention" the "Greatest Product" and the "Biggest Year." In 1936, Chevrolet sales came to 930,250, surpassing the previous record set in 1929 of 807,300. The 1936 record was not eclipsed until 1949. (G.)

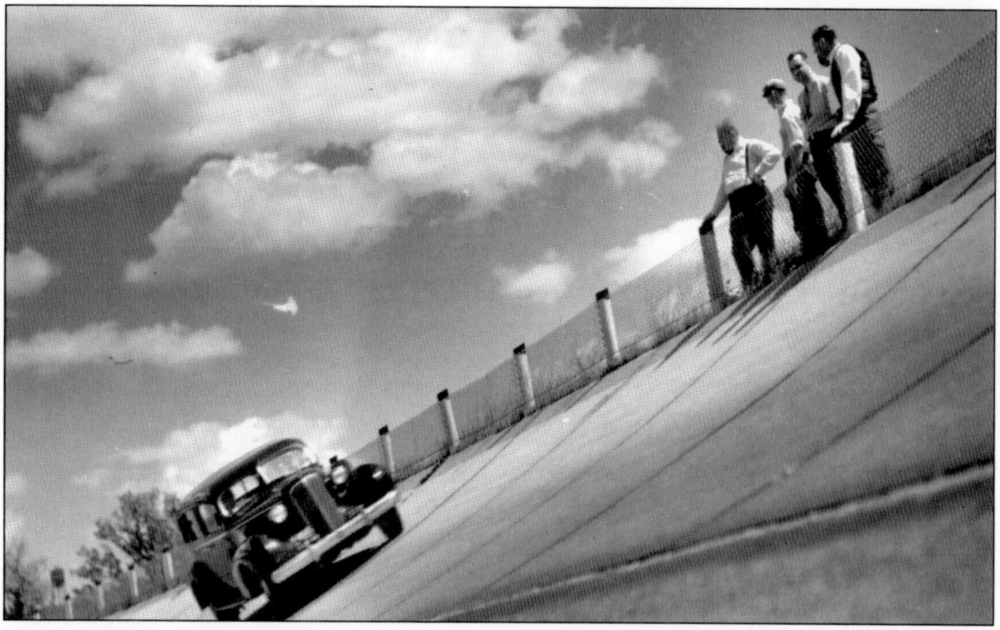

Here a 1937 Cadillac whizzes by onlookers on the proving ground's high-speed track. A low fence to protect people and inhibit animal crossing has been added from the time of earlier photographs a decade before. Today people are not allowed so close to a high-speed track, but deer continue to be a problem, attracted by the ample vegetation and easily capable of leaping even higher fences. (N.)

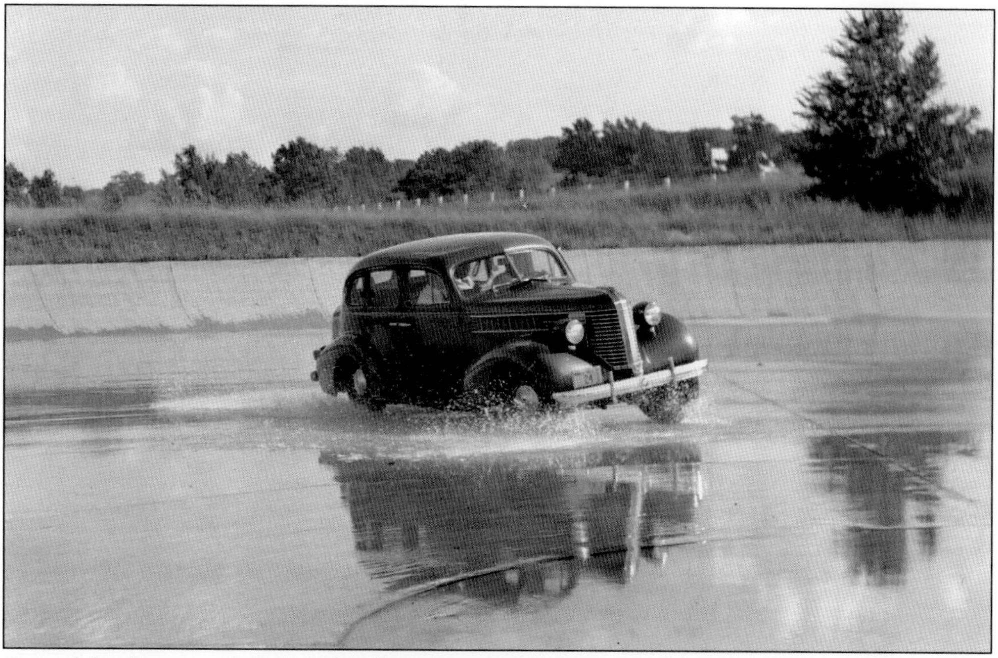

One of the features of GM's Milford Proving Ground was a large skid pad where cars could be tested in steering and handling on both dry and wet surfaces, as shown here with a 1938 Pontiac. None of the other Detroit automakers had such a facility at the time but eventually came to build them. (N.)

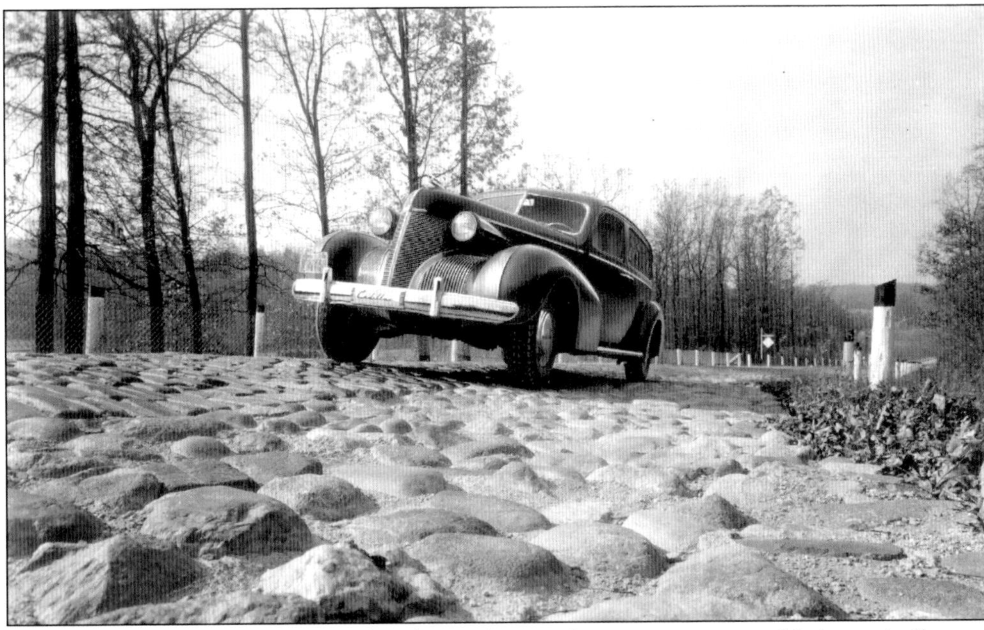

All automotive test tracks featured replicas of particular paving patterns likely to challenge a car's suspension, steering, and handling. Here a 1939 Cadillac is shown driving over a section of Belgian Block roadway at the GM Milford Proving Ground. Repeated circuits over such roadways are designed to accelerate durability testing of prototype cars and verify designs of new cars selected from assembly lines. (N.)

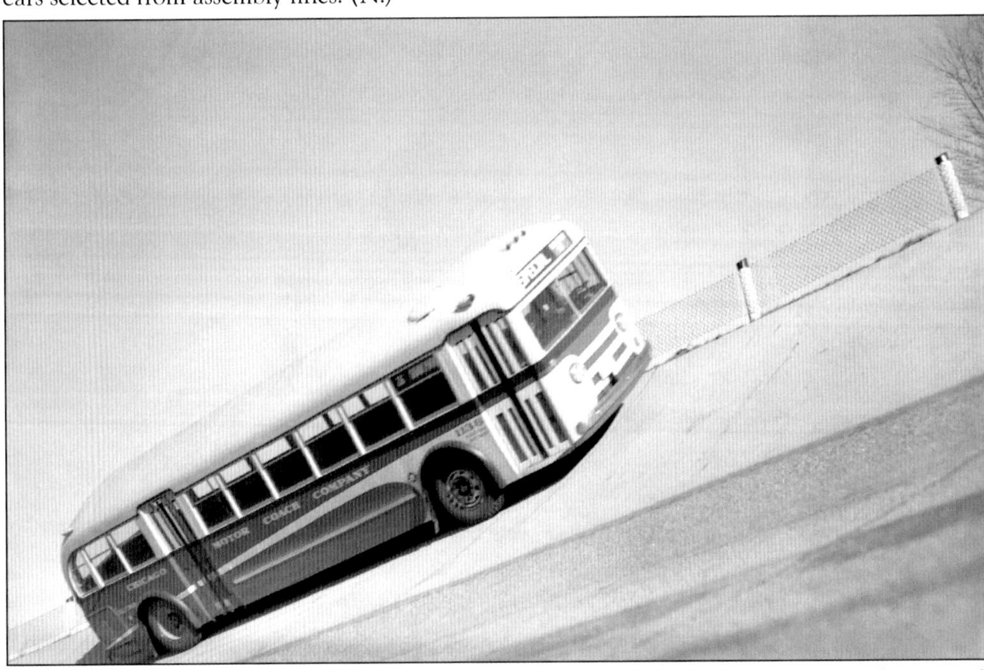

When this photograph was taken in 1940, GM was preparing to integrate the Yellow Coach Manufacturing Company of Chicago into its GMC Truck Division. Thus it began testing city transit buses, such as this one, as well as larger inter-city highway buses on the Milford Proving Ground. The merger of Yellow and GMC was completed in 1943. (G.)

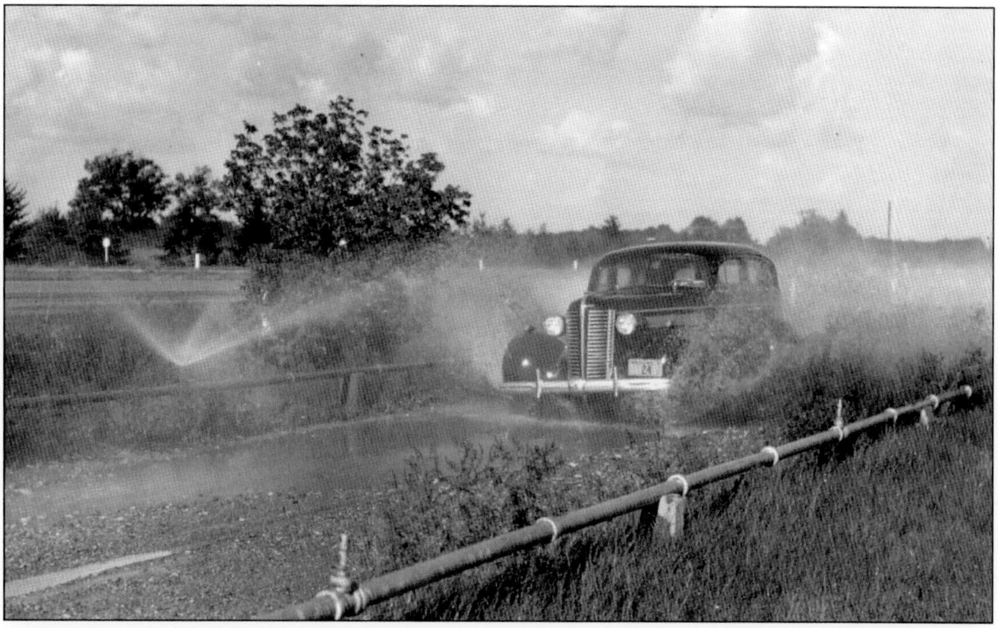

To test its imperviousness to body leaks and engine and brake reliability, this 1938 Buick was being driven through a bath of mud and water at the proving ground. Such a facility was a common test fixture at all automotive test tracks, and such tests were universal even for those companies that lacked dedicated proving grounds. In those cases, automakers had to improvise on convenient owned or leased land. (G.)

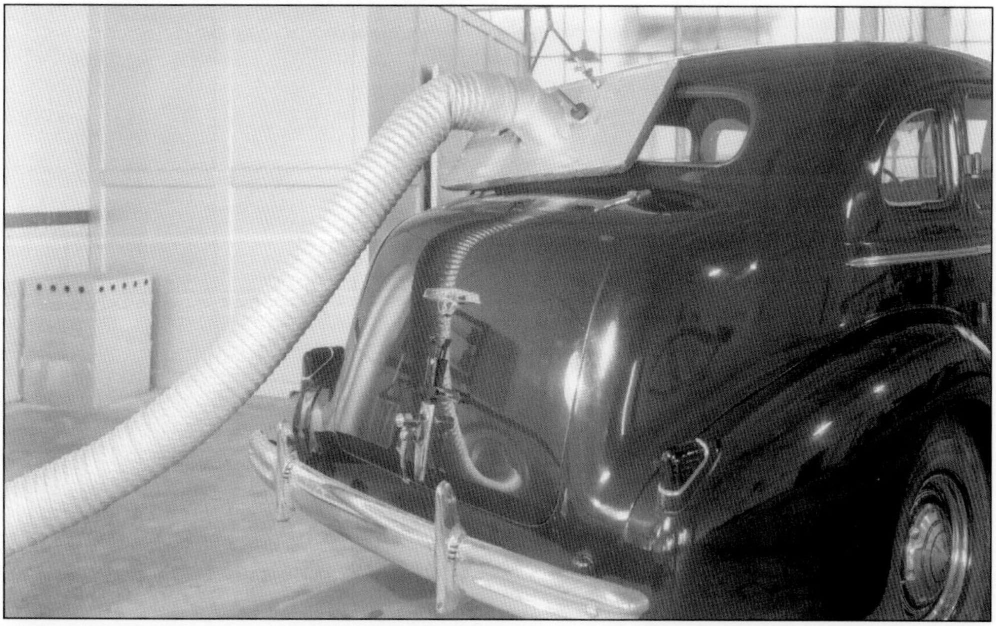

If the above test was an outside-to-inside measure of a car's body integrity, this unusual test measures the inside-to-outside body tightness. Here a large hose forces air into the sealed rear window of a 1938 Buick to find out if there are any unexpected leaks around windows, doors, brake- and clutch-pedal openings in the floorboard, and other possible portals for air to escape or water and dust to enter. (G.)

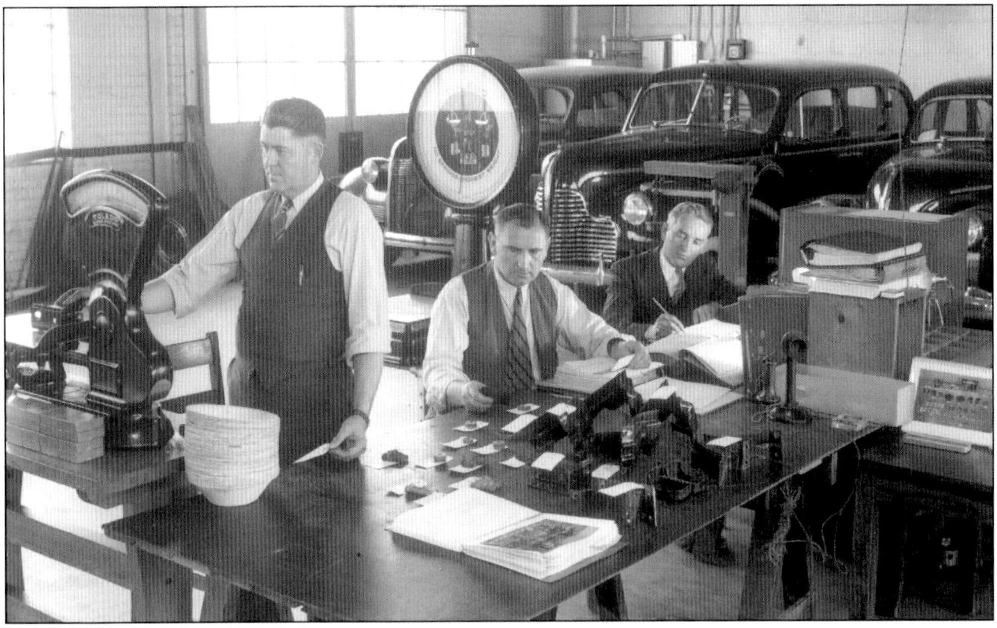

In this test laboratory, located in one of the GM proving ground garages, engineers are carefully analyzing the weight of two cars, a 1939 Chevrolet (left) and a 1940 Buick. It was important for accurate weights to be determined, first as a measure of economic manufacture and second for state motor vehicle licensing purposes. Standards set by the Society of Automotive Engineers specified how a car was to be weighed. (G.)

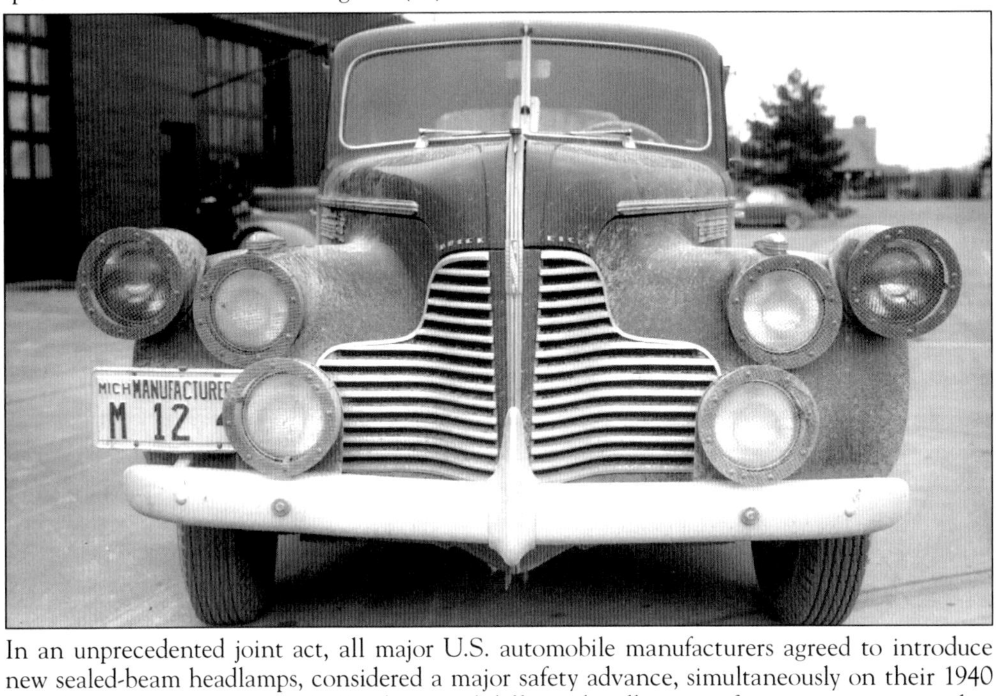

In an unprecedented joint act, all major U.S. automobile manufacturers agreed to introduce new sealed-beam headlamps, considered a major safety advance, simultaneously on their 1940 models. On this test car, a 1940 Buick, several different headlamp configurations were rigged to assess their relative advantages in night driving. Sealed beams had a much longer life and more consistent beams than the bulb lamps they replaced. (G.)

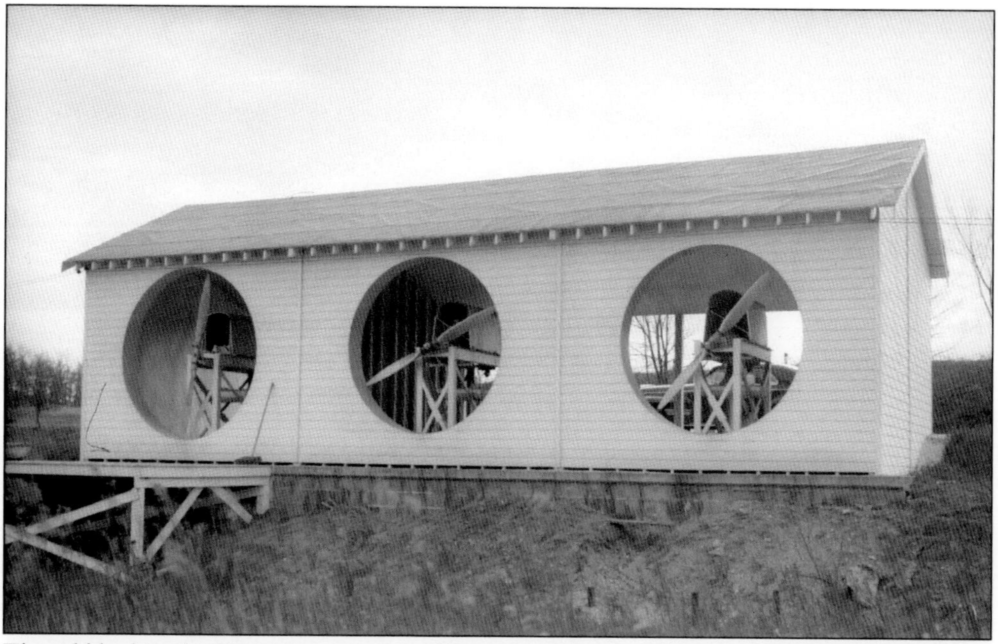

The odd-looking building above was, in effect, an outdoor wind tunnel GM built at its proving ground before World War II. Below, three airplane engines and their propellers were mounted in the shedlike building with round cutouts to control airflow. When turned on, the propellers' wash simulated winds blowing across the path of cars driven behind, such as the 1941 Pontiac seen below. Such a test was helpful in determining a car's handling in strong winds, especially gusting crosswinds. In this way, consistency and repeatability of wind force could be obtained, which was otherwise impossible in nature. (G.)

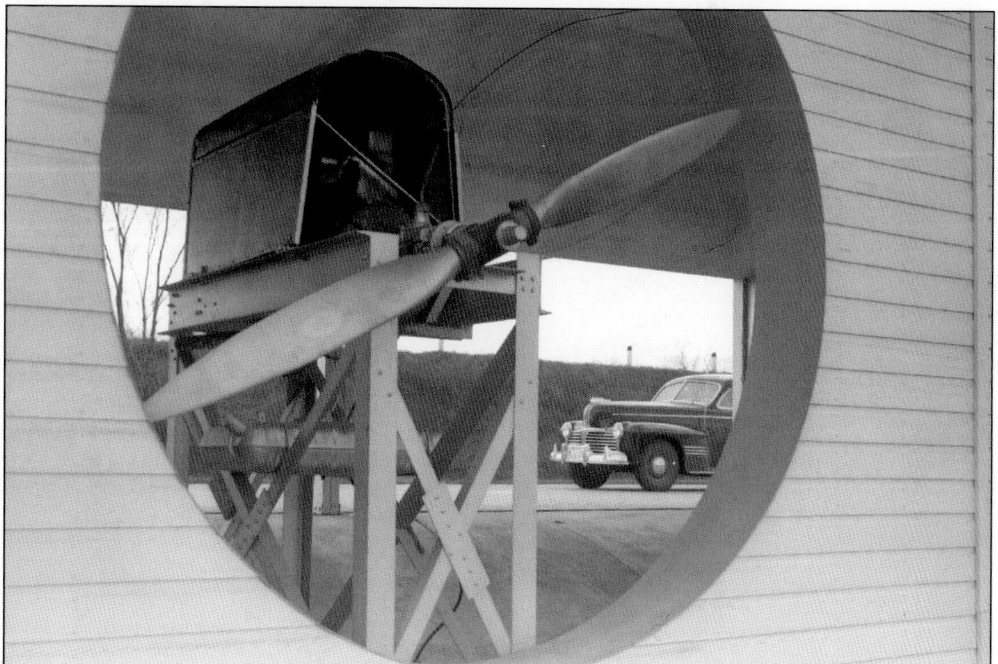

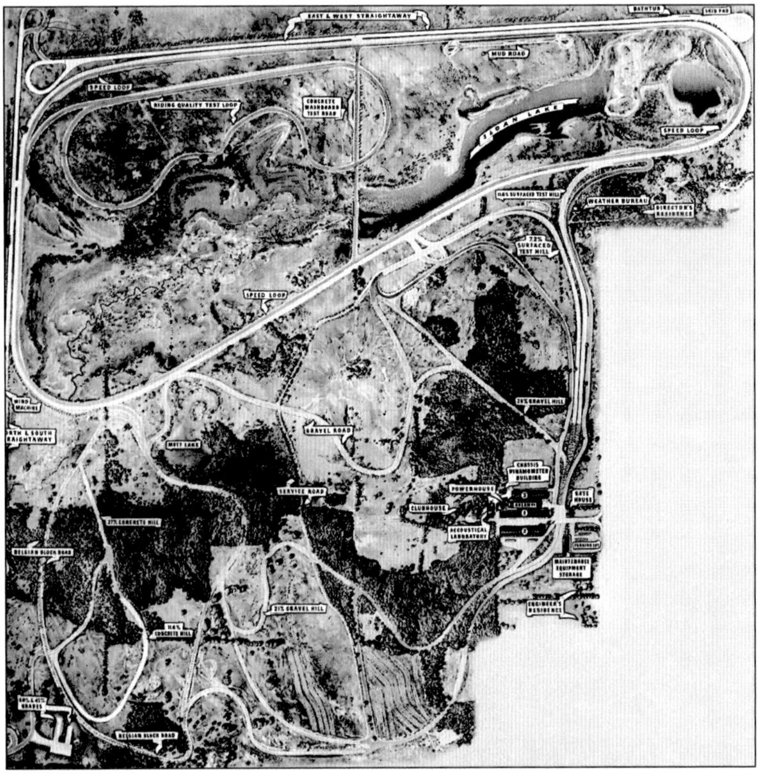

This diagrammatic map of GM's proving ground, created in 1941, shows many changes from the previous map from 1928 (see page 63). The infield of the high-speed track has been partly filled in with test roads, many roadways have been added in the southwestern corner of the property, and additional buildings are apparent near the eastern entrance. (G.)

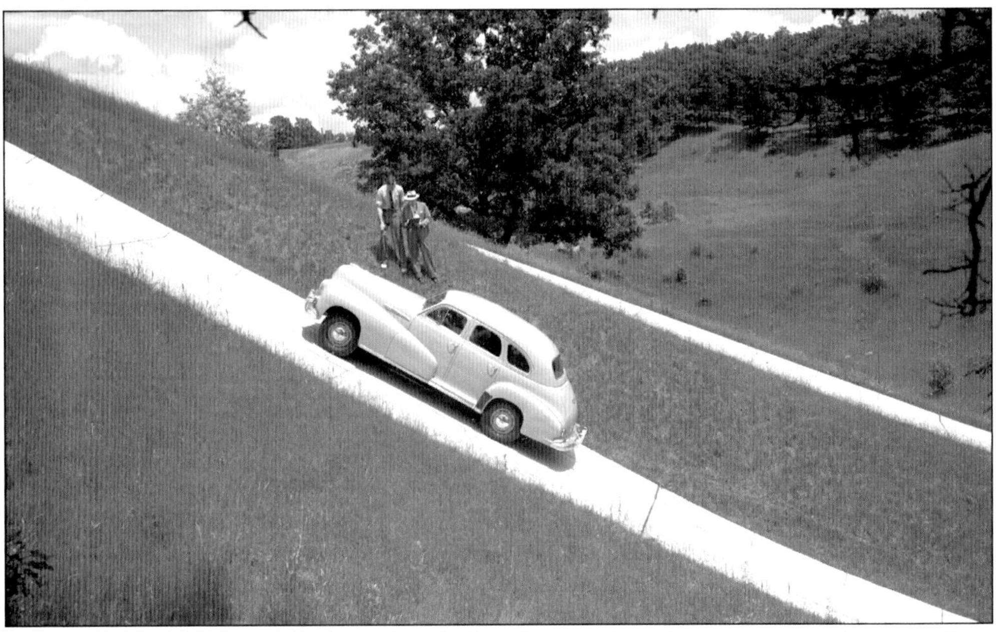

In this photograph, one of the last taken before the complete changeover to military products for World War II, a 1942 Oldsmobile is shown climbing one of the steepest paved roads in the complex. Oldsmobile had introduced the Hydra-Matic two-pedal automatic transmission just two model years earlier, and one of the most serious challenges for such a new development was its performance on such hills. (G.)

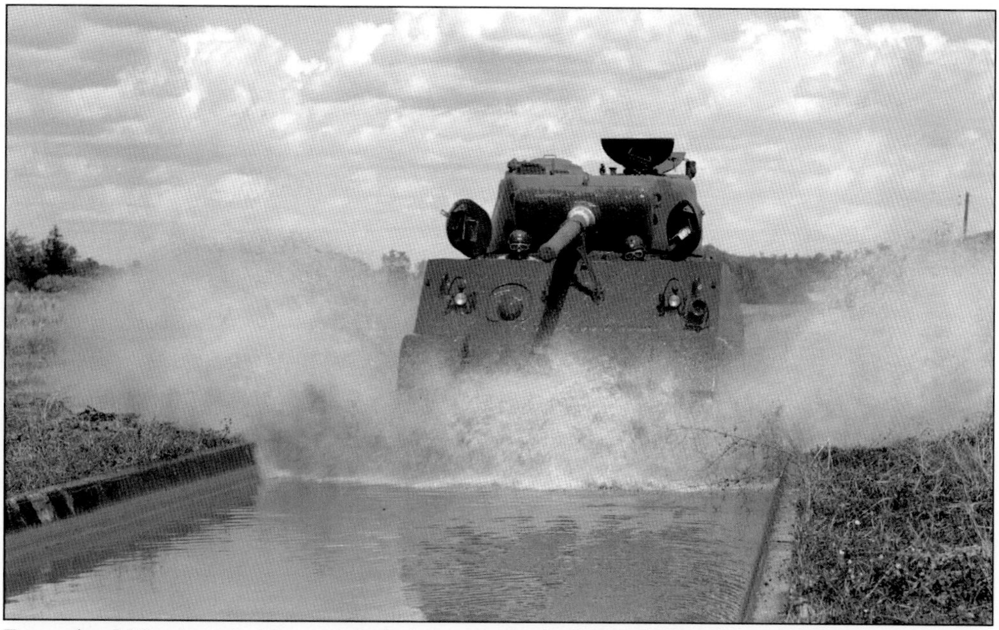

Even the U.S. Army's 15-ton M2 light tank, built by Cadillac during World War II, was tested through the proving ground's bathtub, as shown in this 1944 photograph. GM's biggest contribution to the Allied war effort, however, may have been its president William S. Knudsen, who resigned to become America's dollar-a-year defense production chief in mid-1940, managing the complex job of coordinating military production by all industry. (G.)

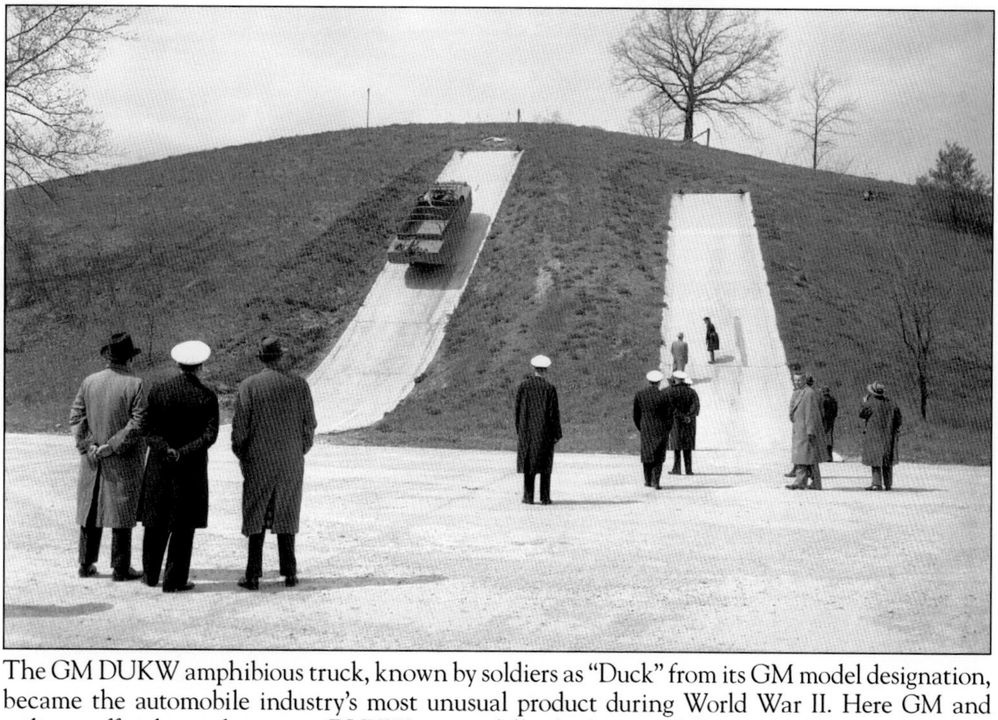

The GM DUKW amphibious truck, known by soldiers as "Duck" from its GM model designation, became the automobile industry's most unusual product during World War II. Here GM and military officials watch as a test DUKW successfully climbs one of the steep hills at Milford. The vehicle aided in Pacific island invasions and river crossings in Europe. (G.)

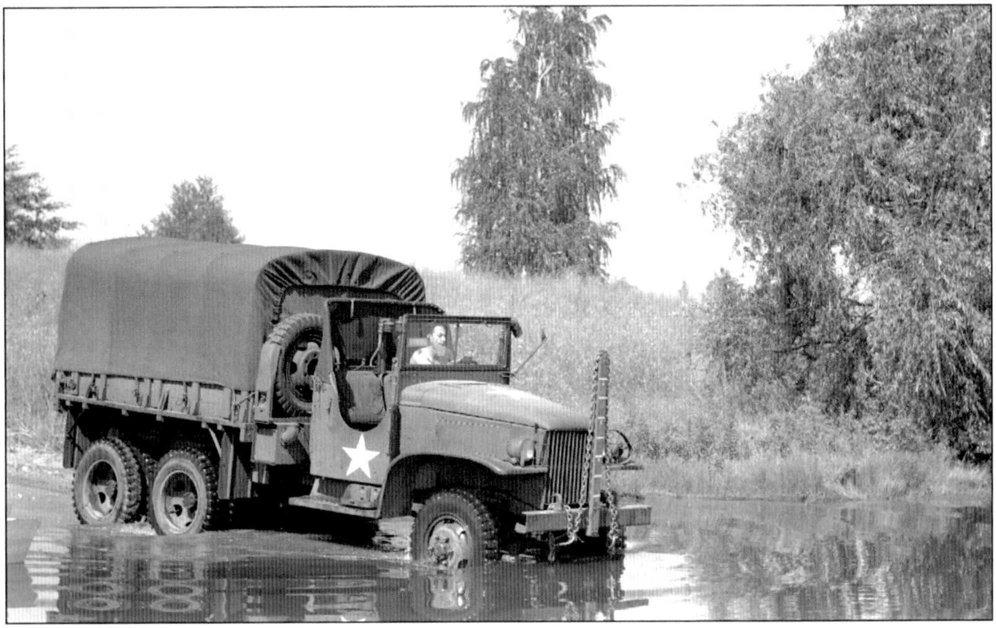

In this photograph, a white-shirted GM engineer drives a U.S. Army GMC Model CCKW six-by-six, two-and-a-half-ton truck into a water test at the proving ground. Passing this test was crucial for military vehicles in order to cope with battlefield conditions. Beginning in 1939, GM produced nearly 563,000 such trucks for the military during the war, forming the basis for supplying rapidly advancing troops, especially in the European theater. (G.)

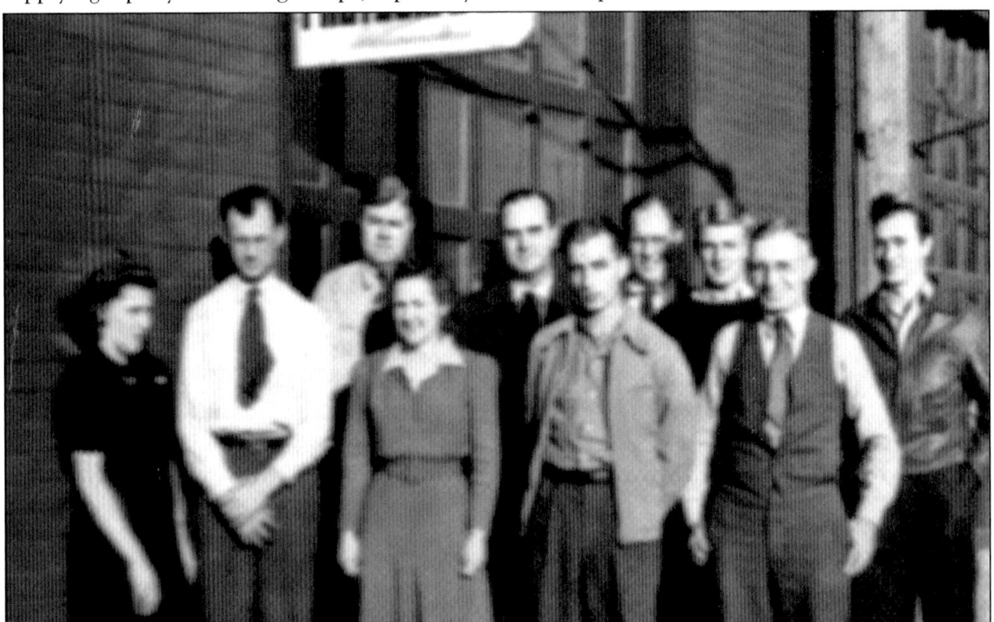

GM maintained a relatively large staff for its photographic department at the proving ground. Here 10 members of the department pose for this 1944 photograph, taken in connection with the facility's 20th anniversary. In addition to collecting a wealth of data from testing, detailed photographic records were gathered. (G.)

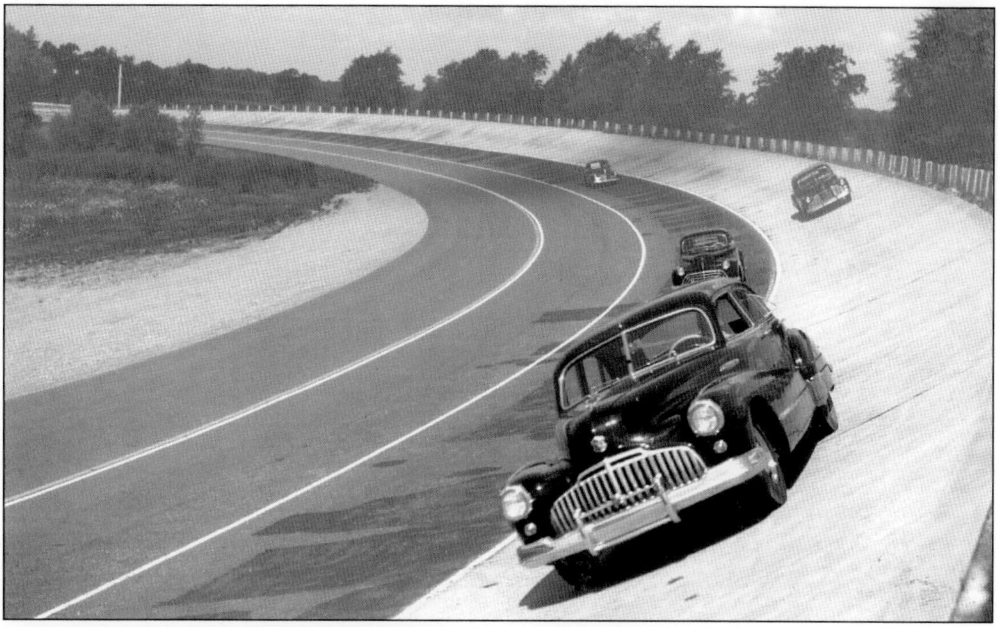

Four of GM's first post–World War II 1946 models are shown here circling the high-speed track at Milford. The Buick in the front and the Cadillac behind it in the same concrete-paved lane are traveling in the 90-mile-per-hour section, while the Oldsmobile and the Pontiac to the left are cruising in the 60-mile-per-hour lane. According to the caption, all four were recording fuel economy at the high speeds. (N.)

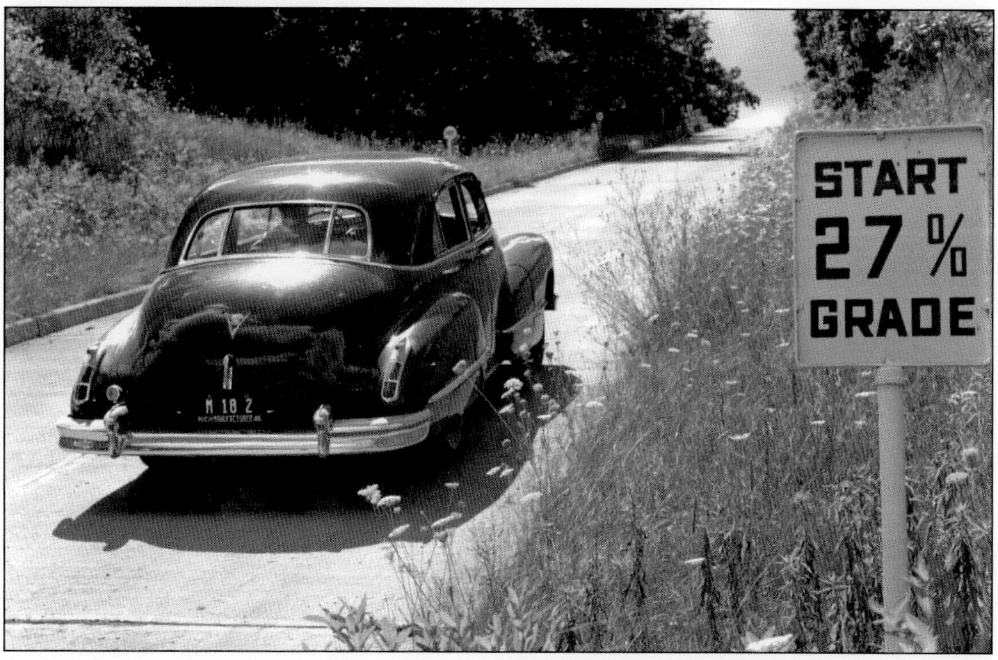

In this photograph, a 1946 Cadillac makes stop and start tests on a relatively steep 27 percent grade at the GM proving ground. (A 27 percent grade means it rises 27 feet in every 100 feet of length.) The Milford track included grades up to 60 percent, the steepest mainly reserved for testing military vehicles, as it was too steep even to walk up in leather-soled shoes. (N.)

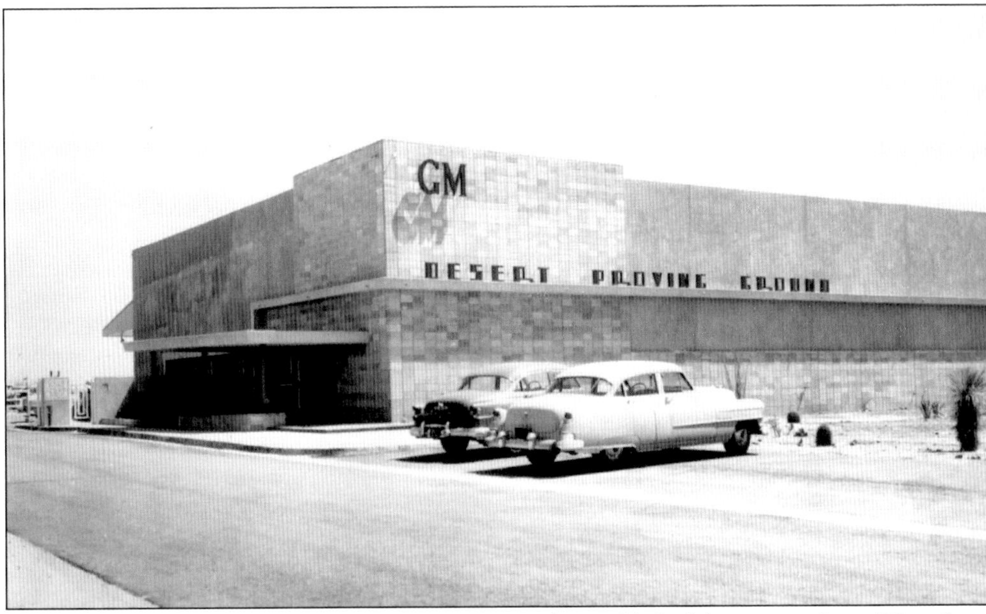

In 1953, GM pioneered the desert proving grounds established by automakers. The above photograph shows the administration building at GM's 5,000-acre Mesa, Arizona, test track near Phoenix. Hot weather testing in the desert was required by rapid acceptance of car air-conditioning and by engine-cooling stresses from automatic transmissions and reduced frontal area forward of the radiator in lower, wider cars. The desert provided a different kind of road testing for GM, pictured in the scene below of a 1964 Chevrolet and a 1964 Oldsmobile (rear), winding along a gravel road past rock outcroppings and saguaro cactus. Rumor says that once a tourist somehow entered the Mesa Proving Ground in error and could not figure out how to escape the circular roads going nowhere. Overwhelmed by the encroaching Phoenix metro area, GM sold the Mesa track and vacated it in mid-2009, moving its desert testing to the U.S. Army Proving Ground at Yuma, Arizona, in the southwestern corner of the state. (N.)

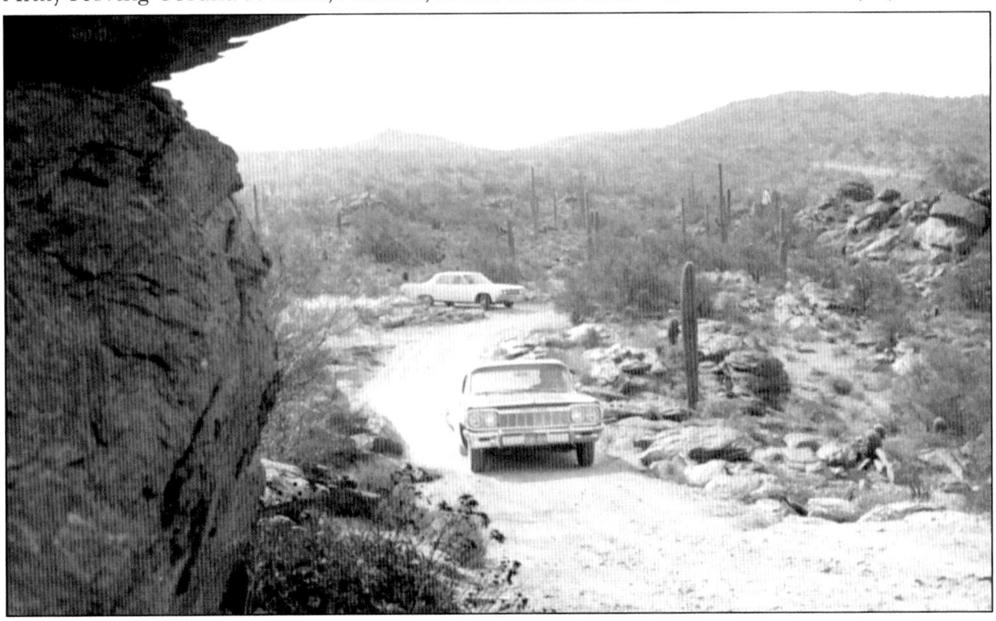

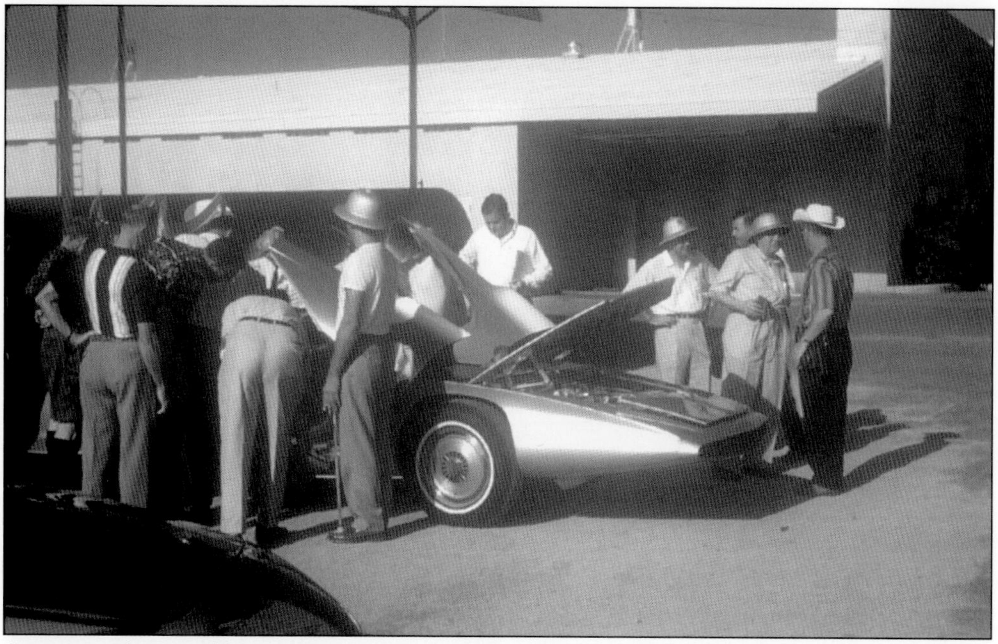

As part of its golden anniversary in 1958, GM unveiled the third in its family of gasoline-turbine–powered experimental cars, the Firebird III. In August 1958, GM flew several Detroit automotive and business writers, including the author, to the Mesa Proving Ground for a preview of the futuristic car. Here reporters are examining the Firebird III before taking a ride down the test track. (D.)

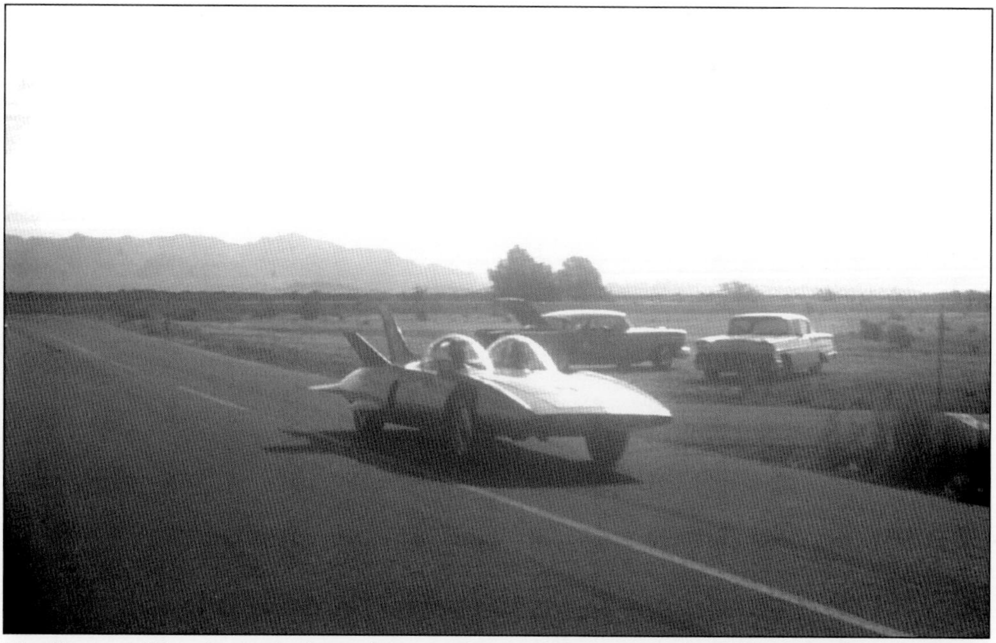

The Firebird III is shown flashing down a Mesa straightaway in the early morning sun, driven by a GM research engineer with an unidentified writer as passenger. Viewing this car today, 50 years later, at the GM Heritage Center in Sterling Heights recalls the fate of automotive turbine engines, which turned out to be irretrievably fuel-thirsty with dubious durability. (D.)

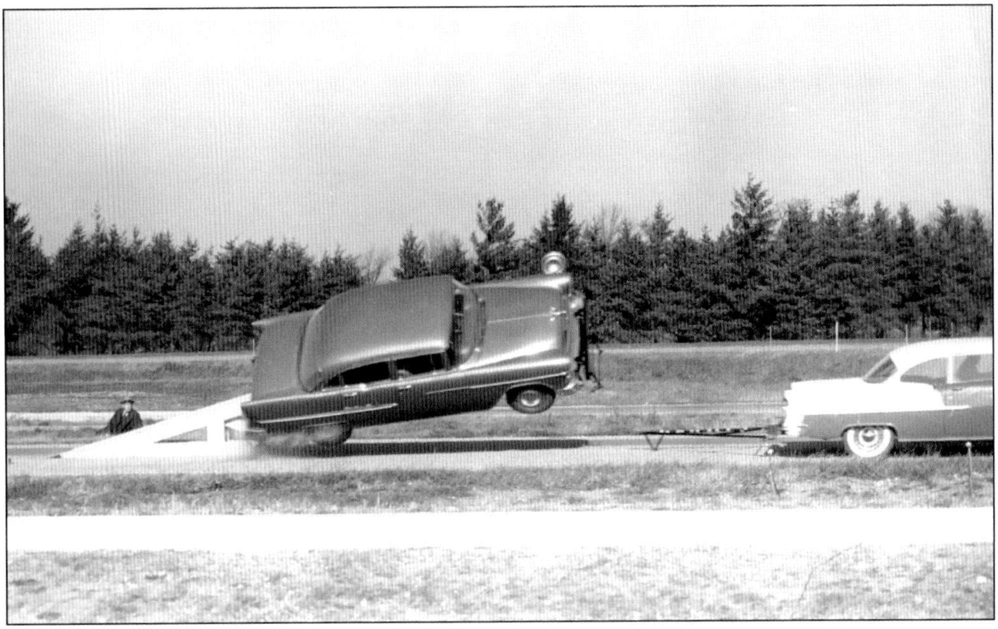

In the mid-1950s, Detroit automakers initiated a new testing routine: crash testing. Little was known about causes of injuries in crashes, and even less was known about staging crashes in a scientific, repeatable way. Safety engineers were especially challenged in trying to create rollovers. Here at the GM proving ground, a 1955 Bel Air Sport Coupe tows a driverless 1955 sedan onto a ramp, causing it to overturn. (N.)

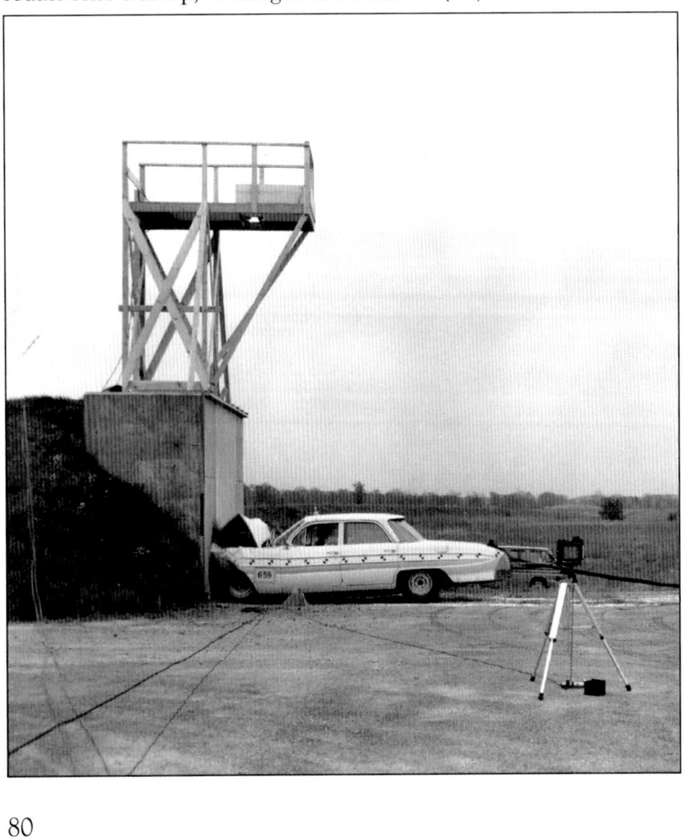

In this photograph, a 1961 Oldsmobile has been impelled into a solid concrete barrier at Milford, simulating a crash into either a wall or another vehicle traveling the same speed. Crash test vehicles were instrumented to record crash forces (deceleration), movement of components, and, using instrumented anthropomorphic laboratory dummies, the movements and impacts that might be encountered by human occupants. (N.)

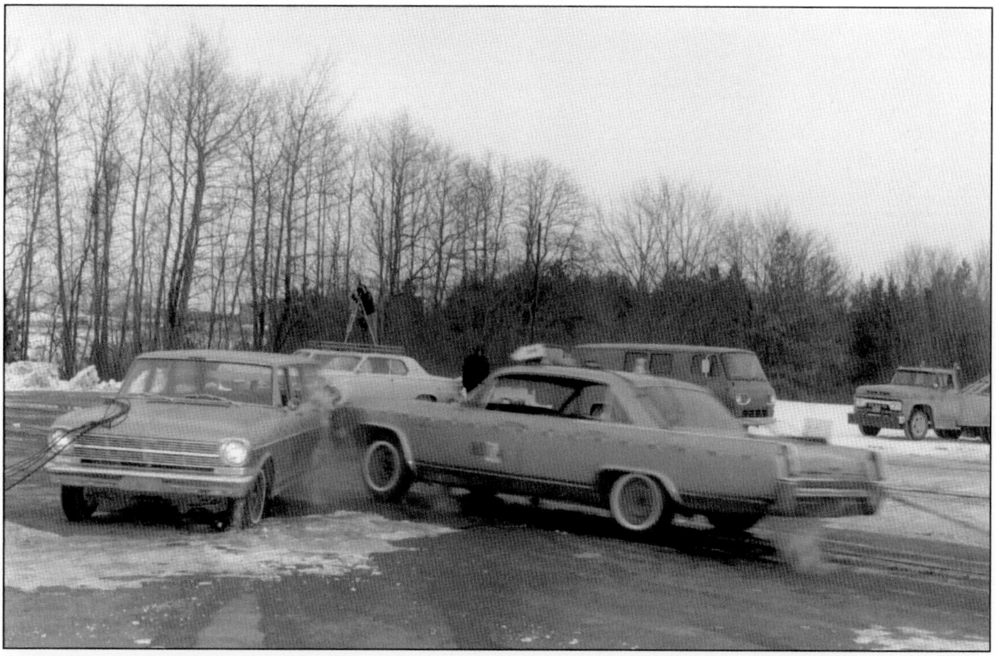

A third type of staged crash was the car-to-car test impact. Shown here at the GM proving ground is a large 1963 Oldsmobile 98 sedan striking the rear quarter of a compact 1962 Chevy II station wagon. Note the Ford Econoline van in the background—GM customarily put competitive vehicles under evaluation to work at routine tasks around the secluded test track. (N.)

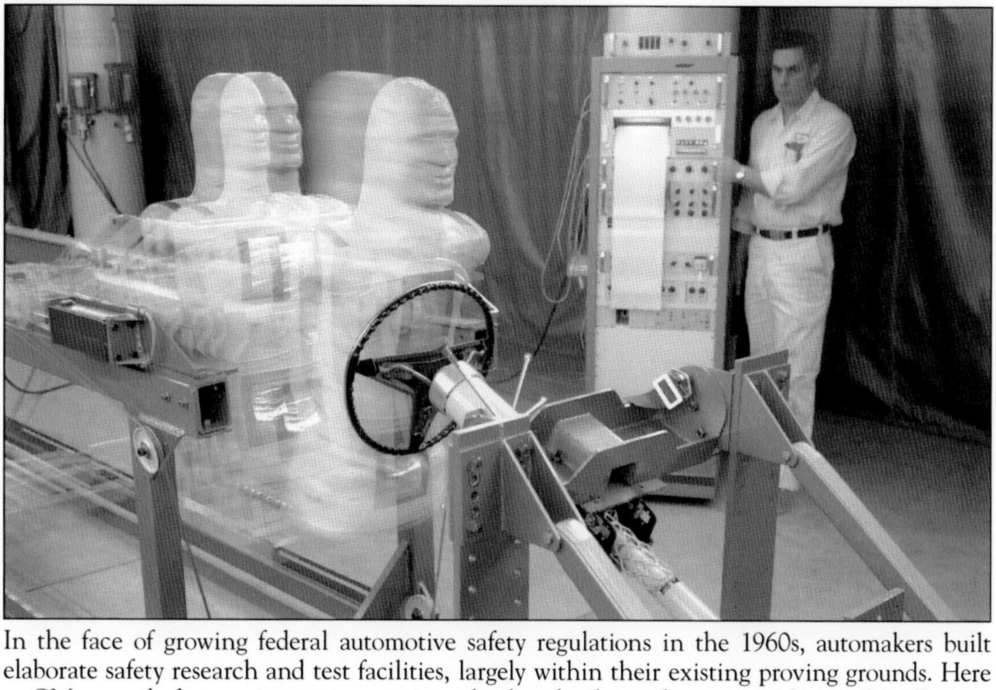

In the face of growing federal automotive safety regulations in the 1960s, automakers built elaborate safety research and test facilities, largely within their existing proving grounds. Here at GM, a crash dummy impacts a steering wheel and column fixture, simulating the effect on a driver dummy in a front-end crash. GM pioneered the telescoping, or collapsible, steering column through such testing. (G.)

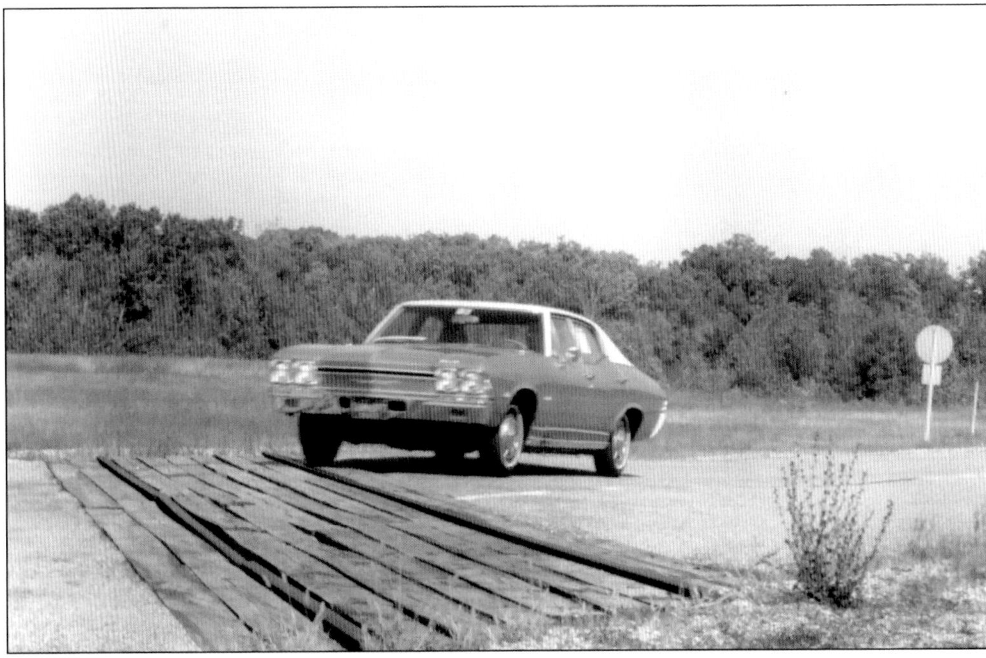

Among the road features built at GM's Milford Proving Ground were two replica rail crossings on the ride-and-handling track to test suspensions and steering components in repeated crossings. A 1968 Chevrolet Chevelle prototype with a new wheelbase and wider tread is pictured as it crosses the tracks, complete with planks and rails, on an endurance test. (N.)

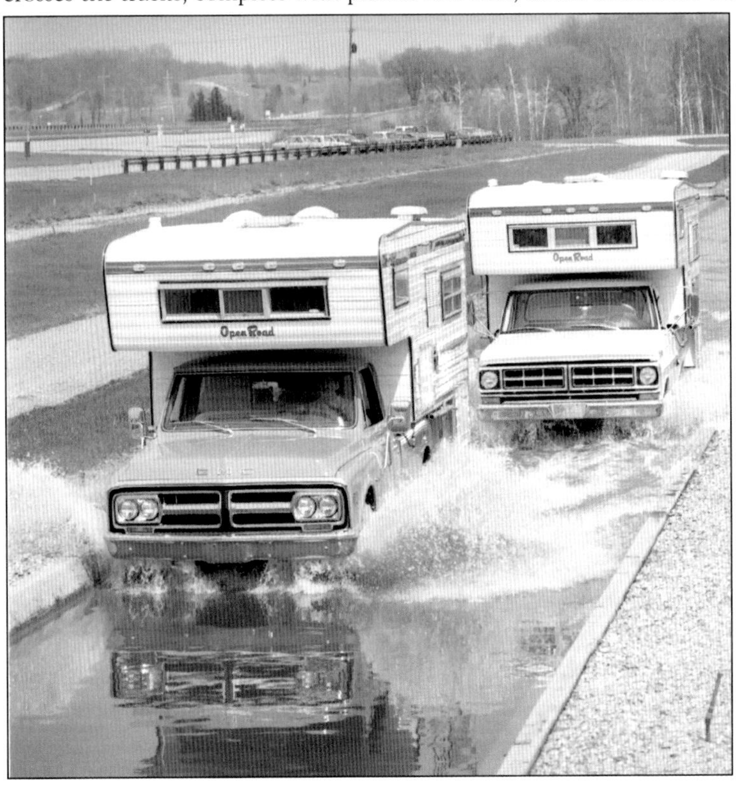

In the late 1960s, pickup trucks with aftermarket bolted-on camper bodies became the rage as Americans embraced the outdoors. Here both a 1972 GMC truck with a camper extension and a rival 1971 Ford pickup with camper are shown splashing through the GM proving ground's bathtub to test for water leaks and mechanical challenges—another example of competitive vehicle testing. (G.)

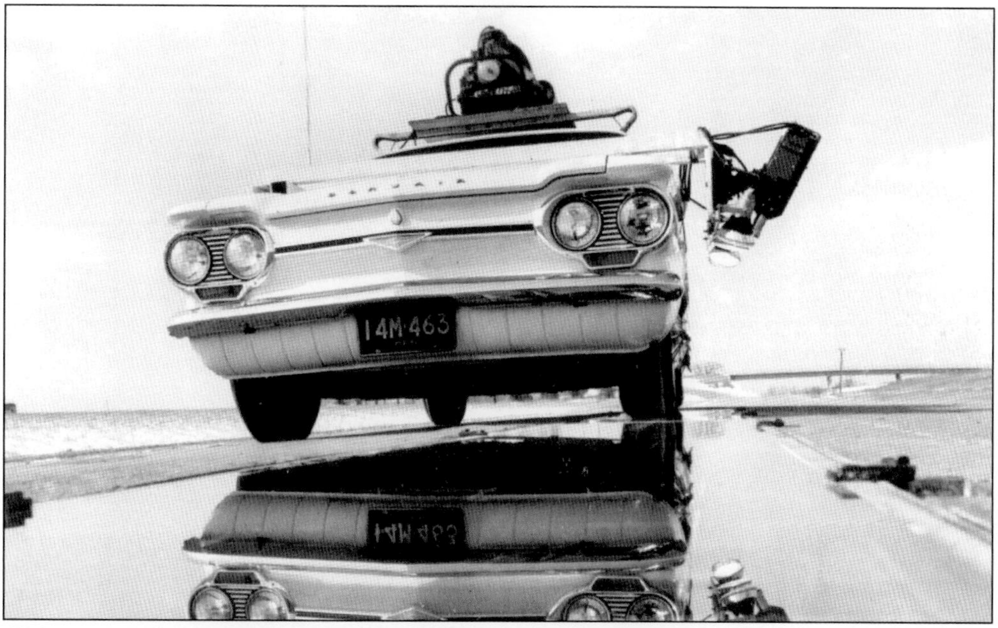

GM continued to experiment with novel testing techniques. This shows a 1964 Chevrolet Corvair to which are attached photoflood lamps and a high-speed camera. The car is rolled onto a mirrored glass surface on a proving ground road, which reflects the tire's "footprint" as the car undergoes various maneuvers, including braking and induced wheel shimmy, for analysis of tire reactions. (N.)

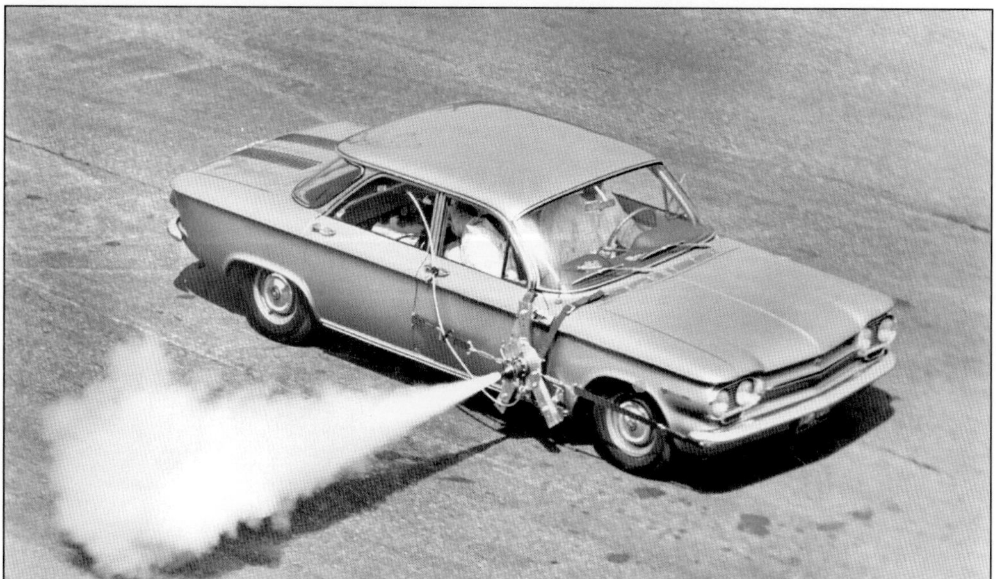

In another attempt to simulate the effect of crosswind gusts on car handling (see page 73), engineers at the GM proving ground equipped this 1963 Chevrolet Corvair with a firehose-appearing apparatus that forced high-pressure steam through a nozzle to the side. This action created the effect of wind gusting against the car as it traveled down the highway but could be easily actuated and controlled by one of the engineers. (G.)

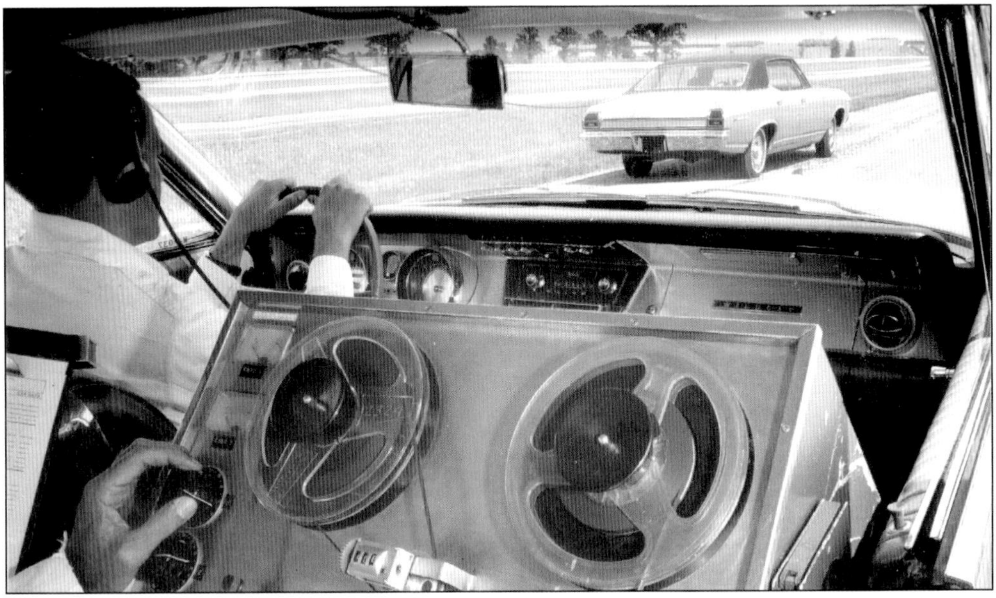

Because California and federal vehicle clean-air rules and safety regulations required much more extensive testing than ever before—for pollution controls alone, 50,000 miles over a prescribed course for each engine, transmission, and vehicle combination—a huge amount of additional data had to be accumulated. Simple hand-recorded or mechanically created records began to be replaced by reel-to-reel tapes, as in this view of a late-1960s test at GM's Milford Proving Ground. (N.)

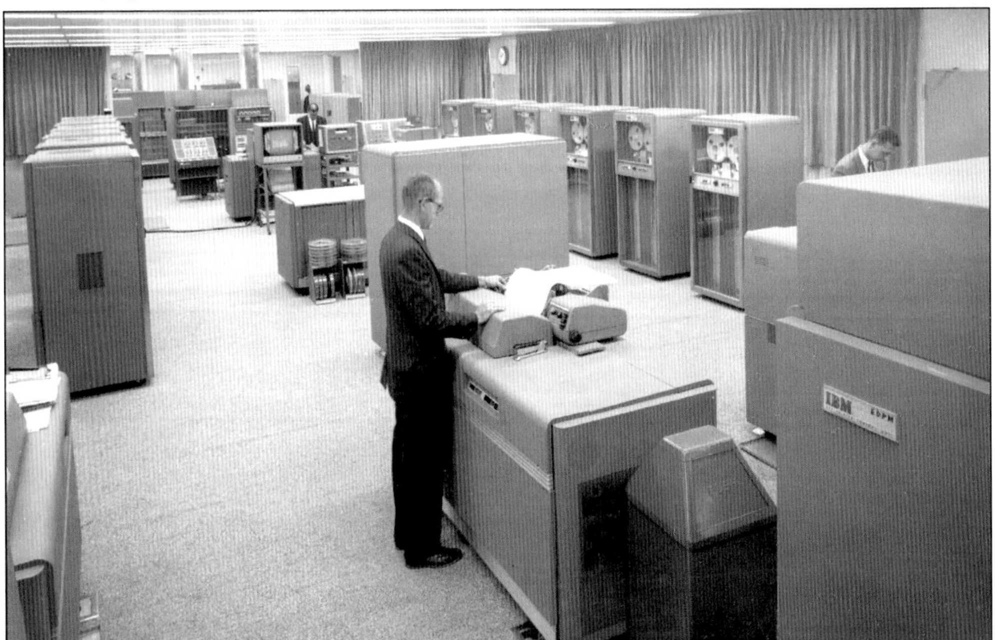

By the 1970s, test data was being analyzed and stored on massive computers in dedicated facilities, such as this computer center at the GM Milford Proving Ground. These buildings required very careful climate control of dust, temperature, and humidity and freedom from being shaken by any outside movements such as heavy trucks passing nearby. (G.)

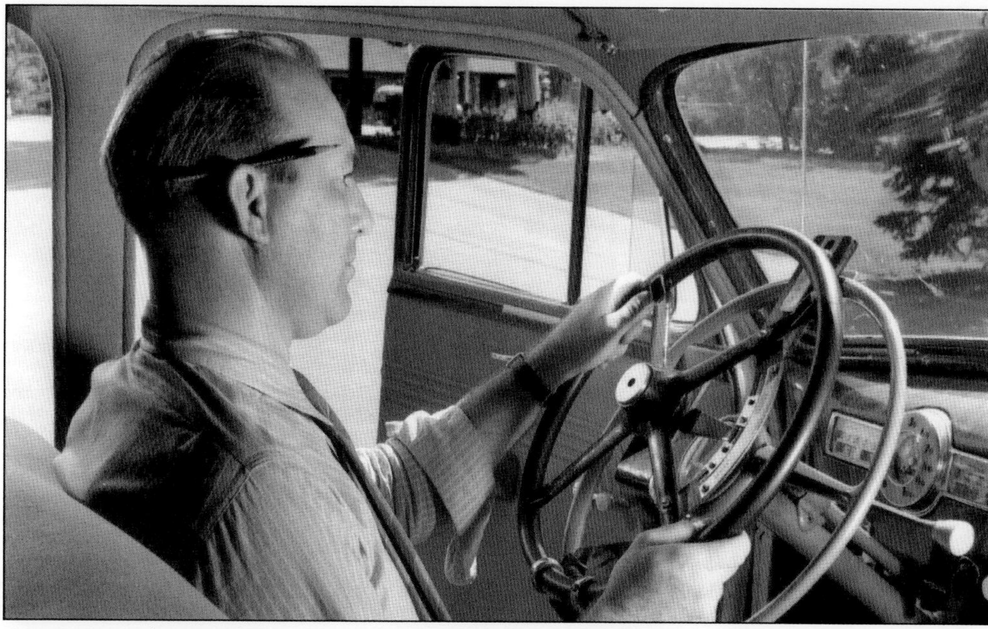

Some testing devices that originated in the first days of the GM proving ground stayed in use for many years. An example was this duplicate steering wheel atop the regular wheel of a pre–World War II Pontiac, a torque gauge used by the test-driver to measure steering effort at a time when power steering was under experimentation. Compare this to the similar, earlier test shown on page 36. (N.)

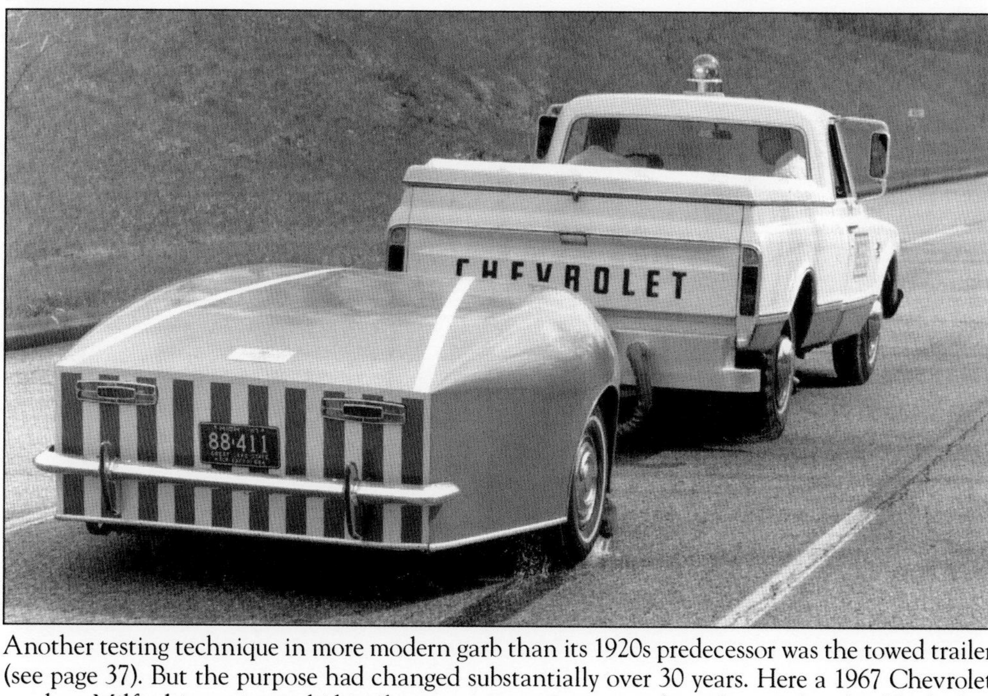

Another testing technique in more modern garb than its 1920s predecessor was the towed trailer (see page 37). But the purpose had changed substantially over 30 years. Here a 1967 Chevrolet truck at Milford is towing a skid trailer up a seven percent grade with its right wheel locked to measure the coefficient of friction between road and tire. The test helped engineers evaluate road surface materials and tire-skid resistance. (N.)

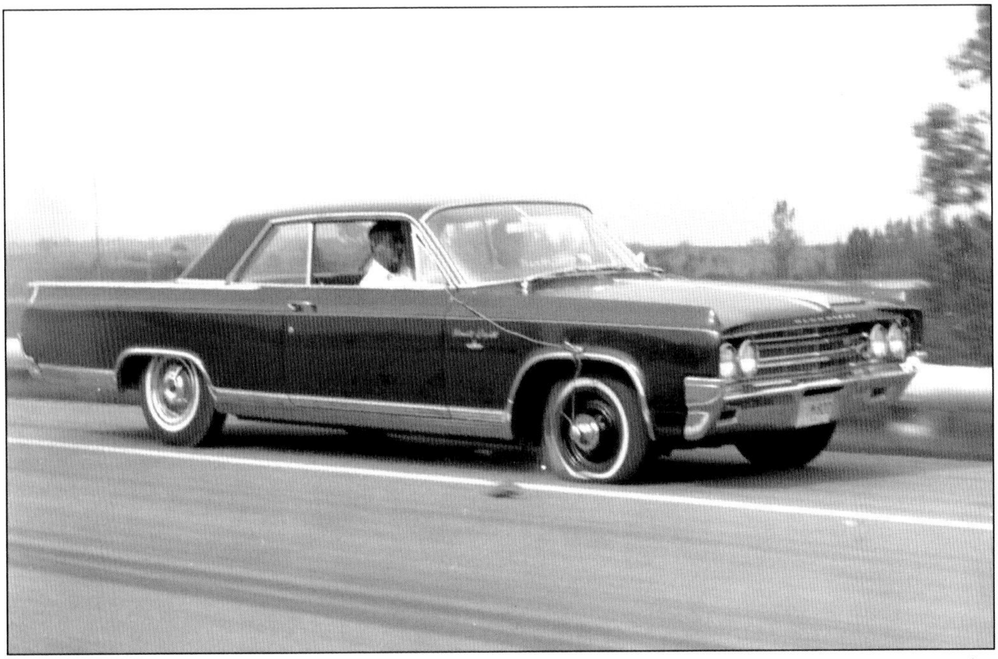

In pursuit of both fundamental knowledge and vehicle improvements, GM test engineers at the Milford Proving Ground continued to try out new techniques. This shows engineers deliberately causing the right front tire of a 1963 Oldsmobile to deflate, as a way of evaluating steering and handling for motorists in a tire-blowout situation. (N.)

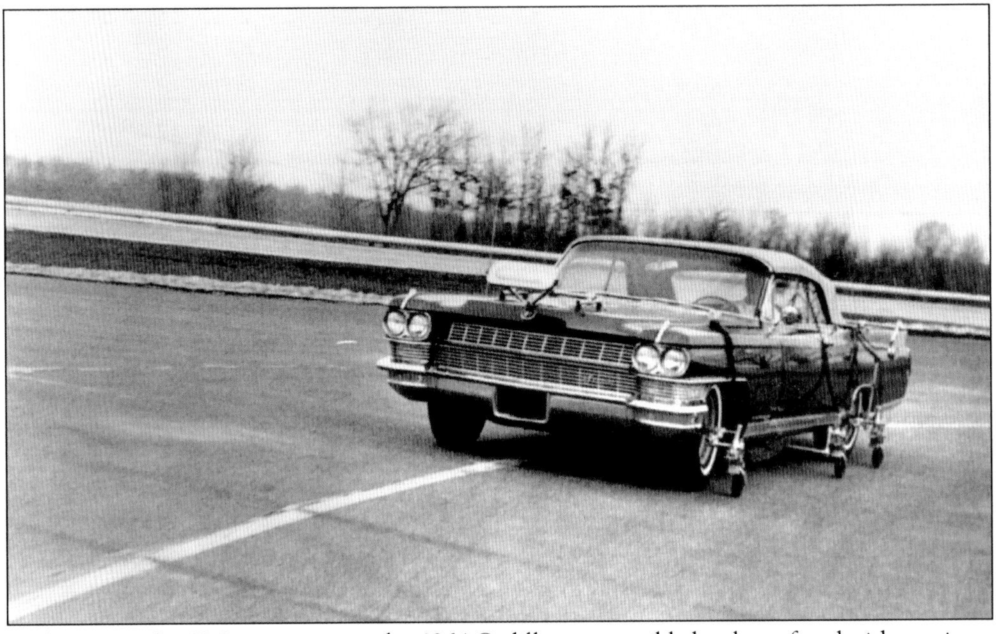

In this test at the GM proving ground, a 1964 Cadillac convertible has been fitted with outrigger dollies along its left-side wheels to help engineers evaluate the car's roadability. By detecting even slight car handling motions, sensors help engineers modify such characteristics as steering slip angles, speed, roll angle, and attitude angle, which was part of the process of developing new suspension systems. (N.)

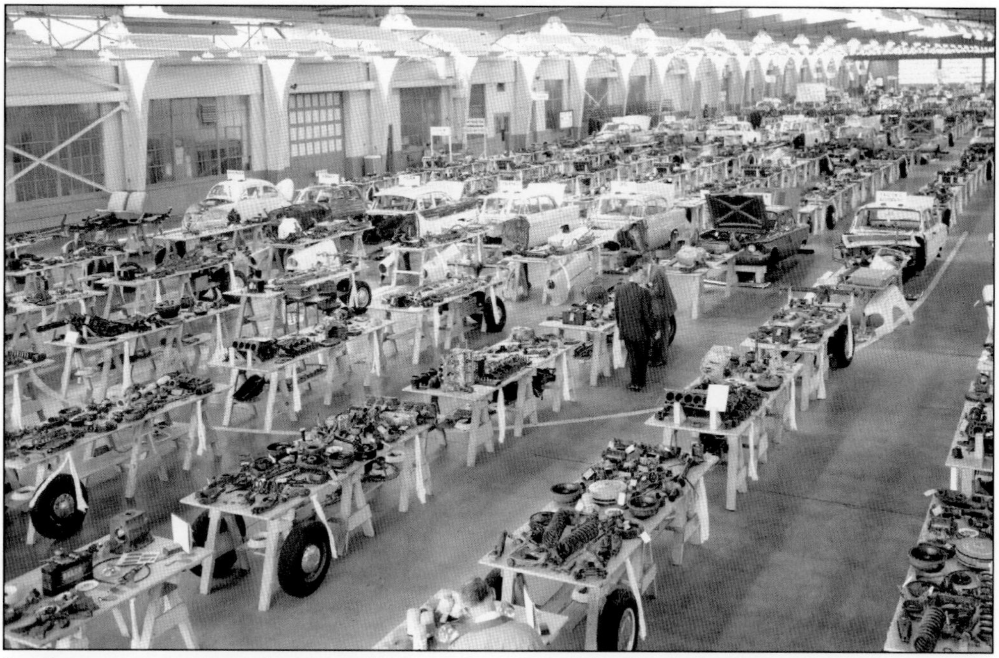

In this competitive-analysis teardown room, GM vehicles and those of competitors are completely stripped down to their component parts for engineering, purchasing, and financial experts to evaluate their features and estimate their costs. In other teardown rooms common at the test tracks, vehicles completing their punishing endurance trials—50,000 miles since the 1960s and now topping 100,000—are stripped, with their parts laid out for wear and failure inspection. (N.)

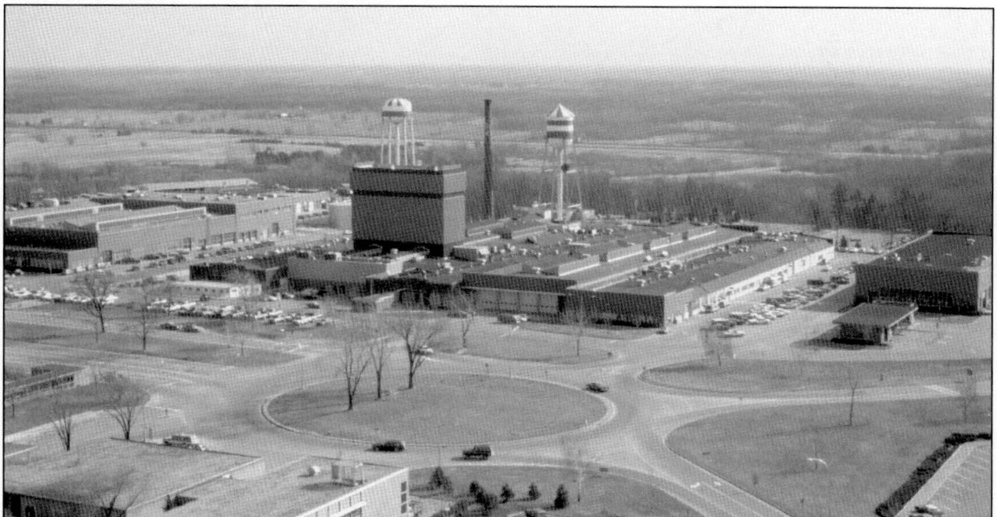

After more than 50 years of operation by the late 1970s, the GM proving ground at Milford presented an extensive array of modern buildings and facilities. These included specialized buildings for automotive safety, emissions, and computers, needs that could not have been foreseen when the track opened in 1924. This 1977 view presents some idea of how Milford has changed over the years. (G.)

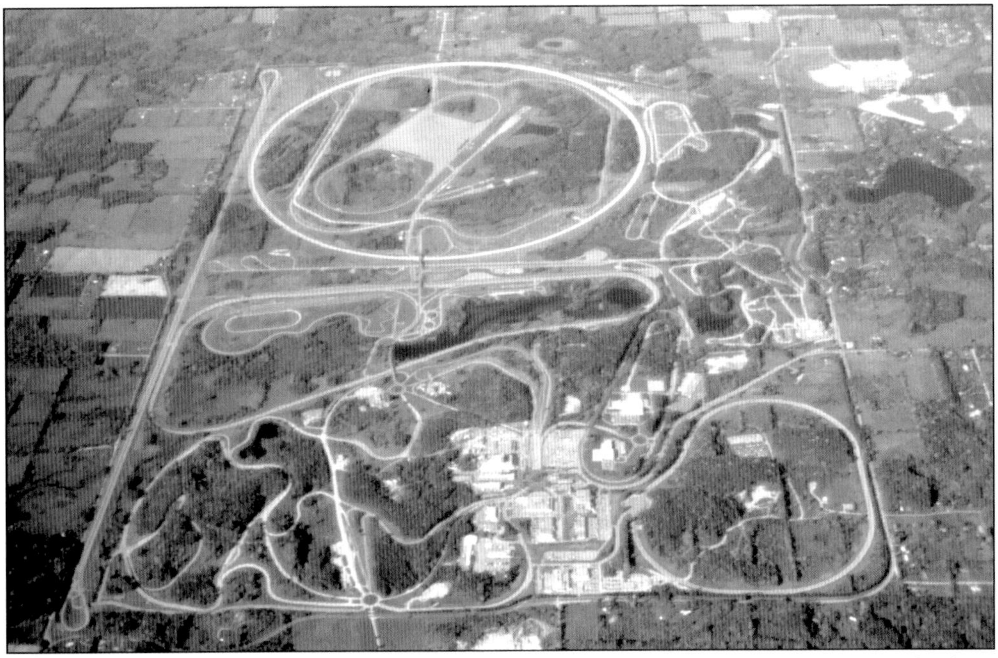

This 1982 aerial north view of GM's proving ground shows the growth of road networks from the simpler facilities of 1924 (see page 31), 1928 (see page 63), and 1941 (see page 74). Property acquisitions have squared off the land at the southeast corner, and there is a large northern addition. Even without regulatory requirements, more extensive facilities would have been needed due to the growth of different models made by GM. (G.)

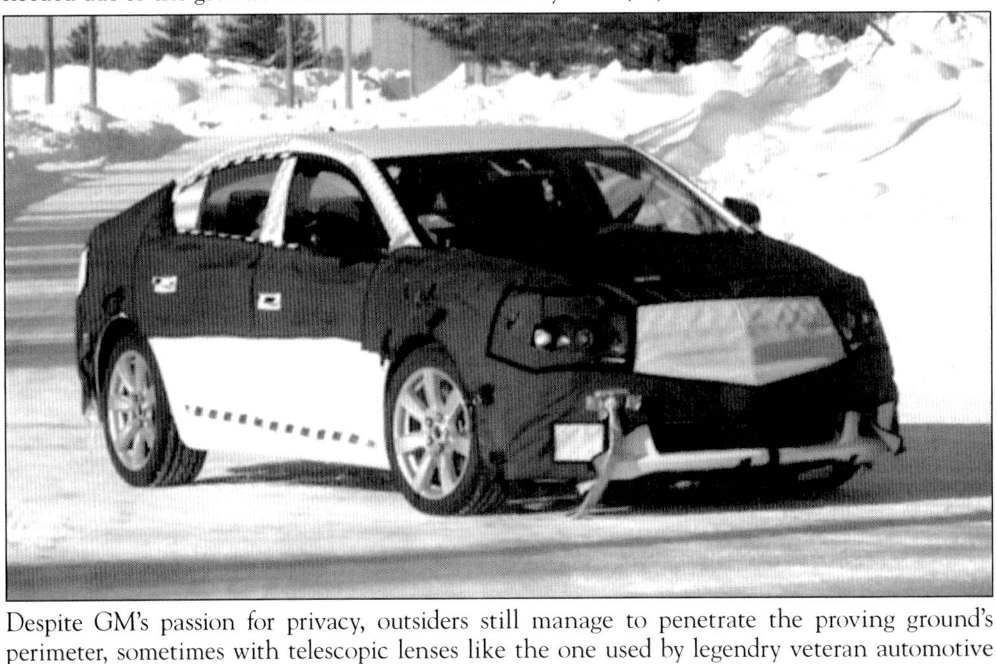

Despite GM's passion for privacy, outsiders still manage to penetrate the proving ground's perimeter, sometimes with telescopic lenses like the one used by legendry veteran automotive writer/photographer Jim Dunne, who, with his long-lens camera, captured this heavily disguised future model Cadillac, called a "mule," during winter testing. Spy photographs of future model cars have been currency around Detroit for more than 80 years. (J.)

Seven

Ford Motor Company Dearborn and Romeo Test Tracks

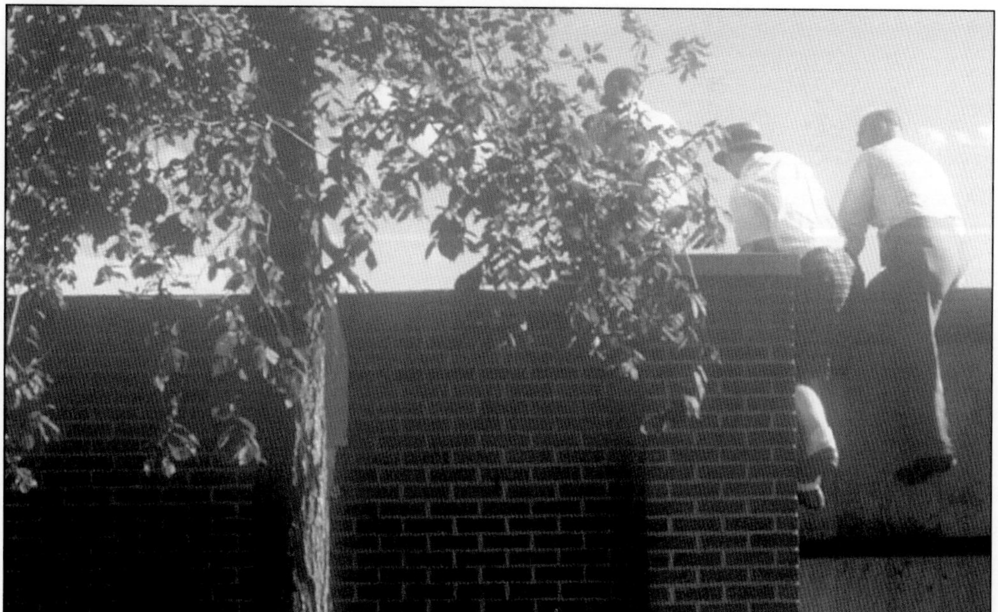

Ford Motor Company's first test track, known for many years as the Dearborn Proving Ground, or DPG, was located adjacent to the Henry Ford Museum and Greenfield Village, Michigan's largest tourist attraction. Millions of people therefore have wondered what lay on the other side of the serpentine brick wall enclosing the adjoining test track. Here in 1958, some tourists, including the author, have climbed the wall to see. (D.)

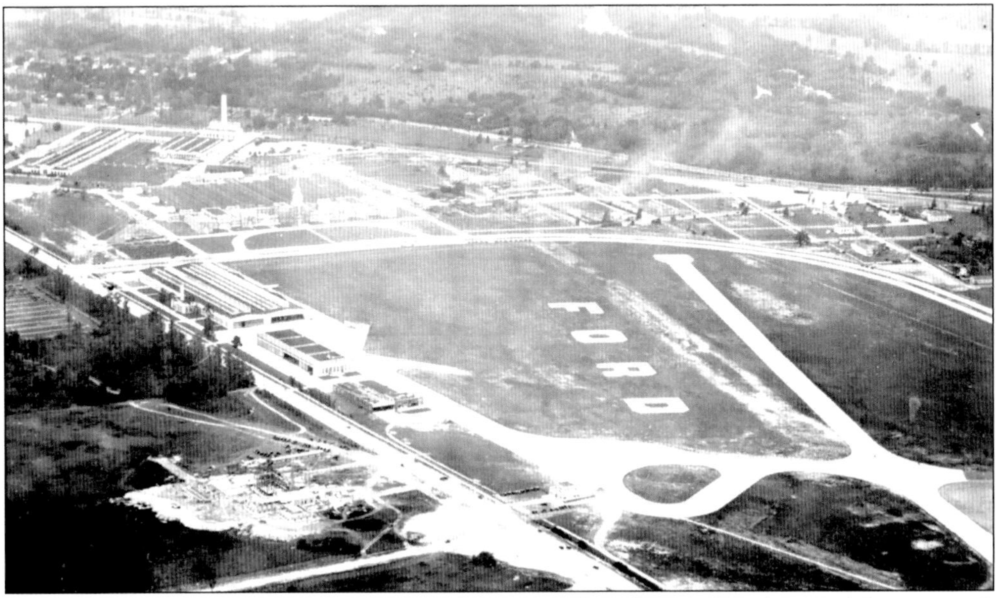

This north view of the Ford Airport in Dearborn was taken about 1930, when Tri-Motor aircraft were still being built at and flown from the site. The Henry Ford Museum and Greenfield Village at the northwest side are brand new, and the Dearborn Inn, the world's first airport hotel, can be seen under construction in the lower-left corner. (D.)

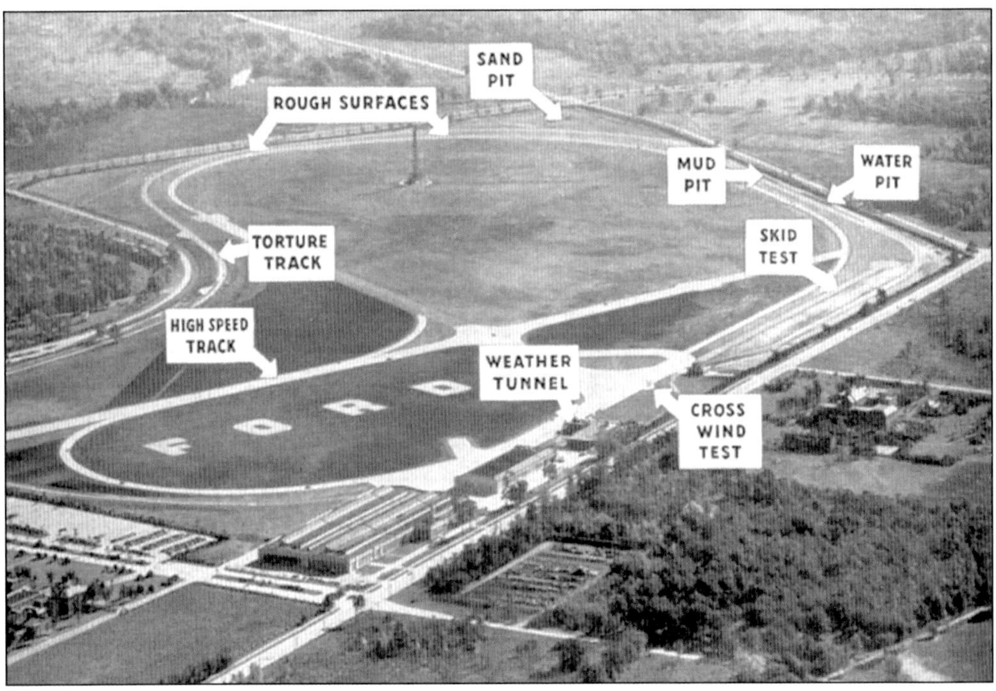

Here is an east view of the former Ford Airport after it was converted to Ford's Dearborn Proving Ground in 1937. The labels show that Ford has installed many features of the other test tracks operating then, including GM, Packard, and Studebaker. At only 360 acres, Dearborn Proving Ground's area was much smaller than the others. Ford converted the airframe factory and hangers to automotive purposes, such as laboratories and garages. (D.)

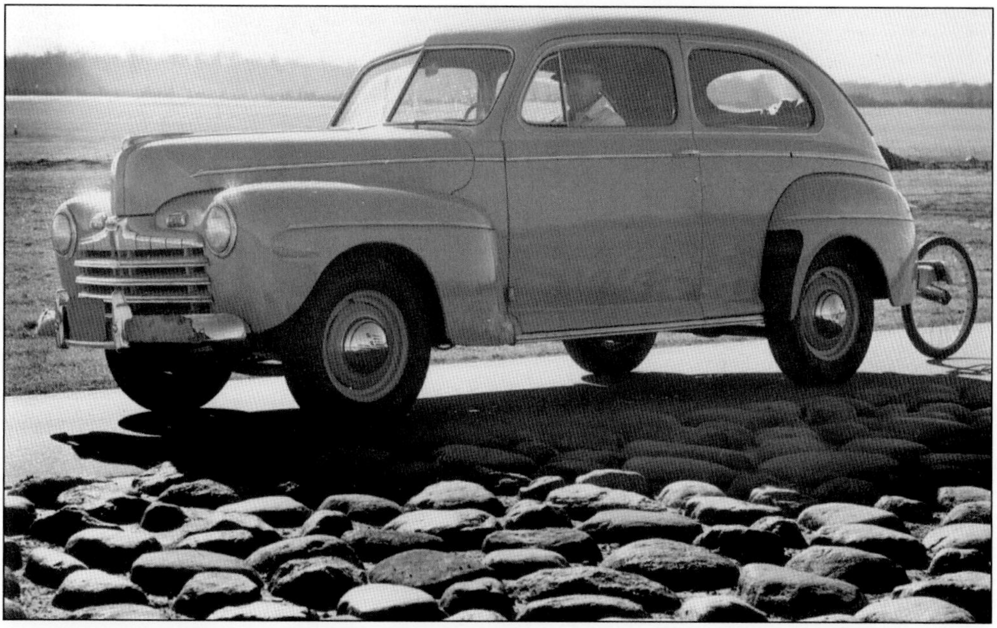

So-called Belgian Block road surfaces were virtually standard at automotive test tracks, designed to stress the test cars' suspensions, tires, steering, and bodies. This shows a 1946 Ford Tudor at Dearborn Proving Ground with a fifth wheel attached on the rear to record distance and speed apart from the car's odometer and speedometer, which had no means for data output. Ford was the first automaker to resume civilian production at the end of World War II. (N.)

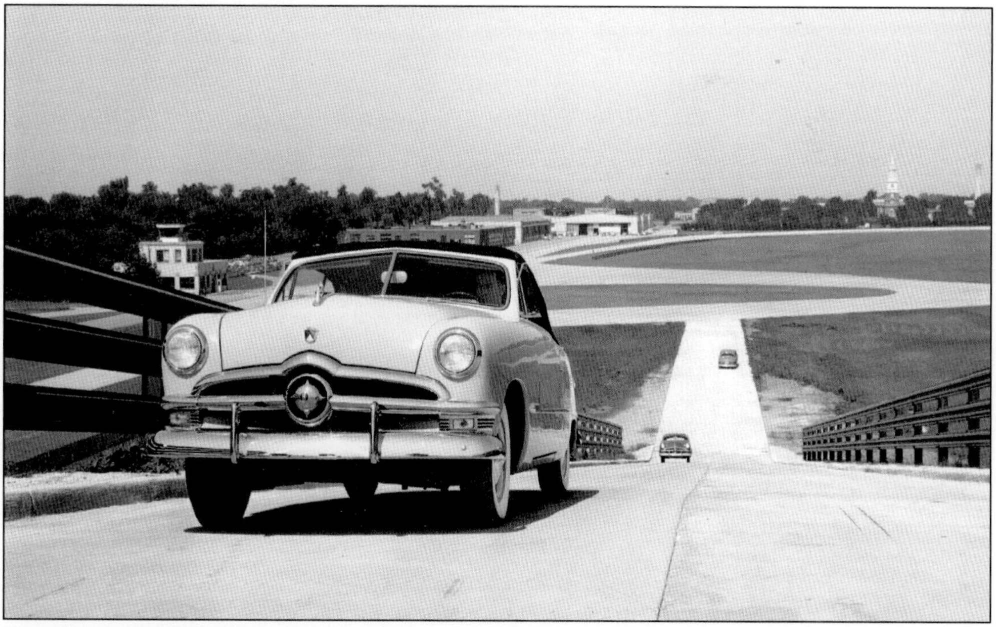

This shows a 1950 Ford convertible climbing a 17 percent grade on the man-made hill at Dearborn Proving Ground. On the opposite side of the test hill, the grade was a steep 30 percent. In the background from left to right are the former airport tower, hangars and airframe building, and the Independence Hall tower at the Henry Ford Museum. The airport's former concrete taxiways and runways have been converted to test roads. (N.)

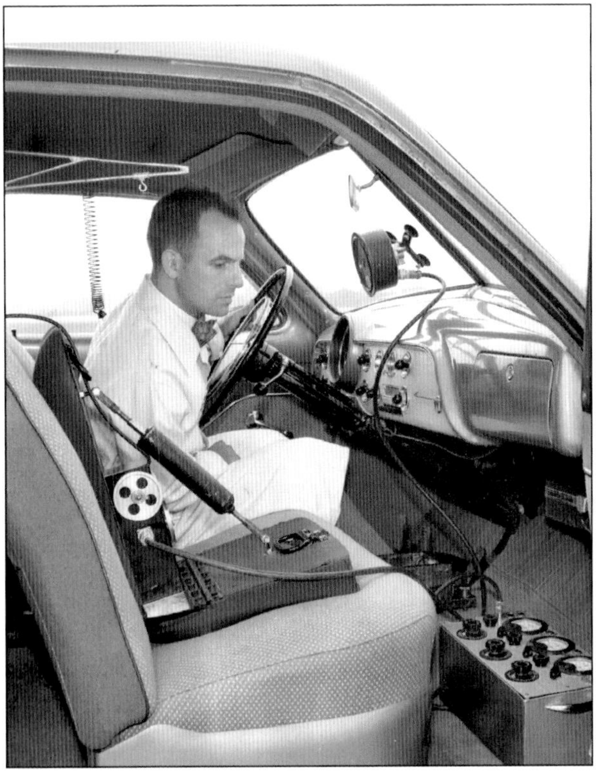

A test-driver in a shop coat looks over the instrumentation in the front compartment of this 1951 Ford at the Dearborn test track. On the passenger seat is a hinged instrument that is calculated to match the weight of a human occupant. Instruments with readouts for the tester are mounted on the floor and the windshield. (N.)

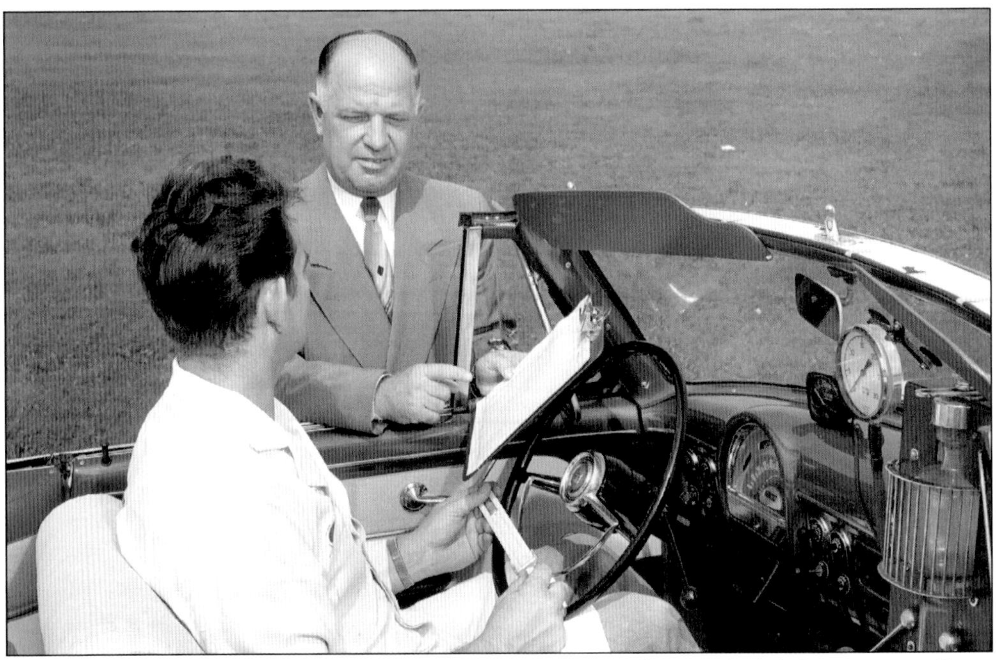

The caption that came with this photograph said in part, "Al Esper (right), known to millions of readers of the Sunday funnies as Ford's chief test driver, checks a report with a member of his staff." The funnies referred to an advertising campaign Ford had run for several years featuring Esper. The test-driver is at the wheel of a well-instrumented 1953 Ford convertible. (N.)

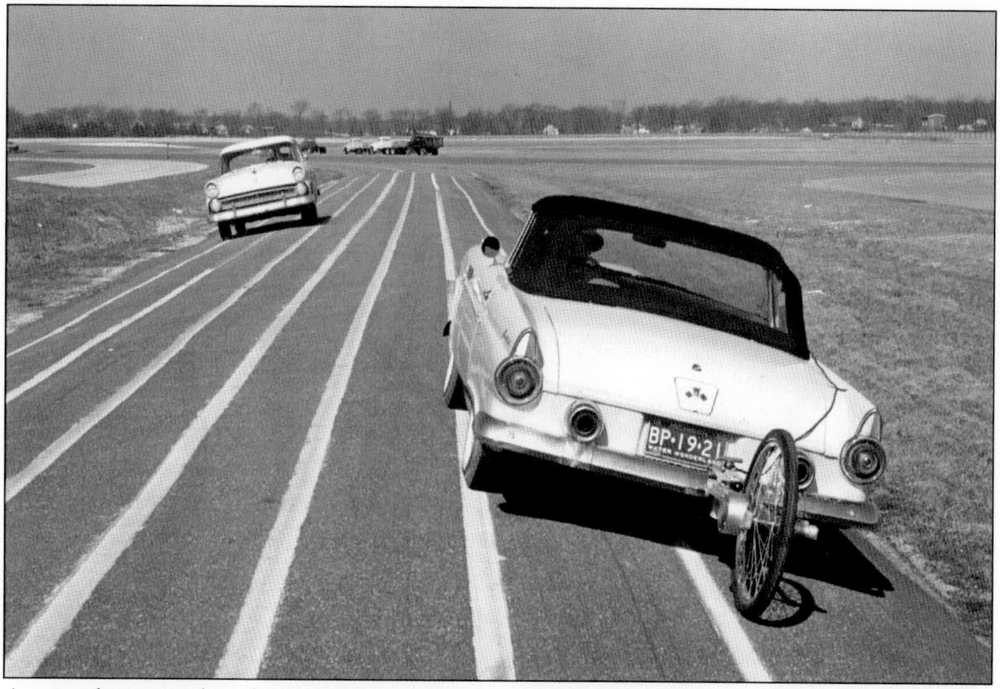

Among the unusual roadways incorporated into Ford's Dearborn Proving Ground was this highly crowned stretch of asphalt pavement, which mimicked many of the rural highways in the United States until construction of the interstate system began in 1957. Pictured are a 1955 model Ford (left) and 1955 Thunderbird undergoing handling tests on the stretch. (N.)

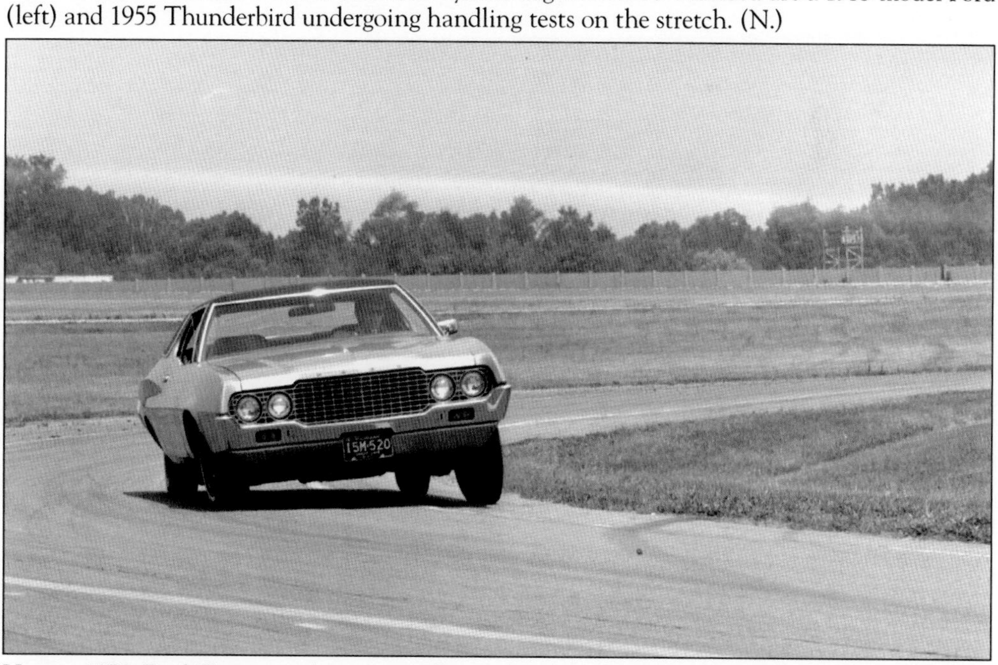

Here a 1972 Ford Torino is shown rounding a bend at high speed on the Dearborn Proving Ground's ride and handling course. This course is used for quick assessment of a car's handling through twisting and ungraded turns. It was frequently used to orient nonengineering Ford executives and outsiders, such as automotive writers and other media to new Ford models. (N.)

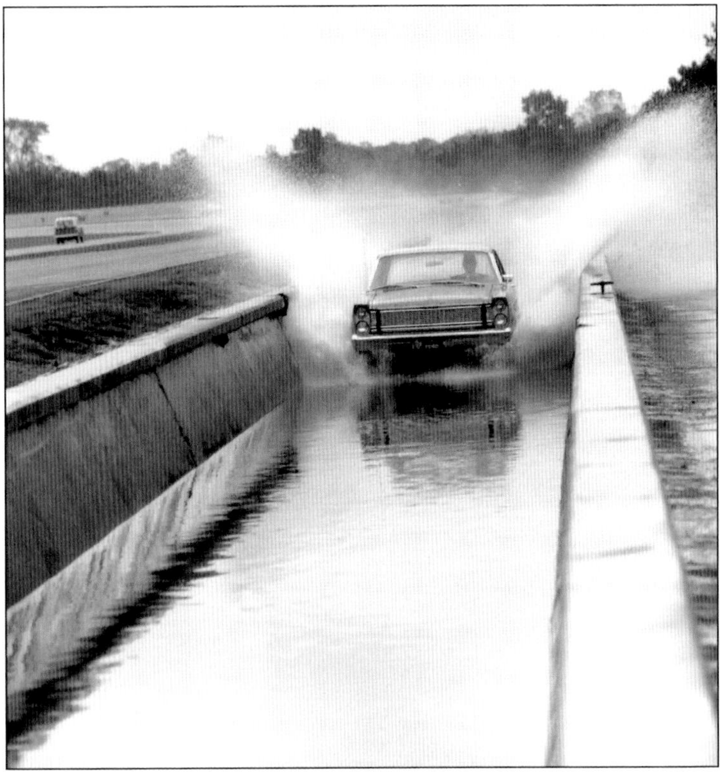

As at other automobile manufacturer test tracks, Ford had its water tank at Dearborn Proving Ground. Here a 1965 Ford Galaxie is shown splashing through the salty mixture. In the 1950s, road commissions began liberal applications of salt to melt snow and ice. However, car manufacturers were not prepared for the resulting car body rust. It took some years to develop test procedures for assessing rust-proofing technology. (N.)

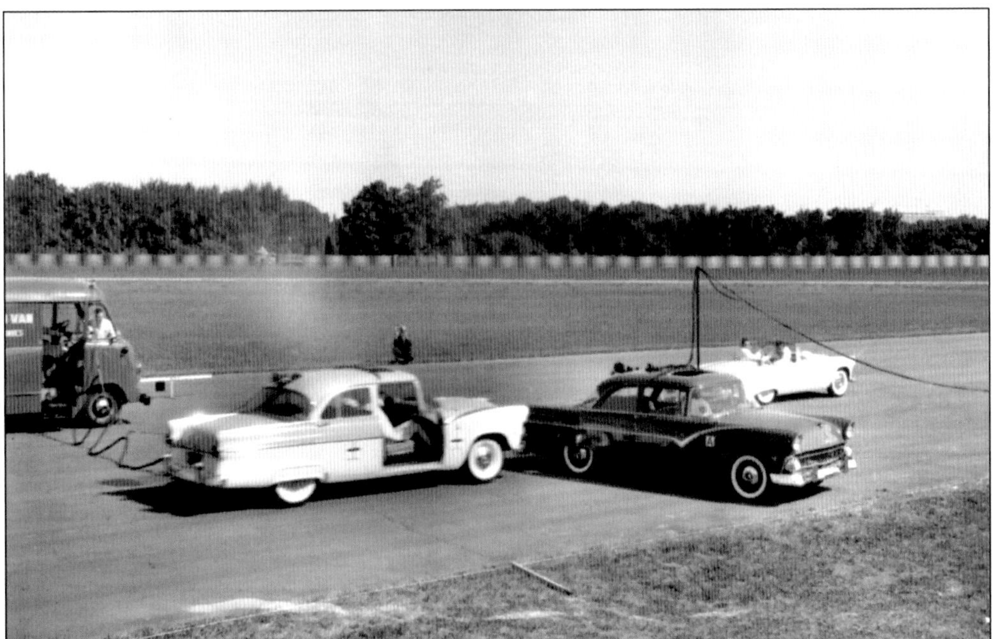

In the early 1950s, drawing on research by the Cornell Aeronautical Laboratory and the Indiana State Police, Ford inaugurated safety crash testing at the Dearborn Proving Ground. This shows a simulated car-to-car crash at 36 miles per hour, staged as part of a national safety forum in September 1955 to announce Ford's pioneering safety package for 1956 models. (N.)

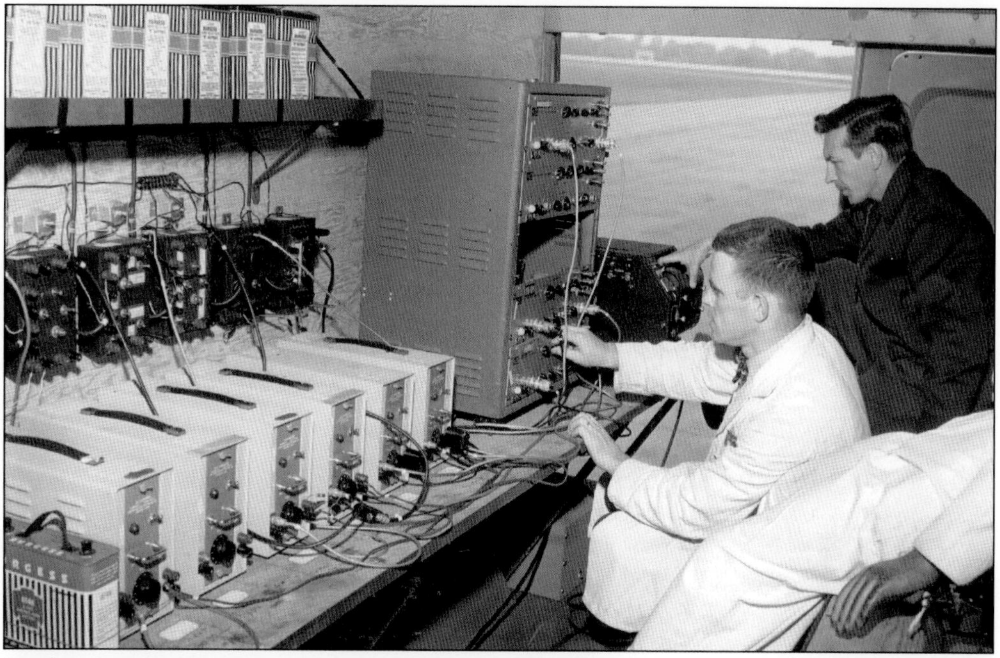

Inside an instrument van, as seen in the bottom photograph on the previous page, technicians at the Ford test track recorded readouts from the cars and the anthropomorphic crash dummies inside the cars. They did this in order to gauge crash forces in car-to-car impact and dozens of other tests carried out at the facility in the 1950s. (N.)

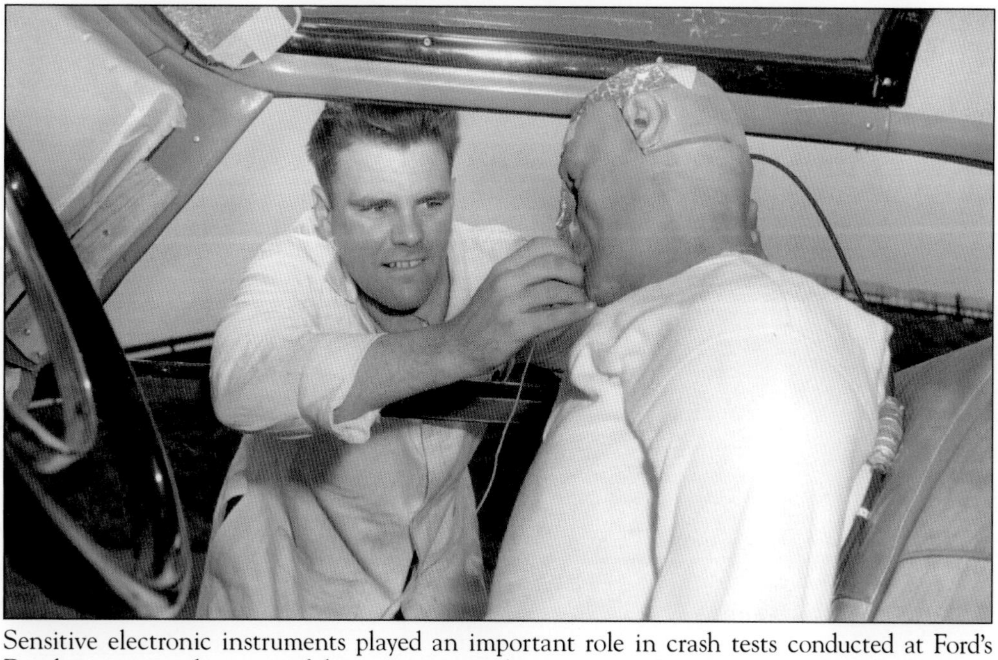

Sensitive electronic instruments played an important role in crash tests conducted at Ford's Dearborn test track as part of the automotive safety program. Here a Ford technician adjusts an electrical connection from aluminum foil on the crash dummy's head. During the crash, the foil closes an electrical circuit if it touches the instrument panel, windshield, or sun visor, producing a signal in the nearby instrument van, recording impact time and force. (N.)

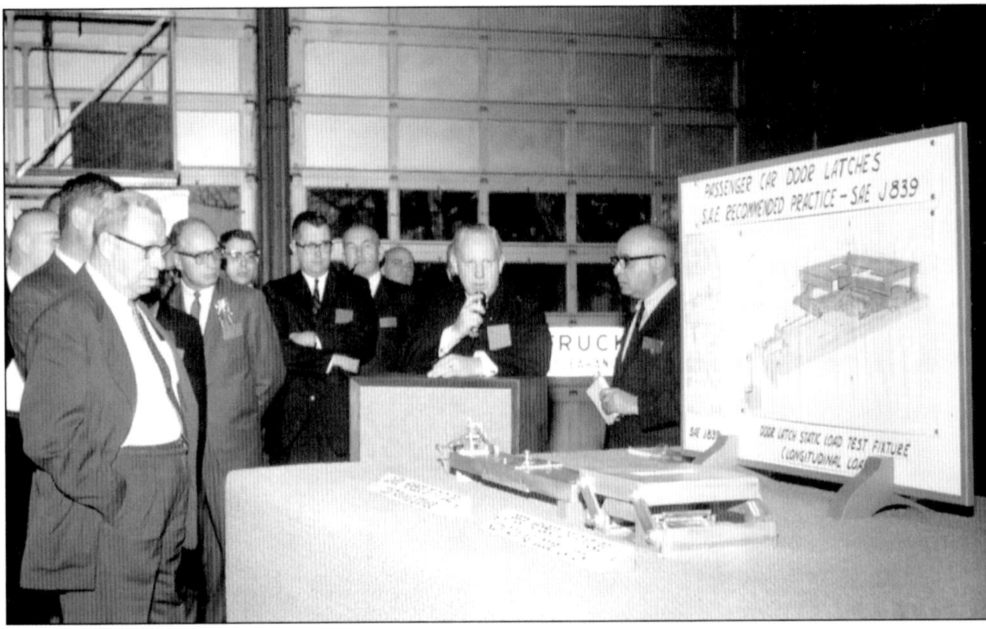

Ford's 1956 safety package that developed out of the early 1950s testing included front seat belts, a padded dashboard, a deep-dish energy absorbing steering wheel, and a vastly improved door latch mechanism. Here a new Society of Automotive Engineers standard for latches is being explained to a group, either press or visiting engineers, at the Ford Dearborn Proving Ground. (N.)

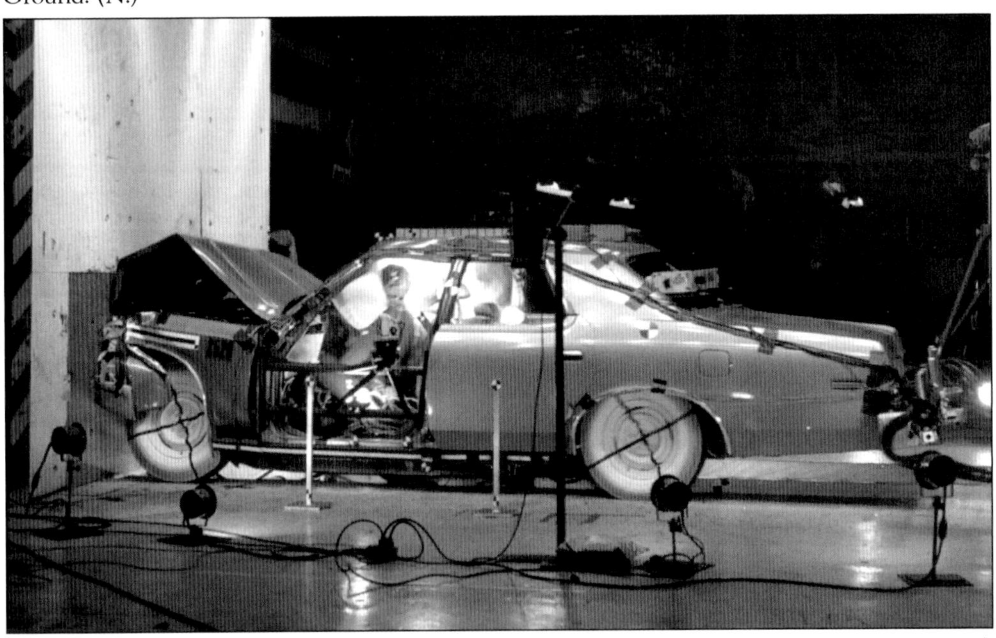

In the mid-1960s Ford opened a new automotive safety center at the Dearborn Proving Ground, which was devoted to safety research with indoor vehicle and component crash testing. In the indoor simulated crash, a hydraulic piston similar to an aircraft carrier catapult propels the test vehicle down a track into a barrier. In this photograph, an instrumented mid-1970s Ford LTD is shown at the instant it strikes the crash barrier at 30 miles per hour. (N.)

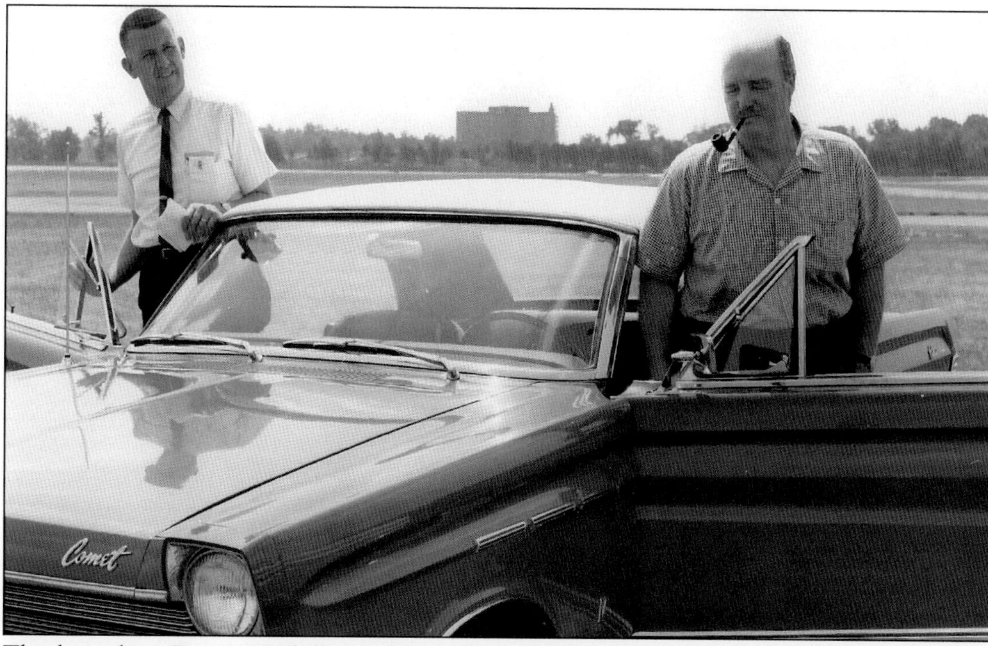

The legendary Tom McCahill, *Mechanix Illustrated* automotive editor and father of spirited automotive writing, is shown here about to test-drive a 1965 Mercury Comet convertible at Dearborn Proving Ground. Accompanying him is Ford engineering executive Howard Freers (left). Ford's world headquarters building can be seen in the distance. The test track was frequently used for such media events. (F.)

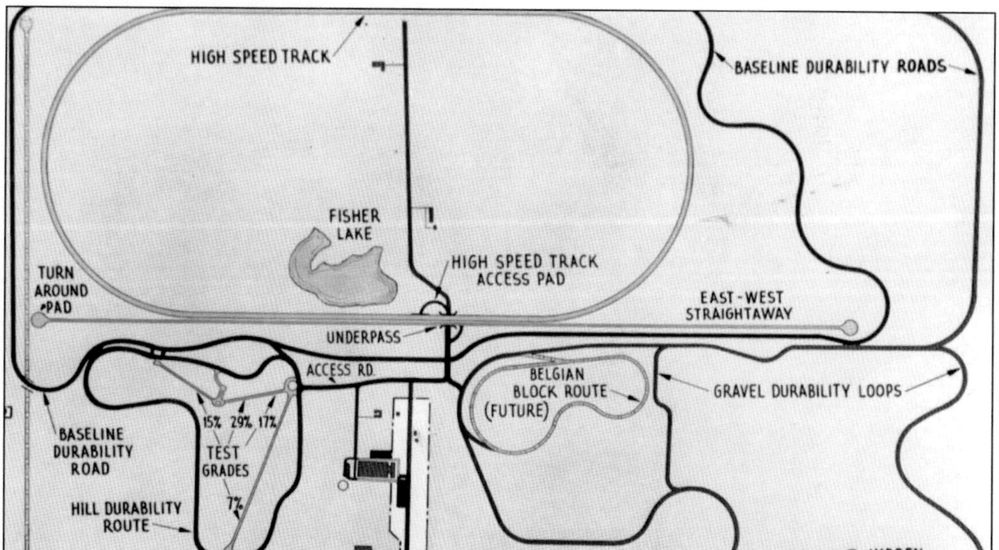

In 1953, finding its small Dearborn facility insufficient for expanding test needs, Ford acquired land northwest of Romeo, located 34 miles north of Detroit in Macomb County. In 1956, it became Ford's Michigan Proving Ground. This diagram shows the layout of the rolling, 3,880-acre site, once a country estate for the prominent Detroit Fisher automotive family. (N.)

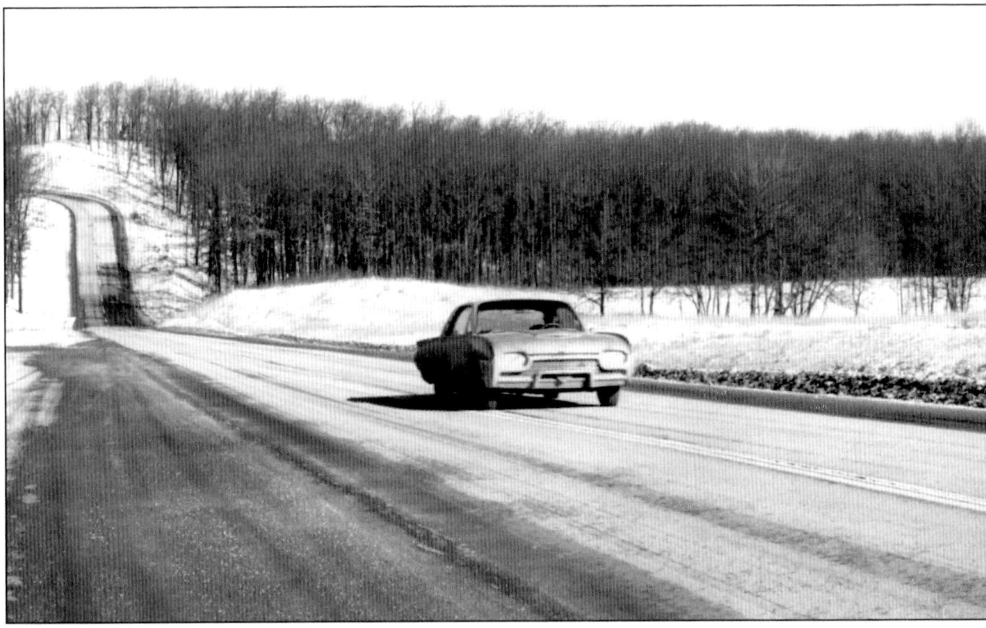

At Ford's Michigan Proving Ground, each hill road of the durability course was designed with a specific test in mind, even though this scene of a 1962 Ford Thunderbird appears like many rural highways in North America—except for the absence of traffic. Some 30 miles of roads were constructed at the Romeo facility, more than twice as many as at the Dearborn track some 90 minutes distant. (N.)

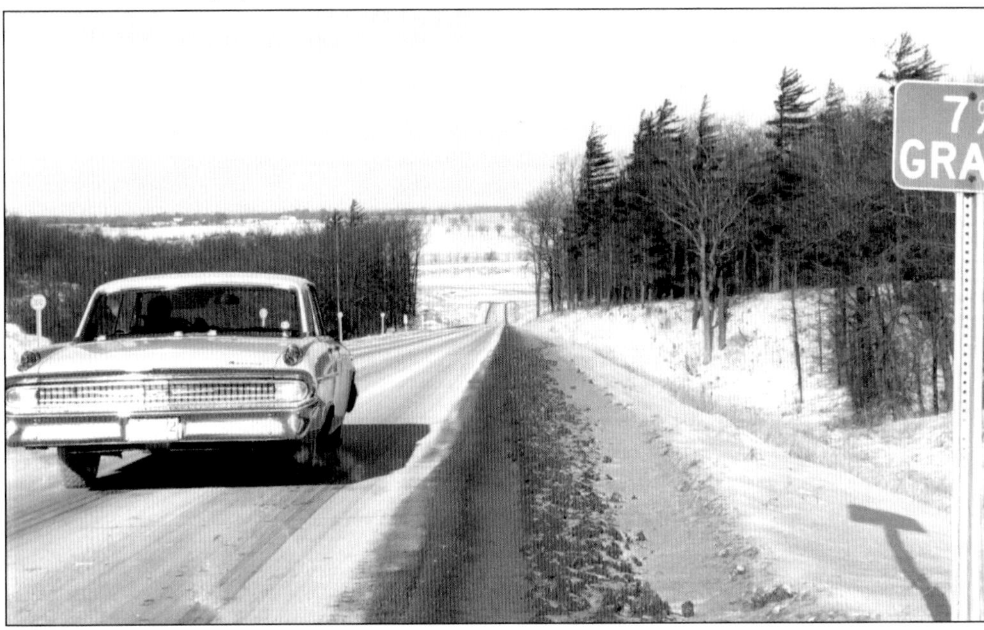

Here a 1962 Mercury Monterey prepares to descend a quarter-mile long, seven percent grade at the Michigan Proving Ground near Romeo. Elsewhere on the hilly property are grades of up to 60 percent and the highest elevation rising 350 feet above sea level. The steeper grades were too much for passenger cars but useful for testing military vehicles of the time and four-wheel-drive vehicles of the future. (N.)

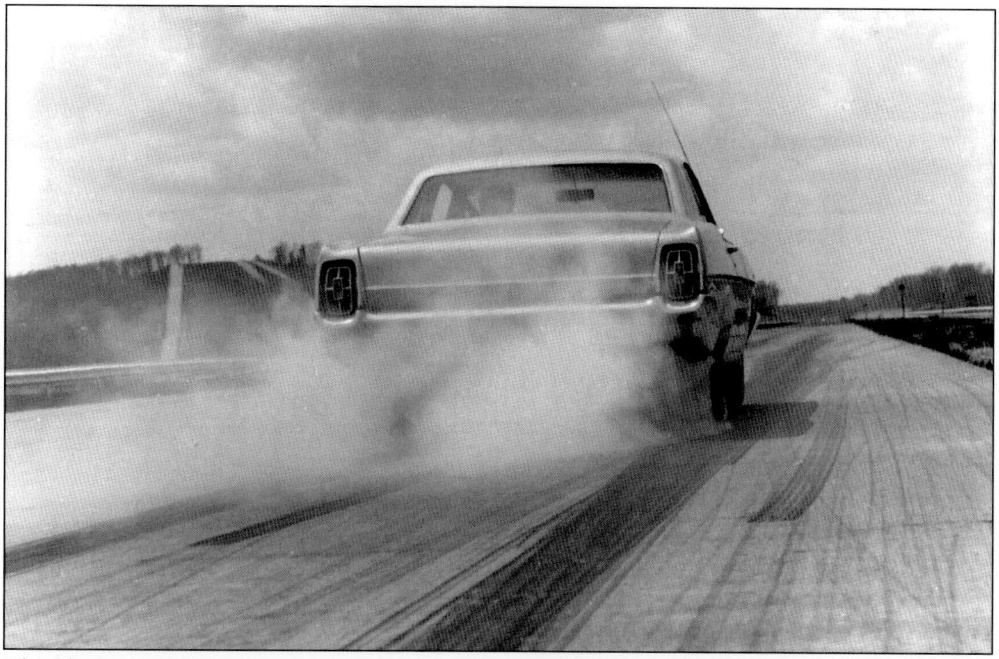

The black streaks seen on the pavement in this photograph resulted from repeated, simulated emergency brake stops, as Ford vehicles were put through their punishing tests at the company's Michigan Proving Ground at Romeo. The car shown here undergoing the test is a 1967 Ford Custom. One of the natural hills of the site and its test roads are seen in the background. (N.)

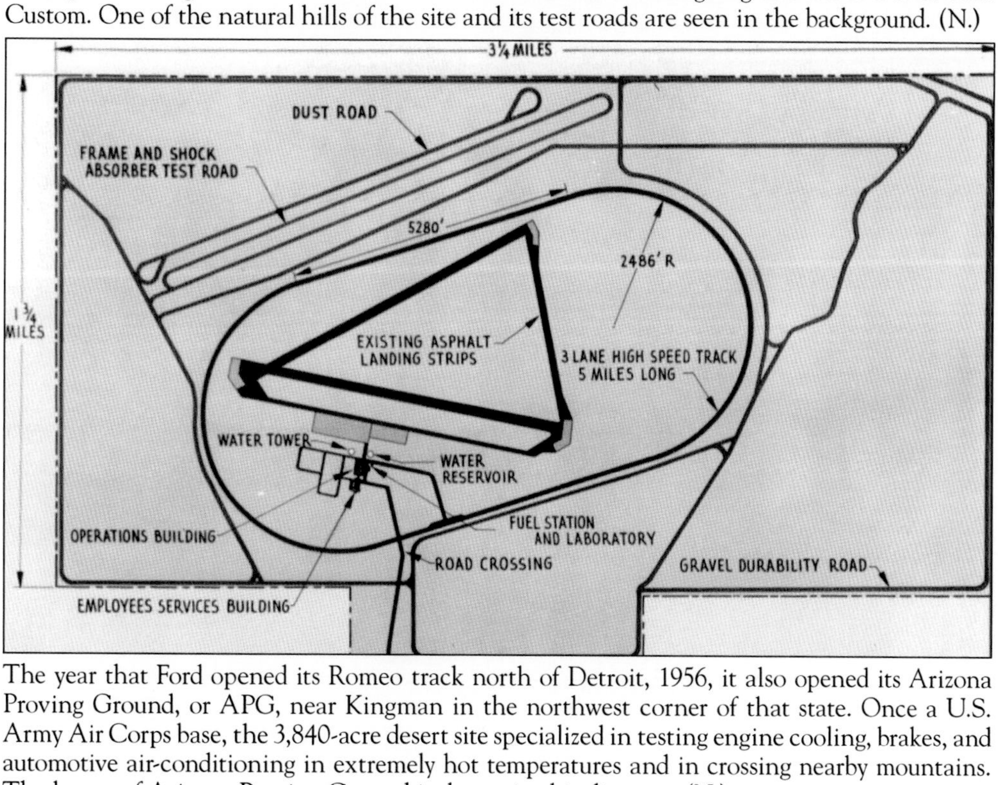

The year that Ford opened its Romeo track north of Detroit, 1956, it also opened its Arizona Proving Ground, or APG, near Kingman in the northwest corner of that state. Once a U.S. Army Air Corps base, the 3,840-acre desert site specialized in testing engine cooling, brakes, and automotive air-conditioning in extremely hot temperatures and in crossing nearby mountains. The layout of Arizona Proving Ground is shown in this diagram. (N.)

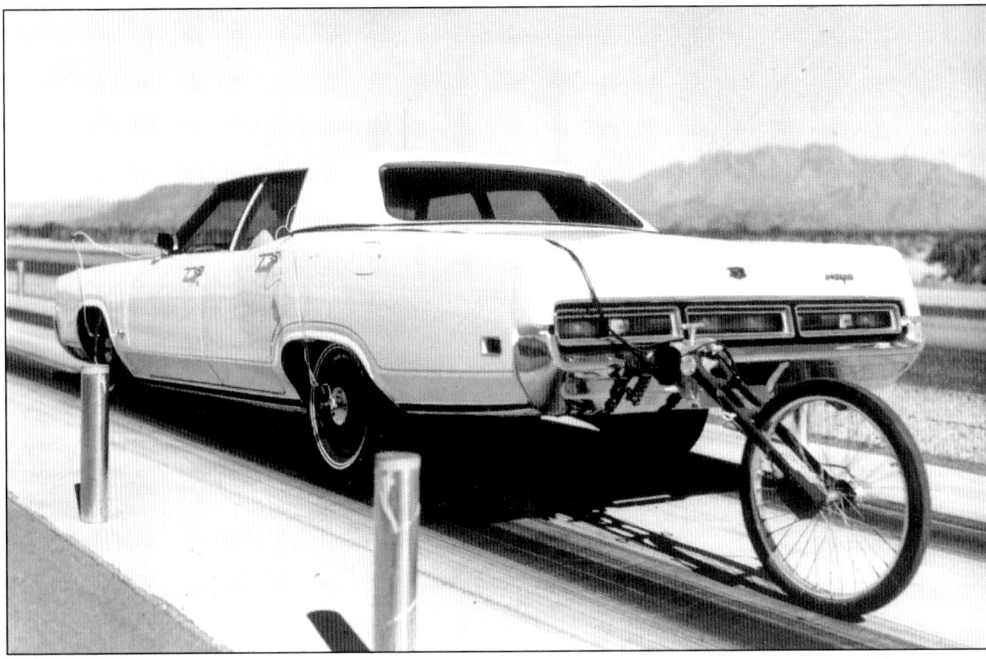

The hard braking test of this 1970 Mercury Marquis at the Arizona Proving Ground has caused the front end to dive. The test car is equipped with a bicycle wheel-like fifth wheel for accurately recording speed and distance. The mountains seen in the distance provided opportunities to test cars and especially trucks climbing the long grades in high temperatures. (N.)

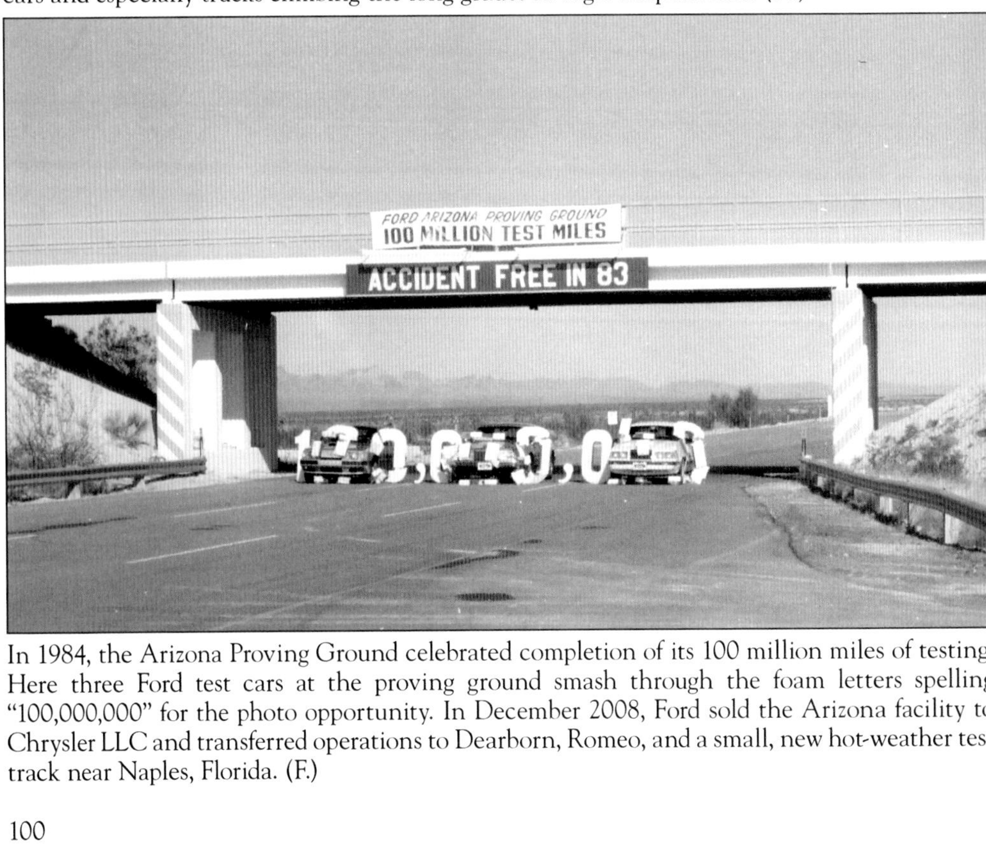

In 1984, the Arizona Proving Ground celebrated completion of its 100 million miles of testing. Here three Ford test cars at the proving ground smash through the foam letters spelling "100,000,000" for the photo opportunity. In December 2008, Ford sold the Arizona facility to Chrysler LLC and transferred operations to Dearborn, Romeo, and a small, new hot-weather test track near Naples, Florida. (F.)

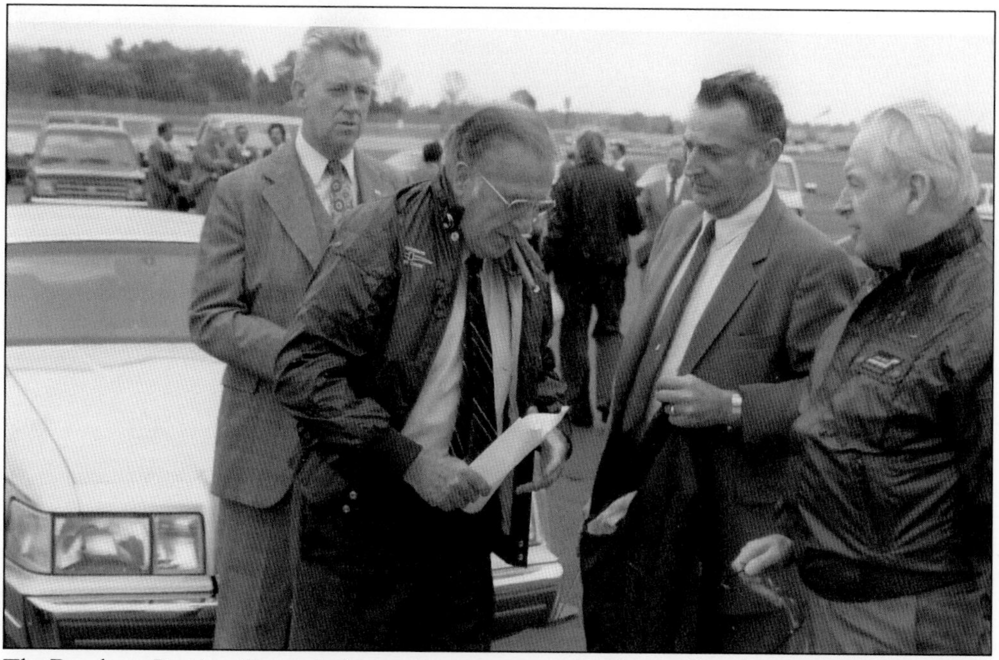

The Dearborn Proving Ground, close and convenient to Ford's world headquarters building, began hosting annual ride-and-drive tests of Ford and competitive vehicles for company executives and members of the board of directors. In this 1983 photograph, former chairman Henry Ford II is shown donning a track jacket, while chairman Phillip Caldwell stands at right. (F.)

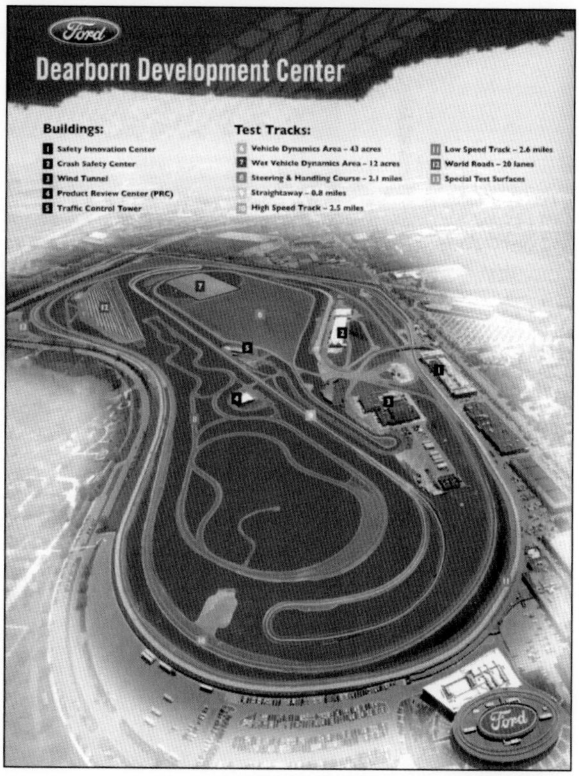

In 2001, Ford announced a complete revamping of Dearborn Proving Ground and changed its name to Dearborn Development Center. This image shows the many features of the rehabilitated one-time airport. Compare this to the 1930s aerial photographs on page 90. There are many more roadways and now buildings in the midst of the site. The old airport tower is long gone, replaced by a traffic-control tower. (F.)

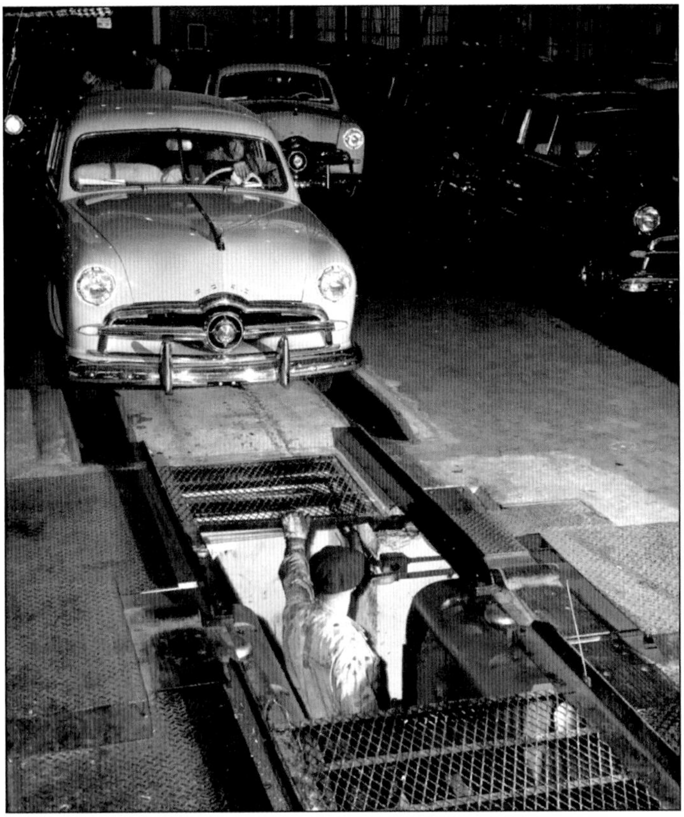

In closing this chapter on Ford's test tracks, one other testing protocol bears mention. It takes place not on proving grounds but in assembly plants before new vehicles are released for shipment to dealers and customers. Here a 1949 Ford is being checked at the old Dearborn assembly plant, where every 20 seconds, cars had their wheels spun at 30 miles per hour by pneumatic rollers before release. This was common industry practice. (N.)

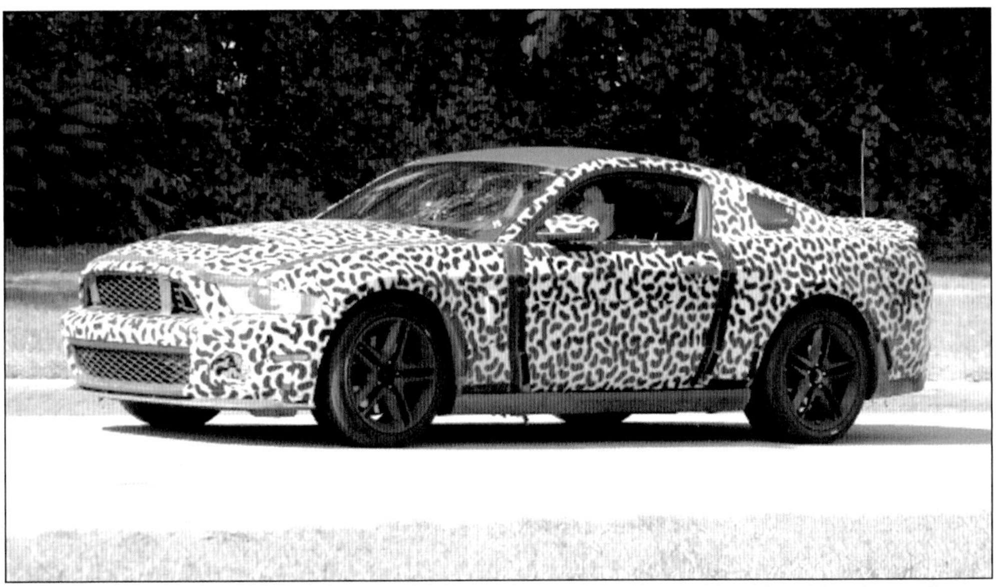

Despite all the security efforts by Ford to keep its future models secret, such as this leopardesque paint job on a future Mustang, ace spy photographer Jim Dunne still manages to catch them when their guard is down, as shown in this shot of a Mustang "mule" on or near one of Ford's proving grounds. (J.)

Eight

Chrysler Corporation Chelsea Proving Ground

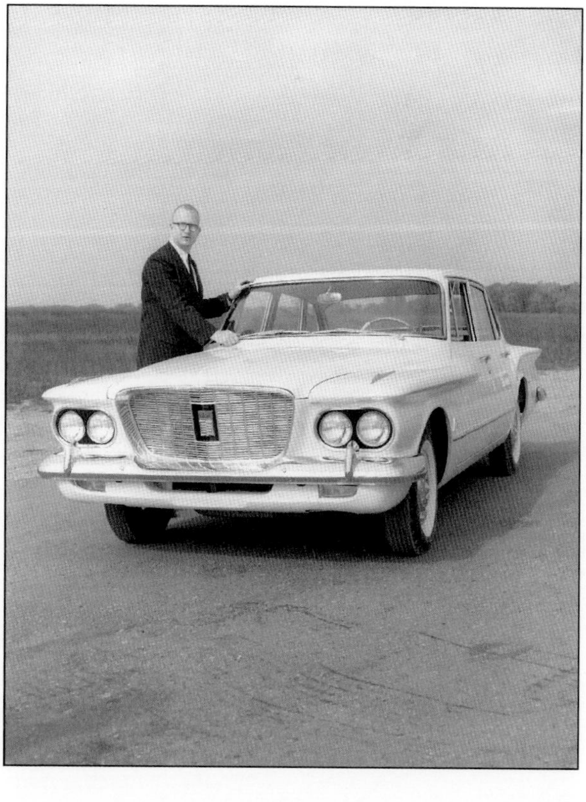

Five years after Chrysler opened its Chelsea Proving Ground some 50 or so miles west of its Highland Park headquarters, this author, then a reporter for *Business Week* magazine, visited the site to test-drive the new 1960 Valiant compact car. Here he poses with the new model at Chelsea. (D.)

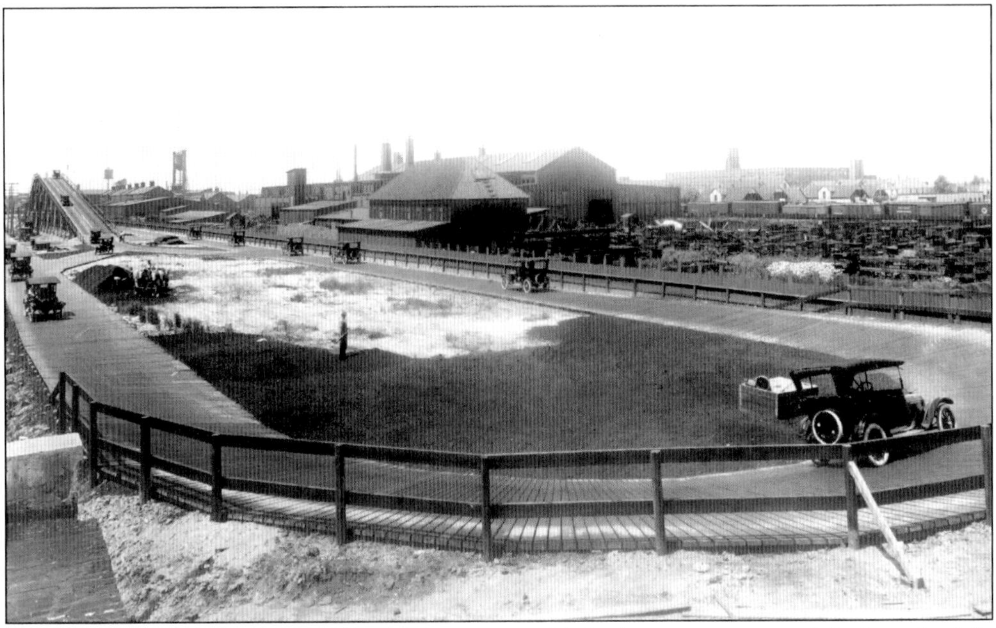

In 1915, after the Dodge Brothers Company established its own automobile brand while continuing to supply major components to Ford Motor Company, it built this pioneering test track behind its Hamtramck factory. It was probably used for some development work but mainly was for testing engines, brakes, and running gear of new cars before they were released from the factory for shipment to dealers. (N.)

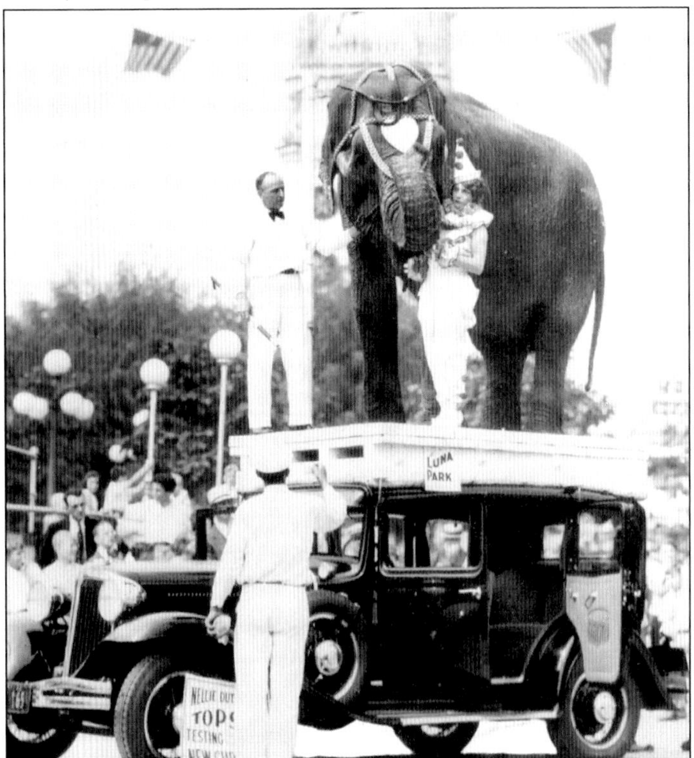

In September 1930, Chrysler staged this stunt, perceived by the public as a test, of putting an elephant atop a 1931 Chrysler. The caption stated, "It was possible to give the [elephant] his first auto spin because . . . Chrysler Eights have all-steel bodies, the latest in motor coach construction. These bodies were designed to support thousands of pounds more than they will ever be subjected to . . . considered the final word in motor car safety." (N.)

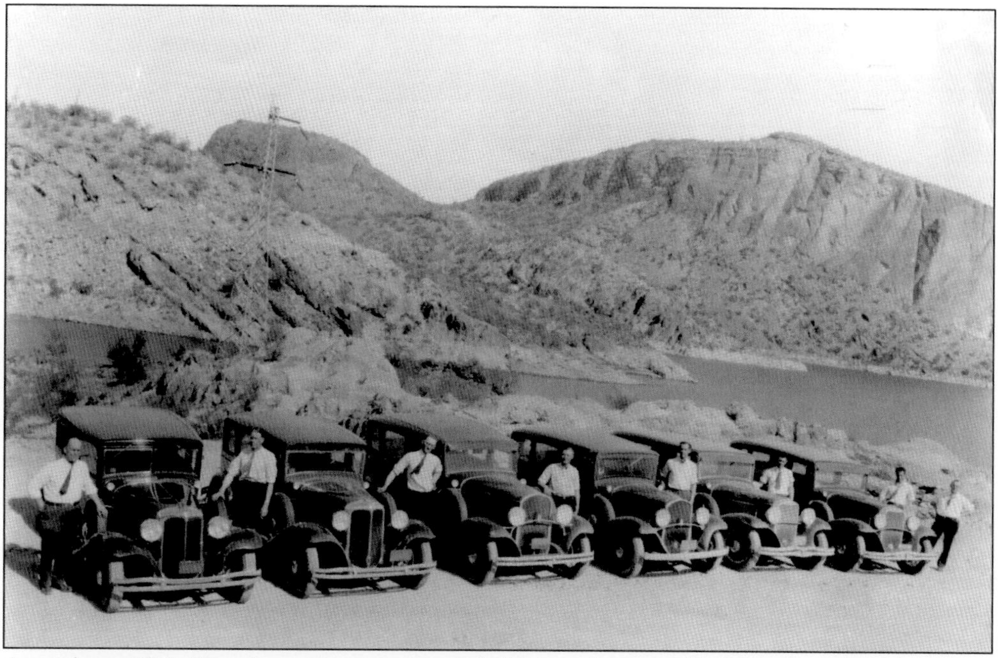

As early as 1930, Chrysler engineers extended their road testing far beyond rural Michigan, in this case to the mountains of Arizona. Here six Chrysler products are lined up with the team at the shore of what could be Theodore Roosevelt Lake, east of Phoenix. The cars include two Chryslers at left, a DeSoto Eight, a DeSoto Six, and two Dodges. (N)

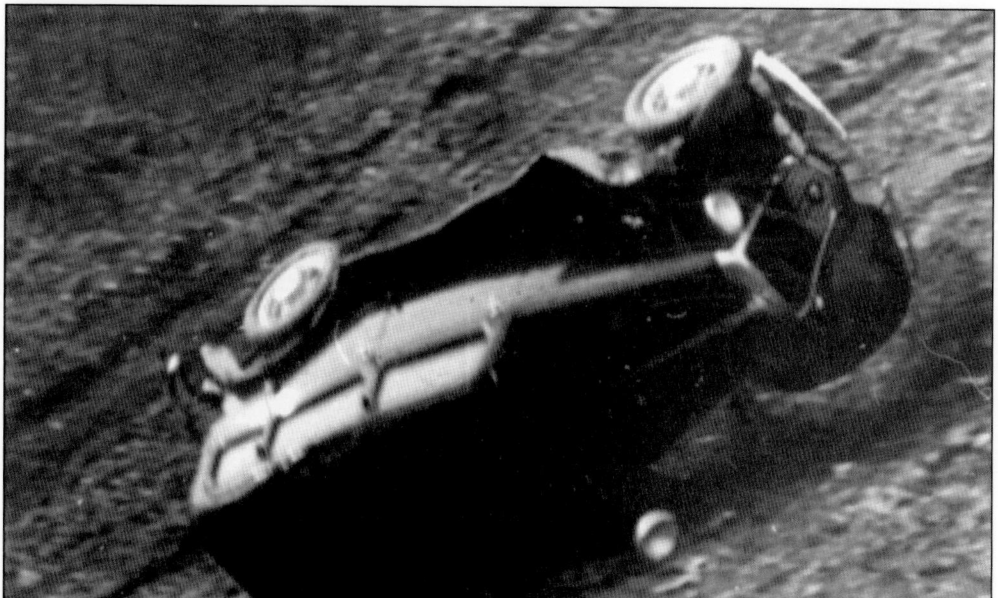

Primitive safety testing took place in the early 1930s, as shown by this 1933 Dodge being rolled down a hill. It is not known who staged the test or why. Unlike post–World War II safety testing, there is no sign of test instrumentation. In similar tests by Chrysler promoters that were recorded by motion picture cameras, body strength was demonstrated by the doors staying closed in the rollover and being operable afterwards. (N.)

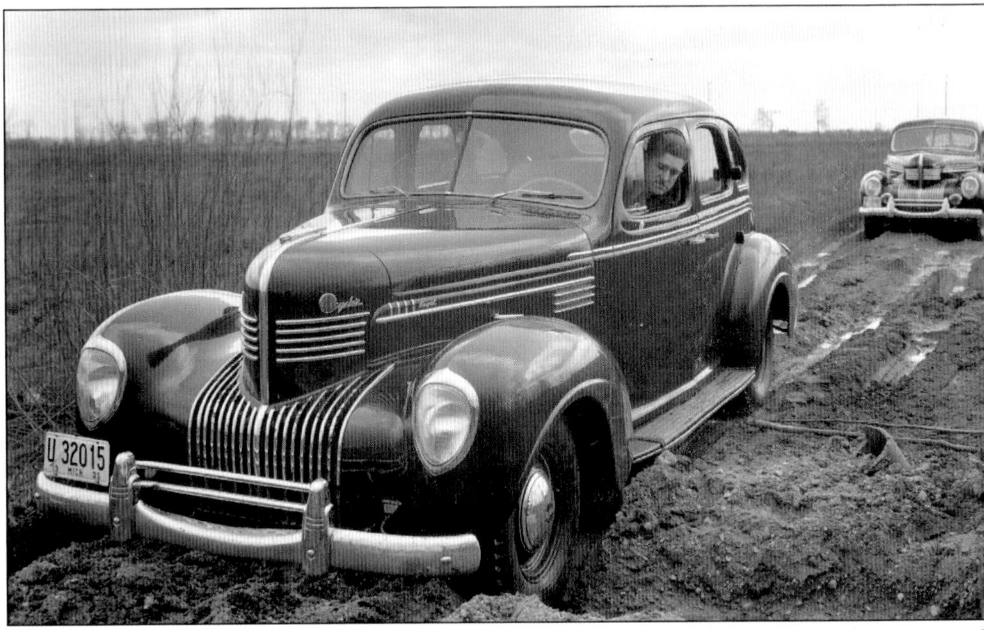

These 1939 Chryslers are being subject to deeply rutted, muddy roads at "the truck test grounds near 9 Mile and Mound," which would have meant adjacent to the Dodge truck plant built in 1938. At a time when Chrysler undertook most of developmental testing on public roads or in laboratories, this could be considered a forerunner of the full-scale proving ground opened 15 years later at Chelsea. (N.)

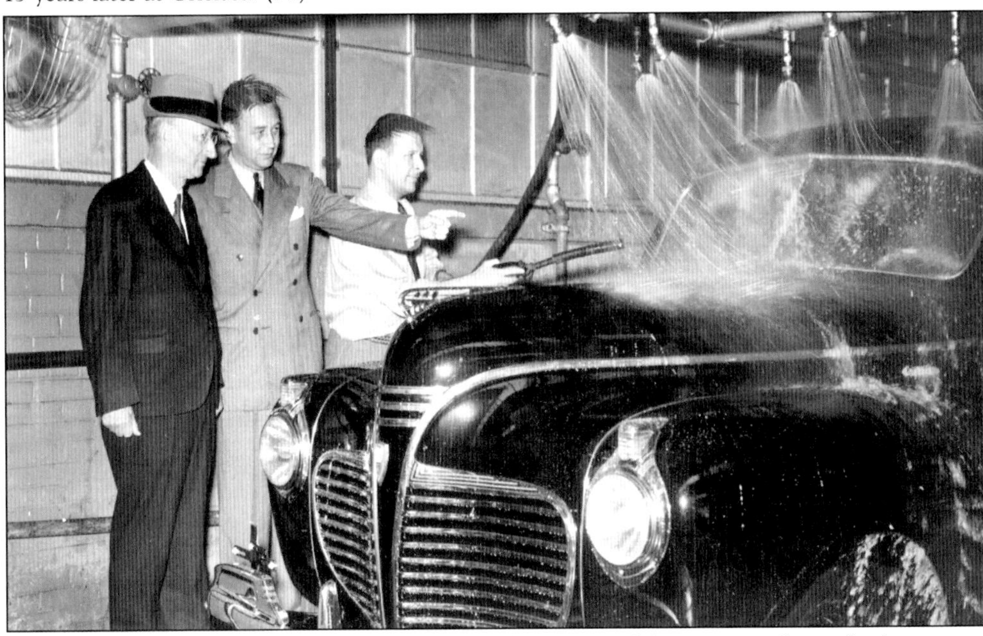

Lacking a proving ground, Chrysler maintained extensive laboratory and test facilities at its Highland Park headquarters. Here a 1941 Plymouth, similar to the car in which the author learned to drive, is bathed by an artificial rainstorm machine while Clarence J. Root (left), the head of the U.S. Weather Bureau in Detroit, looks on. Plymouth general sales manager (center) explains how the car's sealing keeps out the wind and water. (N.)

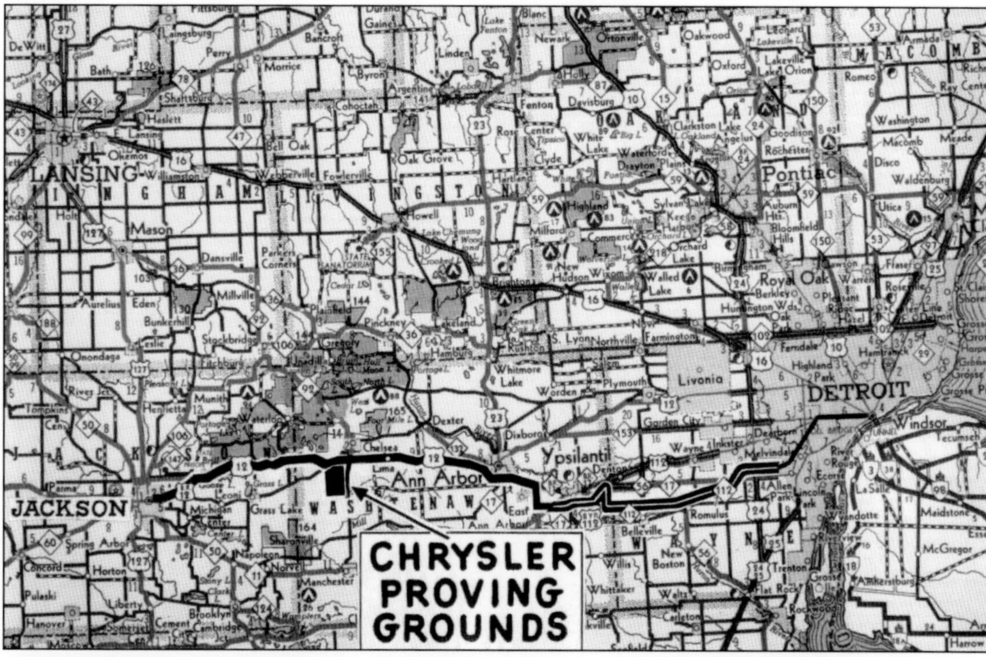

After holding out for decades against building its own test track, Chrysler announced in the early 1950s that it was obtaining land west of Ann Arbor to develop a full-scale proving ground. This map issued at the time shows the location and also that it was some years before the federal interstate highway system replaced the old U.S. highways radiating from Detroit. (N.)

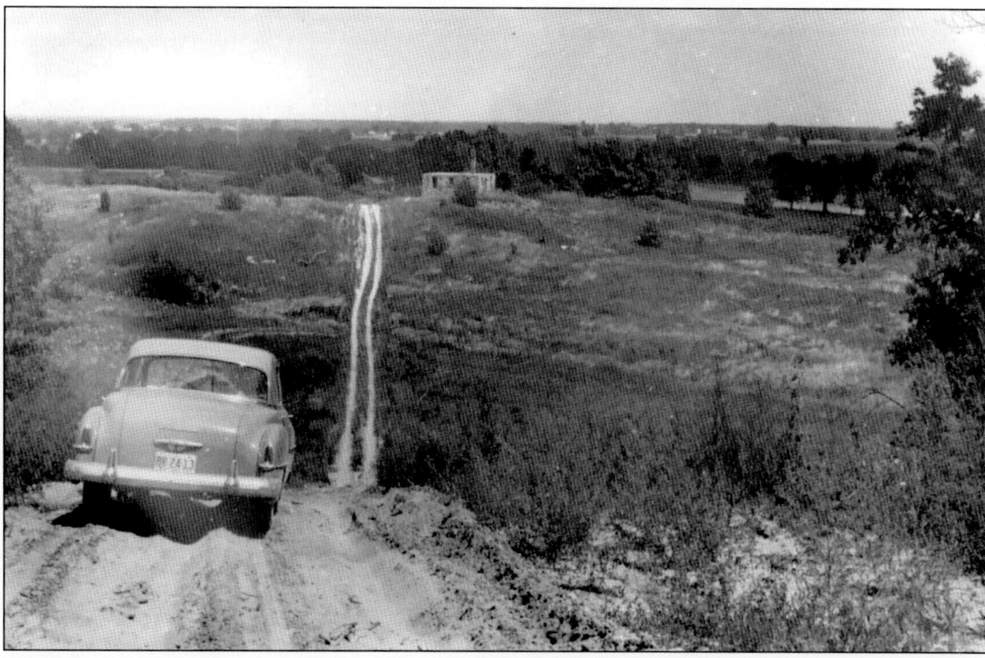
This photograph shows a 1951 Dodge on a country road over what was to become Chrysler's Chelsea Proving Ground. It is not clear whether the car was driven to the site by an official planning the layout of the test facilities or whether Dodge engineers were "pushing the envelope" by testing a car over rough roads on company land. (N.)

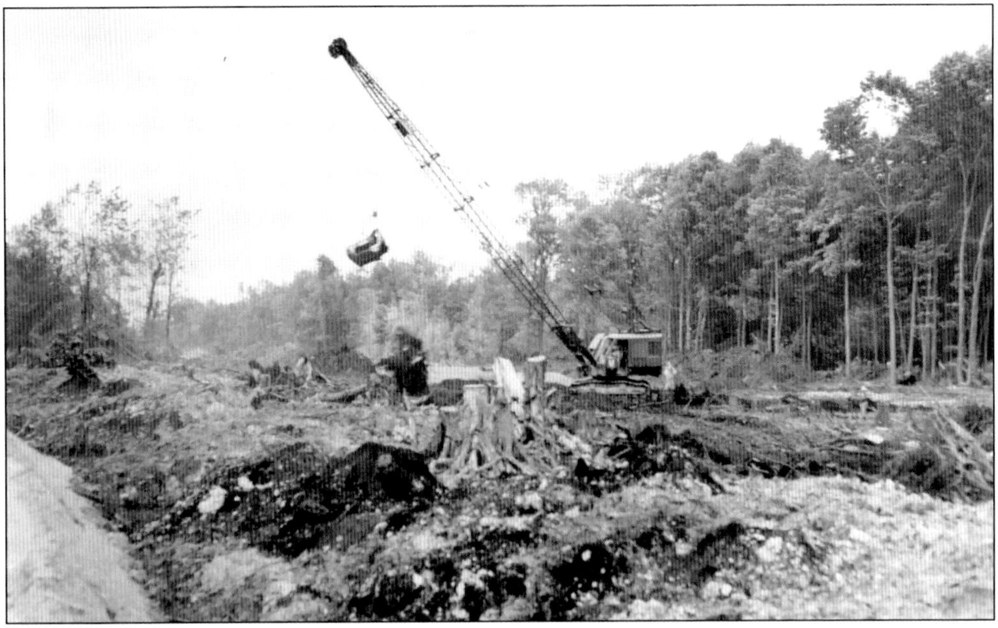

Mammoth site preparation had to precede actual track construction at Chelsea. The caption for this photograph stated, "Trees and stumps were cleared from site of north-south straightaway track at Chrysler Engineering Proving Grounds in the summer of 1952 prior to filling and grading the finished straightaway unit." Located at the edge of Michigan's Irish Hills, Chelsea provided the needed rolling landscape for a proving ground. (N.)

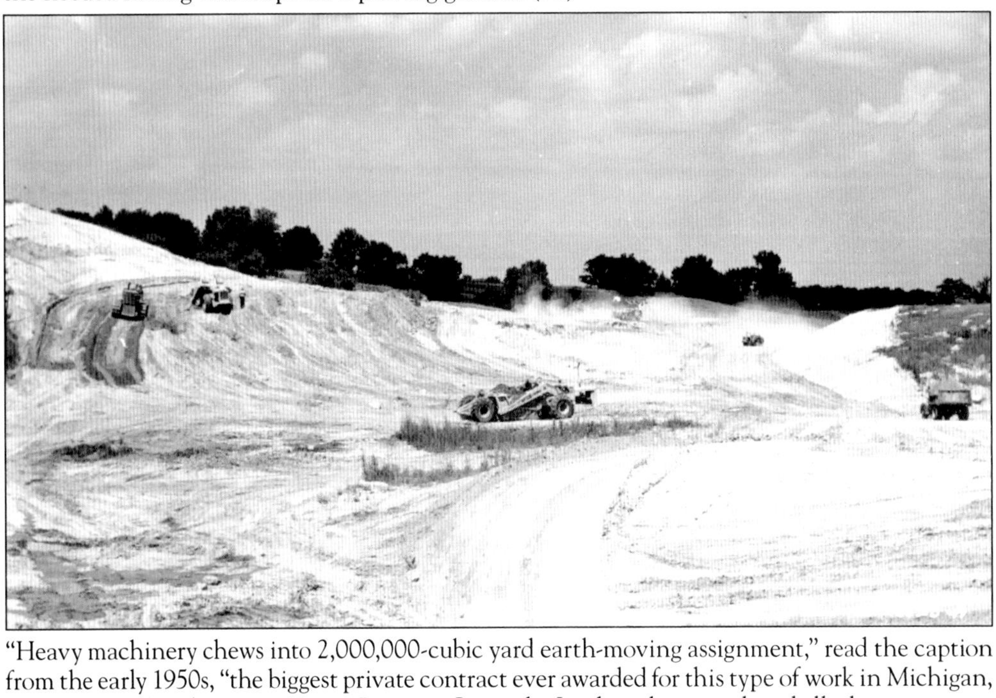

"Heavy machinery chews into 2,000,000-cubic yard earth-moving assignment," read the caption from the early 1950s, "the biggest private contract ever awarded for this type of work in Michigan, at the new Chrysler Engineering Proving Grounds. In this photograph, a hillside is cut away for the 4.7-mile high-speed oval test track, part of the 45 miles of test roads and tracks under construction at the Proving Grounds." (N.)

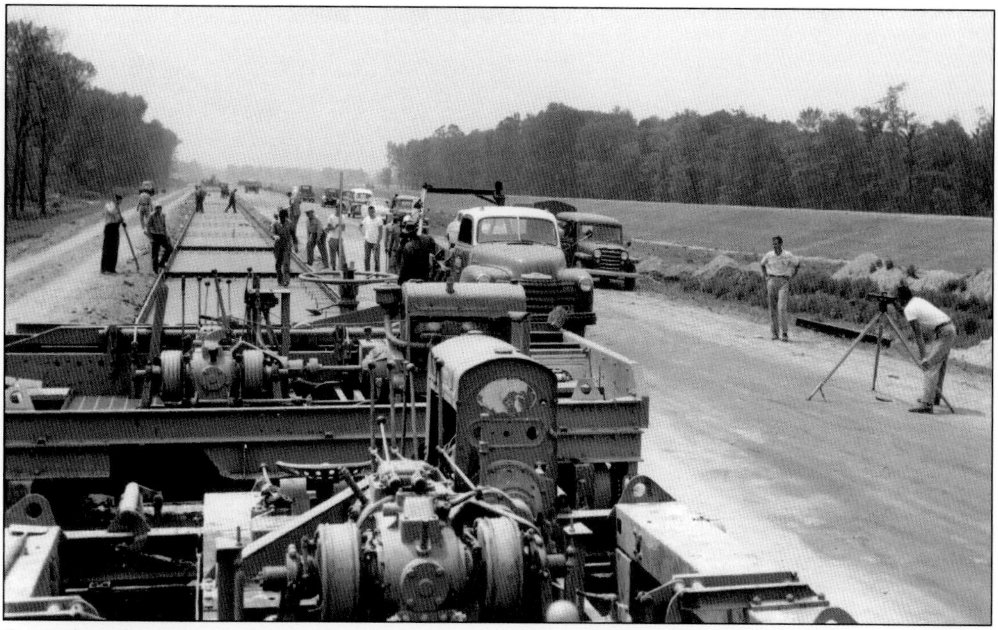

Several work crews can be seen in this view of roadway paving at the Chelsea Proving Ground, using similar concrete-laying equipment to that seen at other industry test tracks earlier in this book and, indeed, at any highway building project—except that here the grading is level for what was probably the 1.59-mile east–west straightaway. The raised edge of the high-speed oval can be seen at right. (N.)

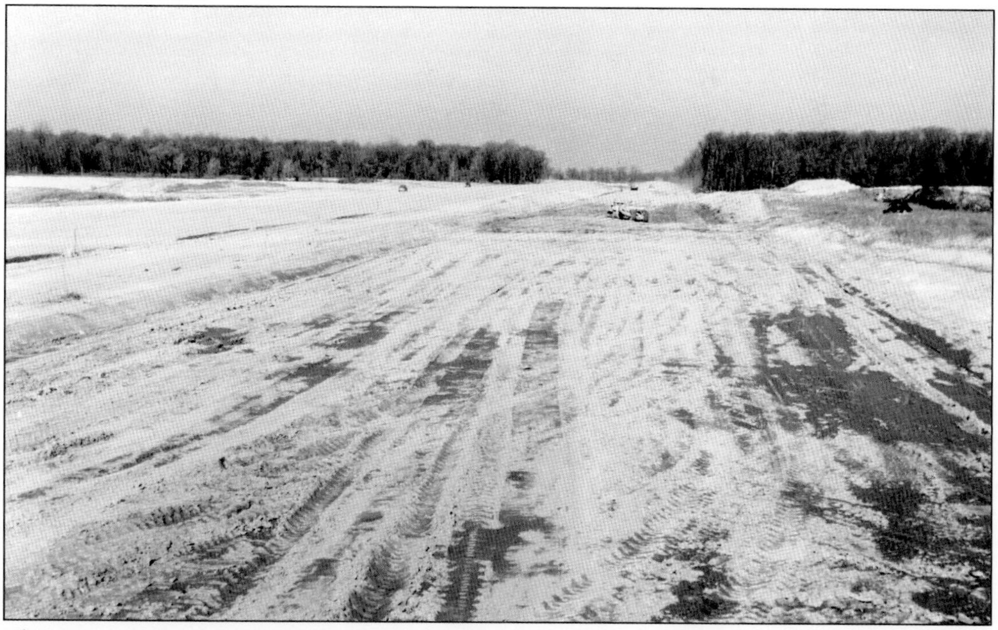

This view is looking north along the 2.23-mile north–south straightaway at the Chrysler proving ground near Chelsea. Stretching into the horizon from the foreground, this separate straightaway track parallels the east leg of the high-speed oval test track at left. From the accumulation of light snow, the photograph likely was taken in the winter of 1953 while construction was ongoing. (N.)

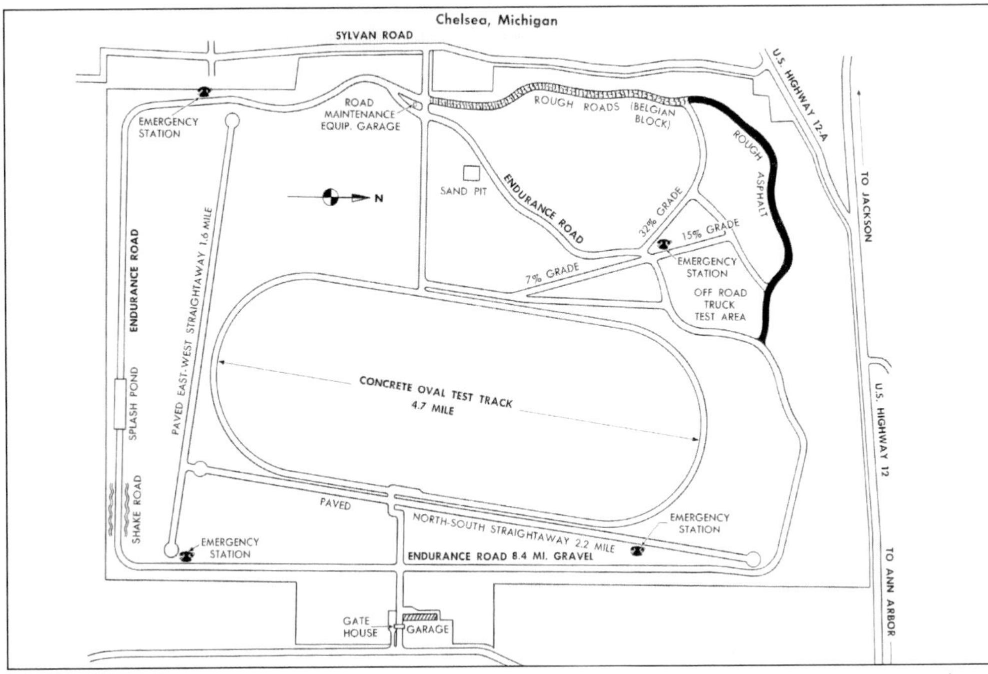

This diagram of Chrysler's Chelsea Proving Ground shows its variety of test roads located just south of U.S. 12, locally called the Jackson Road, a principal route between Detroit and Chicago dating to stagecoach days. The acreage came to 4,000, larger at the time than either GM's or Ford's proving grounds. (N.)

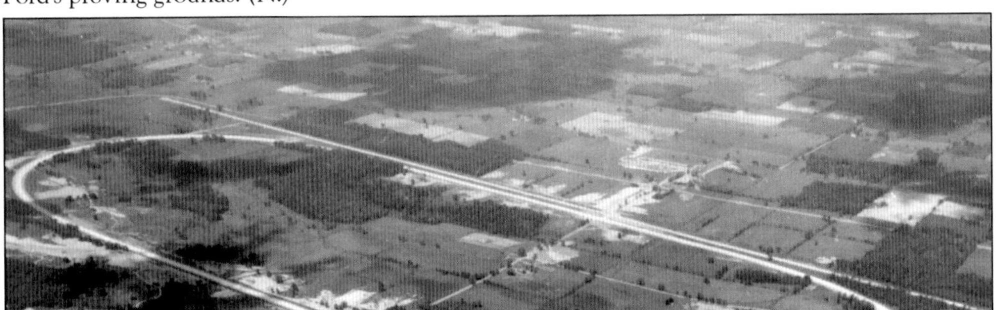

Here is an aerial photograph of the Chelsea Proving Ground, viewed from the southwest. A section of the site's 8.4-mile gravel "endurance road" is visible in the foreground. At the upper right are the 60,000-square-foot test garage and office buildings. The high-speed oval is six concrete lanes wide—two years before Congress passed the law creating the interstate highway system, which provided such superhighways to motorists across America. (N.)

Chrysler formally dedicated the Chelsea Proving Ground on June 16, 1954, with a national press conference to show off its most important facility in many decades. Entertainment for the press included this exhibition of one 1954 Plymouth flying off a ramp over another. Chrysler also showed off dozens of Plymouth taxicabs from around the country to emphasize their reliability. (N.)

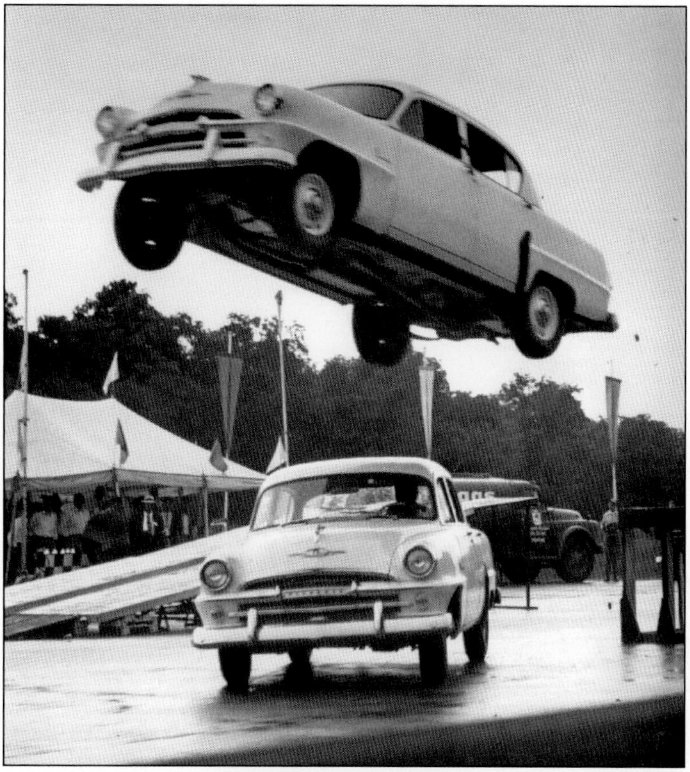

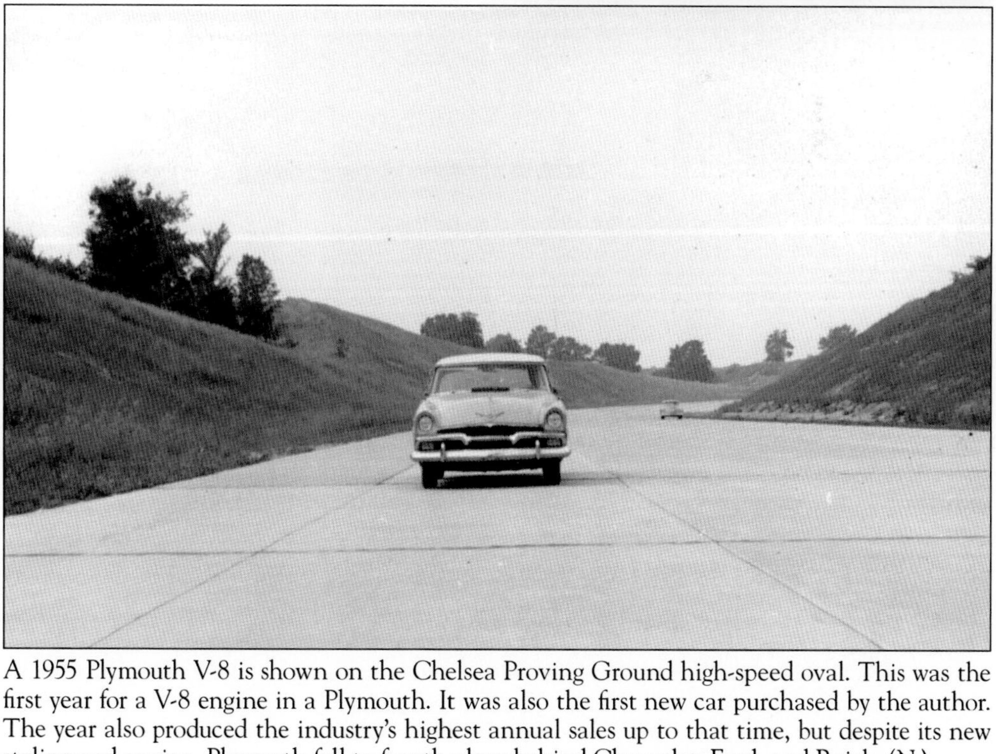

A 1955 Plymouth V-8 is shown on the Chelsea Proving Ground high-speed oval. This was the first year for a V-8 engine in a Plymouth. It was also the first new car purchased by the author. The year also produced the industry's highest annual sales up to that time, but despite its new styling and engine, Plymouth fell to fourth place behind Chevrolet, Ford, and Buick. (N.)

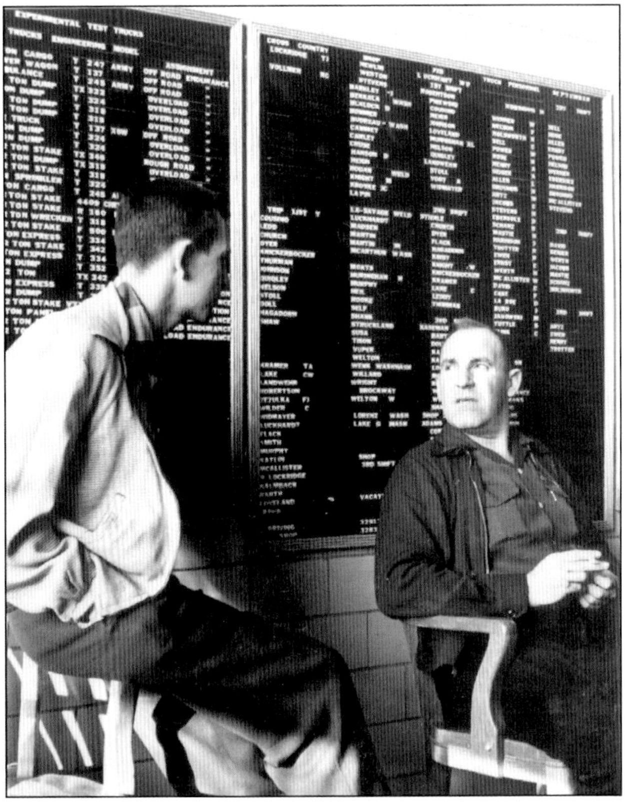

According to the caption attached to this press release photograph, "Test drivers find their assignments posted on these boards in the ready-room of the Chrysler Engineering Proving Grounds . . . Chrysler test drivers will cover more than 2,500,000 miles on Proving Grounds roads during the coming year [1954–1955]." The boards lists truck-testing assignments: off road, rough road, and overload endurance. (N.)

Safety has always been a major concern on automotive test tracks due to the many roadways and intersections, and because many test vehicles have experimental components, some tests call for high speeds, and driving a closed circuit endlessly day and night can be sleep inducing. This sign at the Chelsea test track warns of cross traffic. In more recent years, such crossings have been eliminated as on interstate highways. (N.)

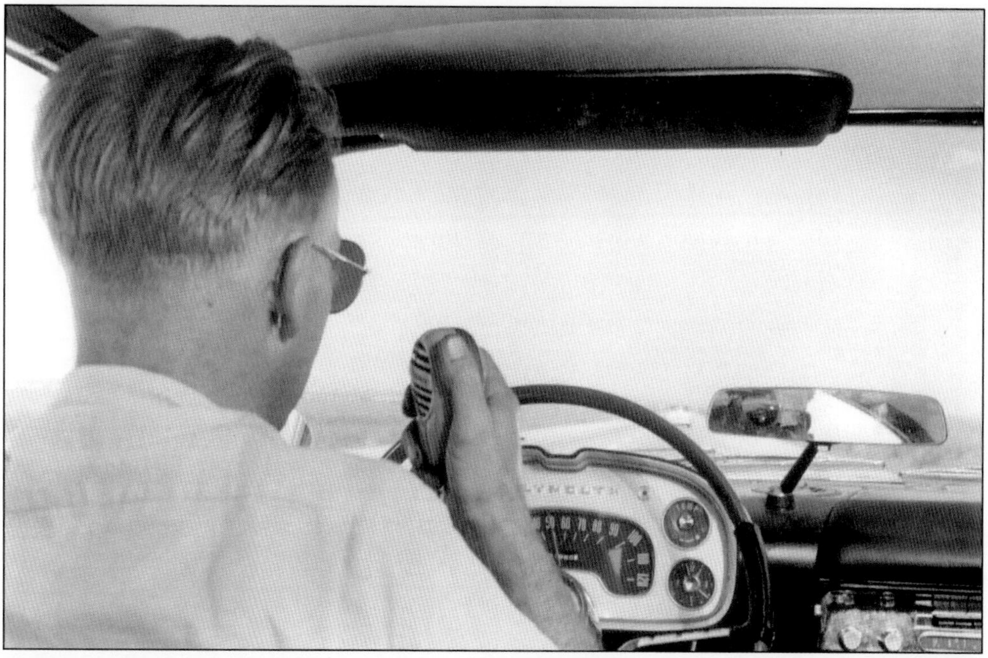

During a 58,000-mile durability test of two 1958 Plymouths, Chelsea Proving Ground drivers used two-way radios, shown here, to arrange for relief drivers to meet them. Four crews of 11 men each participated in the extensive test, working 12-hour shifts with the next 24 hours off. It took 58 days to rack up the desired mileage. (N.)

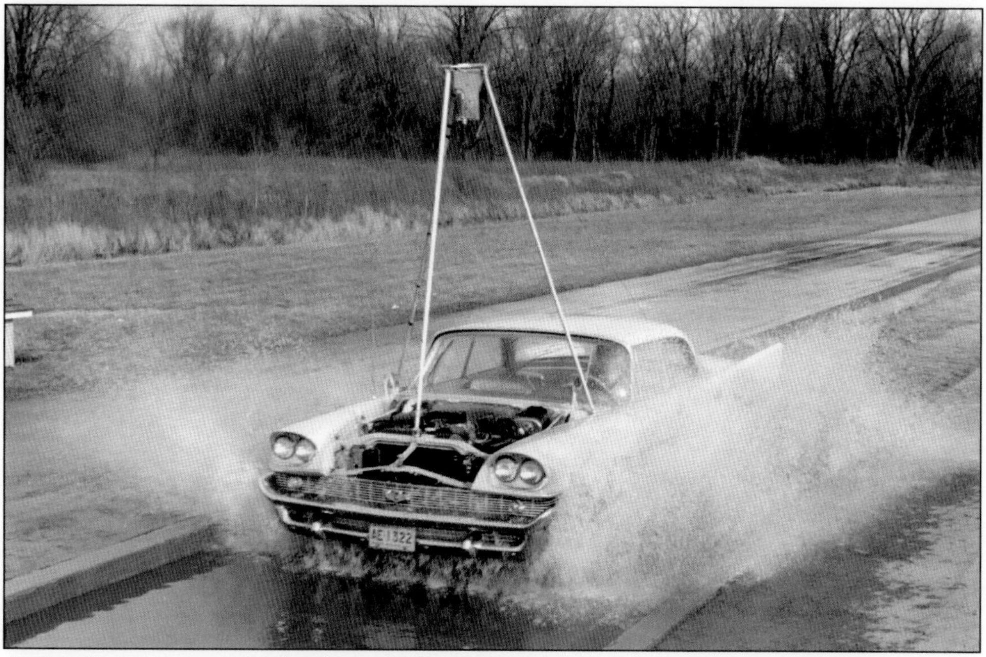

As the illustrations in this book amply demonstrate, every automotive test track seems to have its water pit, and photographers like them because they show movement. This view of a 1958 Chrysler is different because a movie camera is mounted over the open engine compartment to film water splashing on components that might result in the engine misfiring or stalling. (N.)

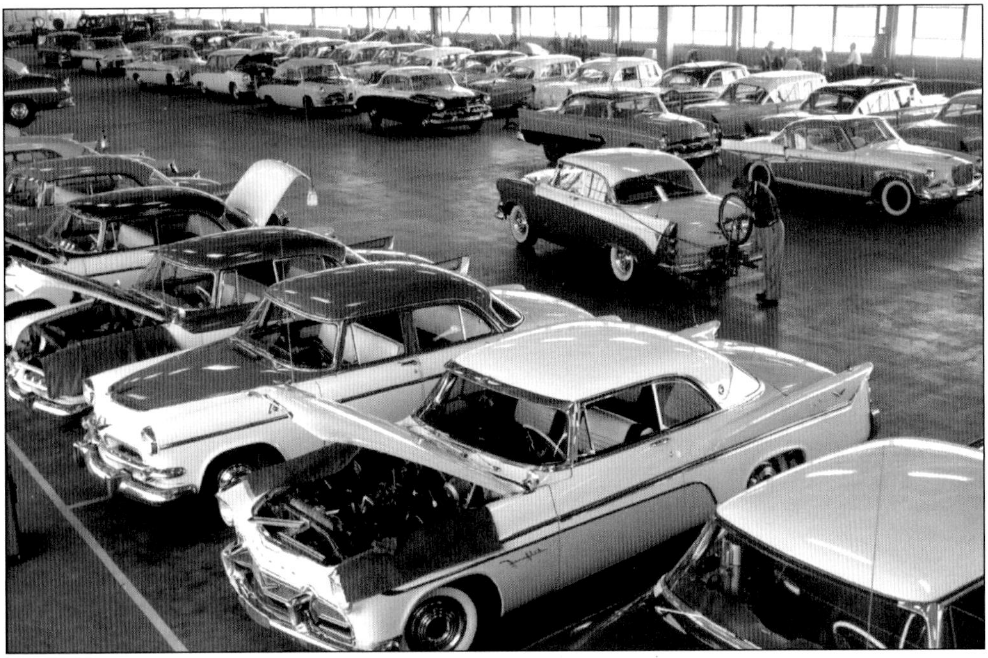

This view of the engineering garage at the Chrysler Proving Ground shows a variety of 1955 and 1956 model Chrysler cars, as well as at least two identifiable competitors—a Studebaker and a Lincoln. A typical fifth wheel test device for accurate recording of speed and distance is mounted on the 1956 Dodge in the center, facing away. (N.)

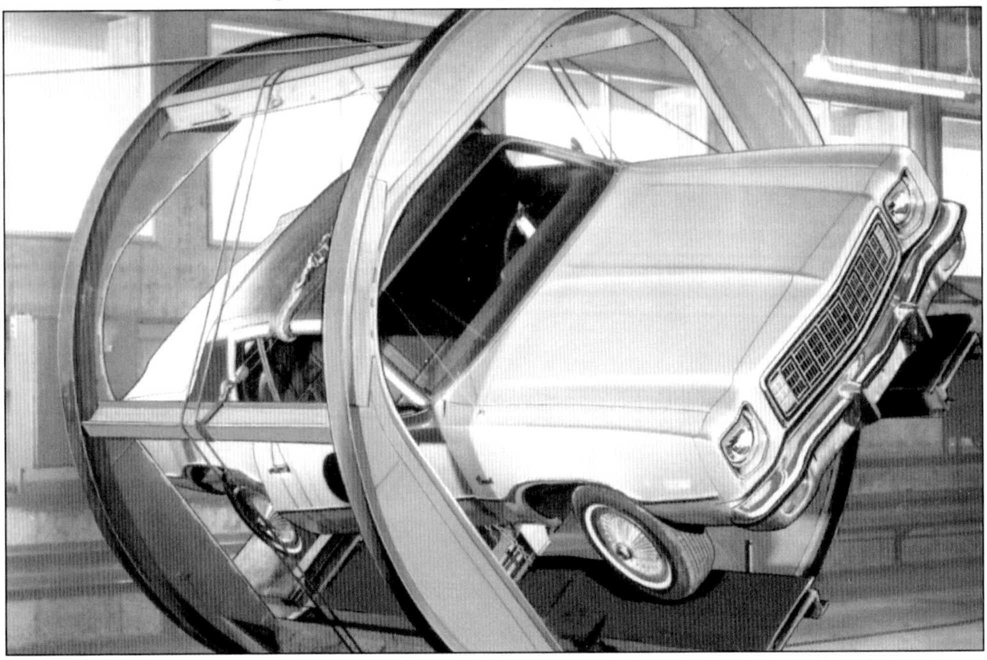

This bizarre-looking rig was developed by Chrysler engineers in the 1970s to measure fuel leakage from an upside-down car in order to comply with National Highway Safety Administration vehicle safety standards limiting such leakage after impacts up to 50 miles per hour. The car in the double hoop is a 1976 Plymouth Fury. (N.)

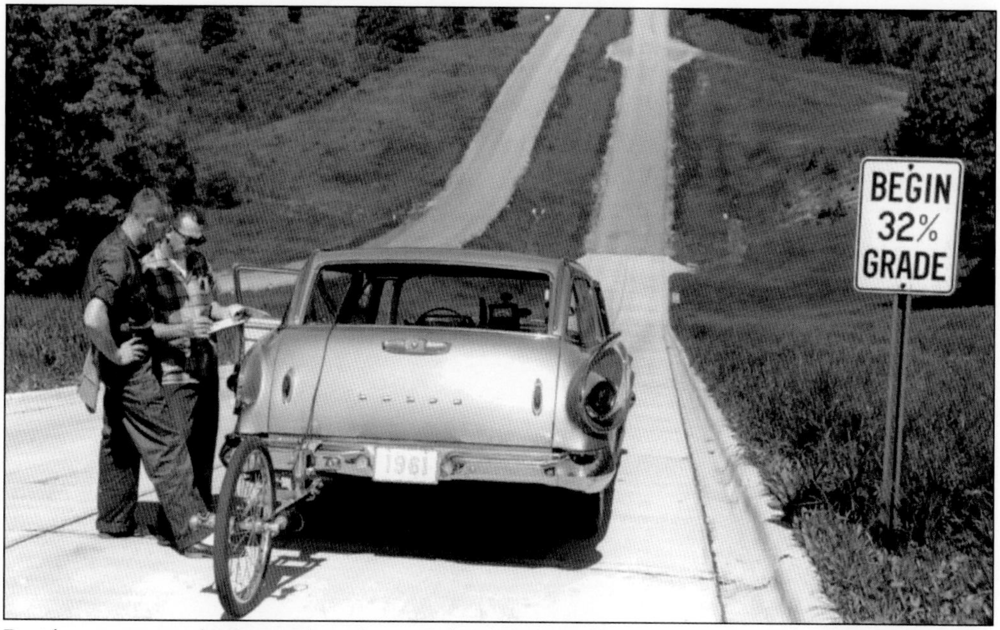

Besides water pits, high-speed tracks, and durability roads, all automotive proving grounds also have specified steep grades, like this 32 percent grade at the Chrysler Chelsea Proving Ground. What is different about this one is that it is dual laned, perhaps to allow some vehicles to climb at the same time others are descending, as this 1961 Dodge Polara station wagon is about to do when the conferring drivers are ready.

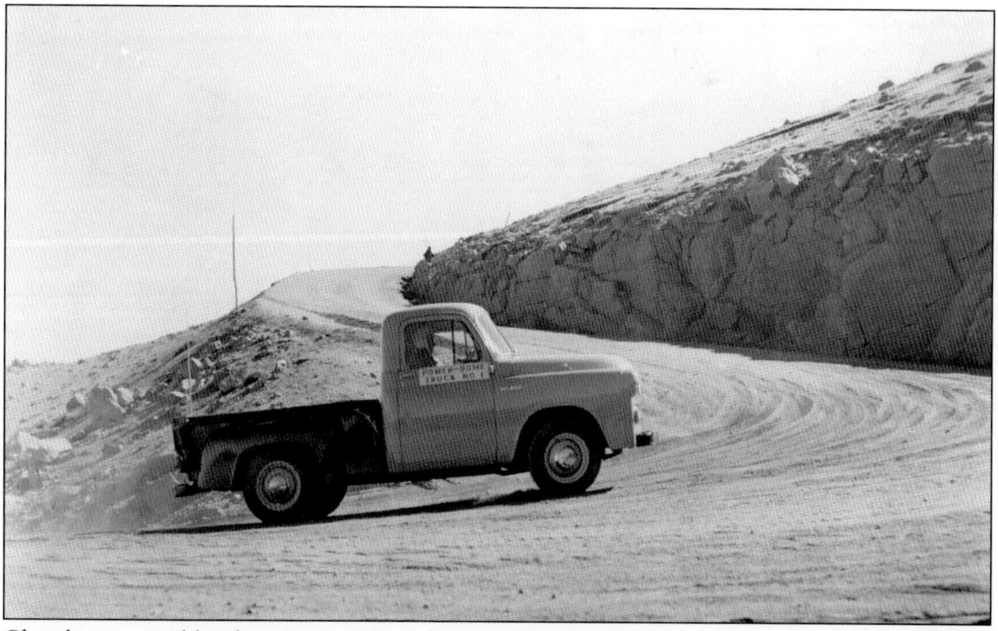
Chrysler acquired land in Arizona for a desert-and-mountain proving ground in the mid-1980s, some 30 years after the other two surviving Detroit automakers. The Chrysler track was a giant 5,555-acre tract northwest of Phoenix and was sold to land developers in 2005. All along, however, automakers utilized the steep grades and high elevations of Pikes Peak, Colorado, for strenuous testing, such as this prototype 1955 Dodge pickup climbing the mountain. (N.)

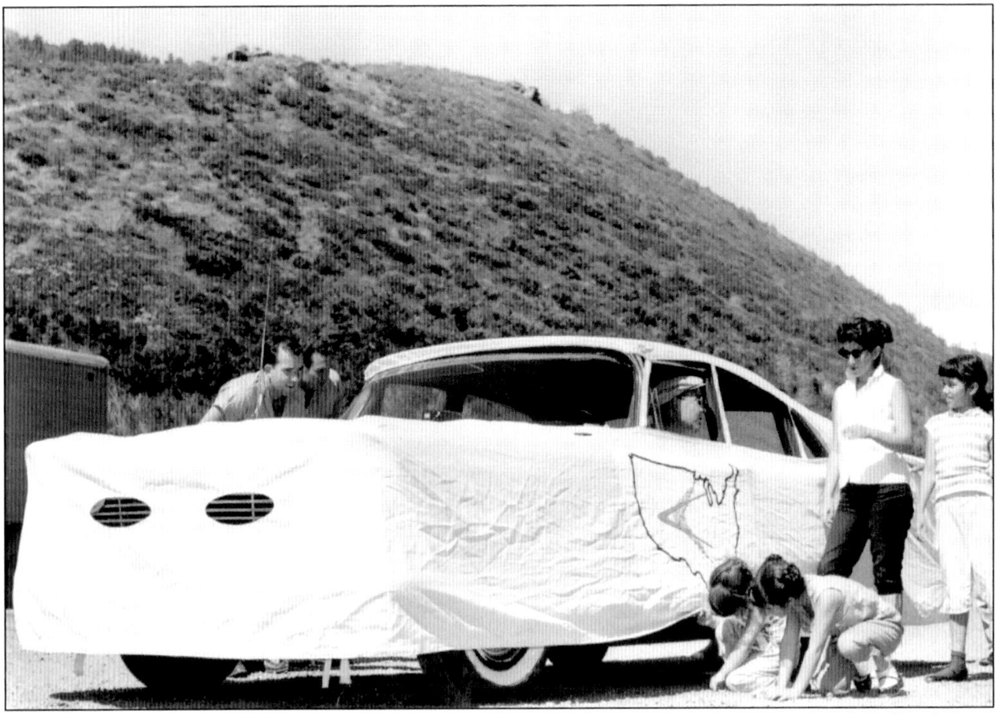

As a promotion for 1958 models, Chrysler sent this Plymouth and others, disguised under sheets, on cross country 58,000-mile durability runs around the United States. The cars attracted the hoped-for curiosity, especially from children, who could not resist peeking under the shrouds covering the cars. Car companies also disguised radically new-appearing future models on public road testing to frustrate the competition and journalists. (N.)

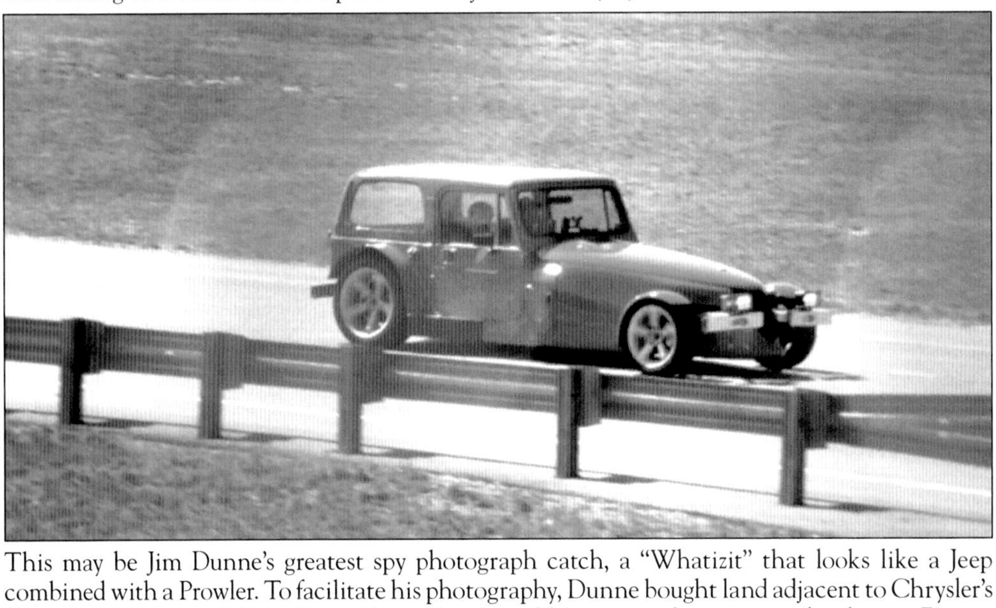

This may be Jim Dunne's greatest spy photograph catch, a "Whatizit" that looks like a Jeep combined with a Prowler. To facilitate his photography, Dunne bought land adjacent to Chrysler's desert proving ground. Years later, when Chrysler sold its test track acreage to developers, Dunne did likewise, pocketing a huge profit where he had expected nothing more than a place to mount his outdoor studio. (J.)

Nine

Other Automotive Test Tracks

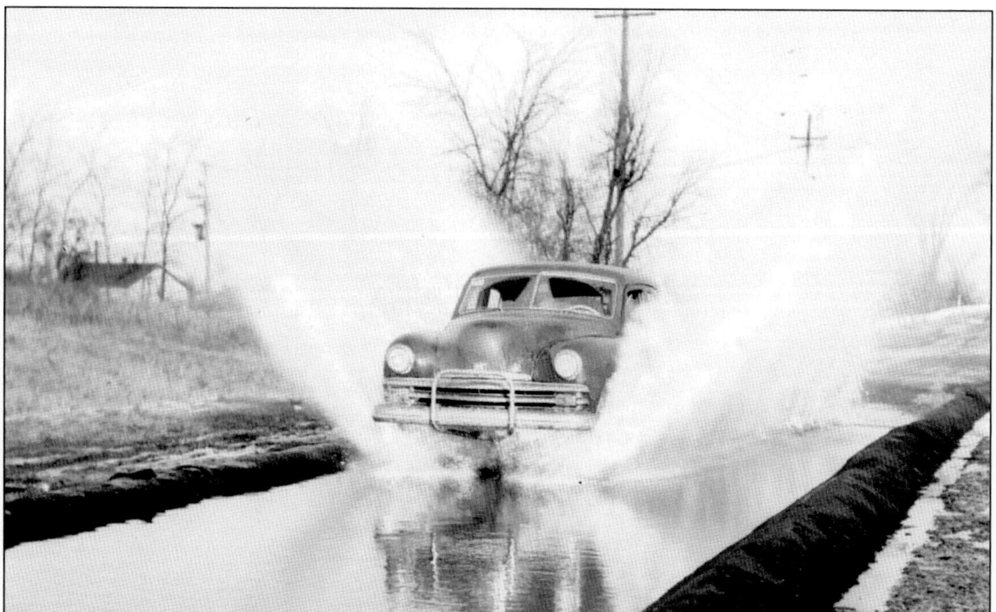

Kaiser-Frazer was an automobile company formed after World War II from the former Graham-Paige Motors and Henry J. Kaiser's shipbuilding empire. It assembled cars in the wartime Ford Willow Run B-24 bomber plant at Ypsilanti, west of Detroit. It was not known to have had a test track; nevertheless, this 1947 photograph shows a 1949 Kaiser prototype splashing through a water test, perhaps somewhere on the Willow Run airport. (N.)

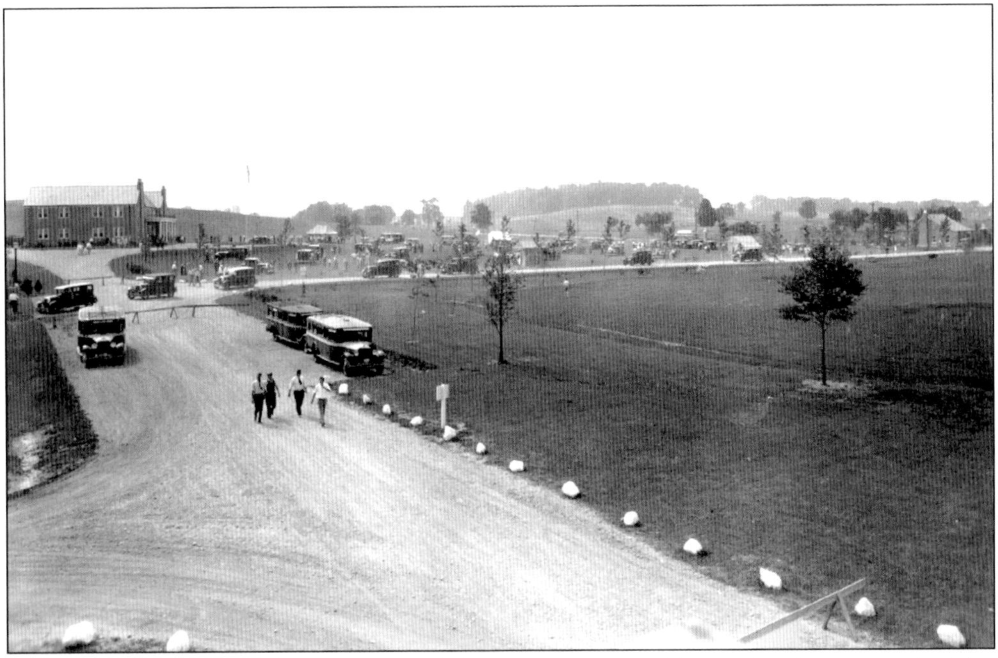

Studebaker was the third main automobile company to build a full-scale test track. This photograph shows the 1927 dedication of the Studebaker facility near its factory and headquarters in South Bend, Indiana. Studebaker began as a wagon maker before the Civil War and once had a large assembly plant in Detroit before consolidating in Indiana. (N.)

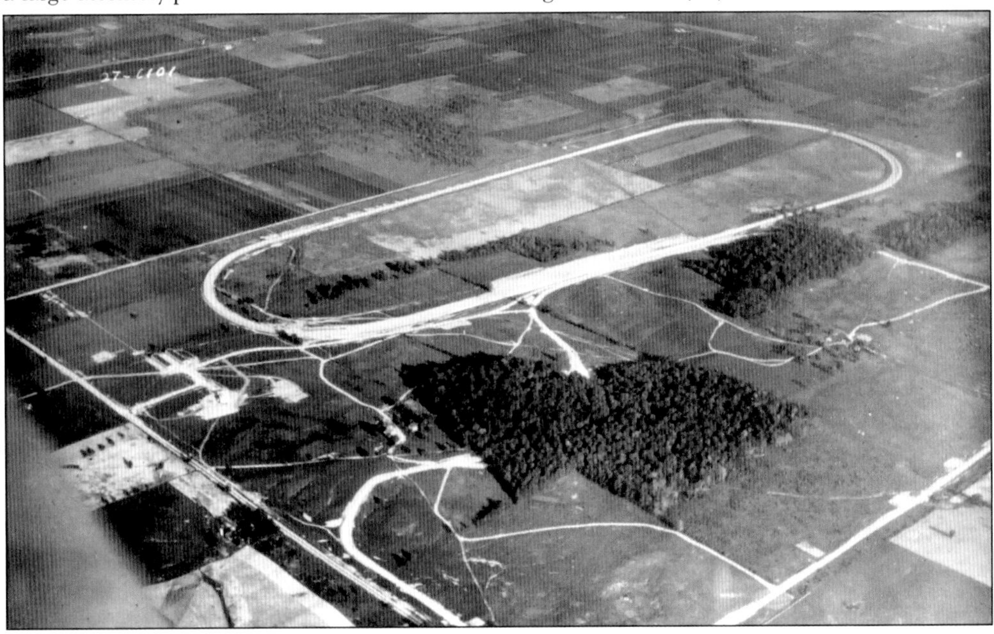

Although not clear from this 1927 aerial photograph of the Studebaker Proving Ground, the site was relatively small at 840 acres. Studebaker planted a grove of trees in the middle, spelling out its name when seen from the air, and was said to be the world's largest signboard. When Studebaker ceased to exist as an automaker in the 1960s, the test track was sold to automotive supplier Bendix Corporation. (N.)

This winter scene at the Studebaker Proving Ground shows a 1942 model Studebaker Commander or President approaching a relatively short but steep 30 percent grade, a feature similar to those found on all automobile test tracks. Studebaker rose from bankruptcy during the Depression to be a successful competitor in the postwar years but ultimately failed after merging with Packard in 1954. (N.)

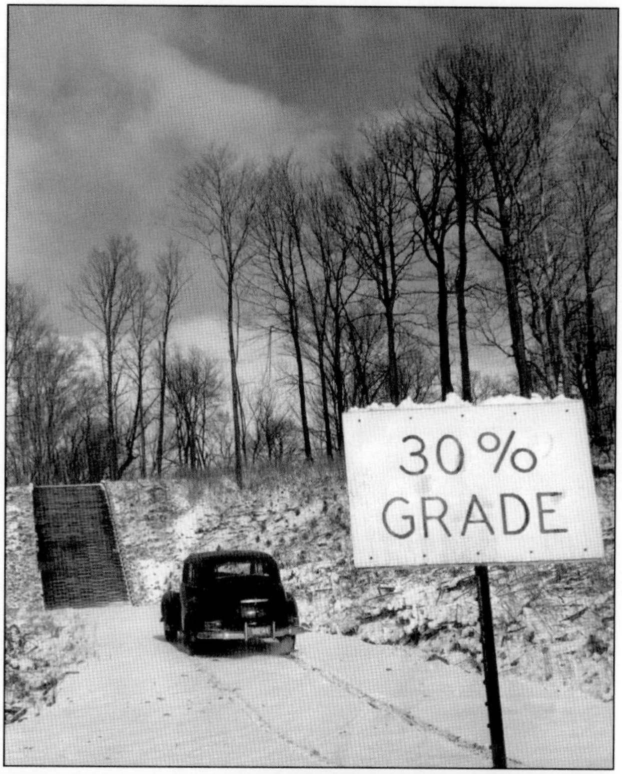

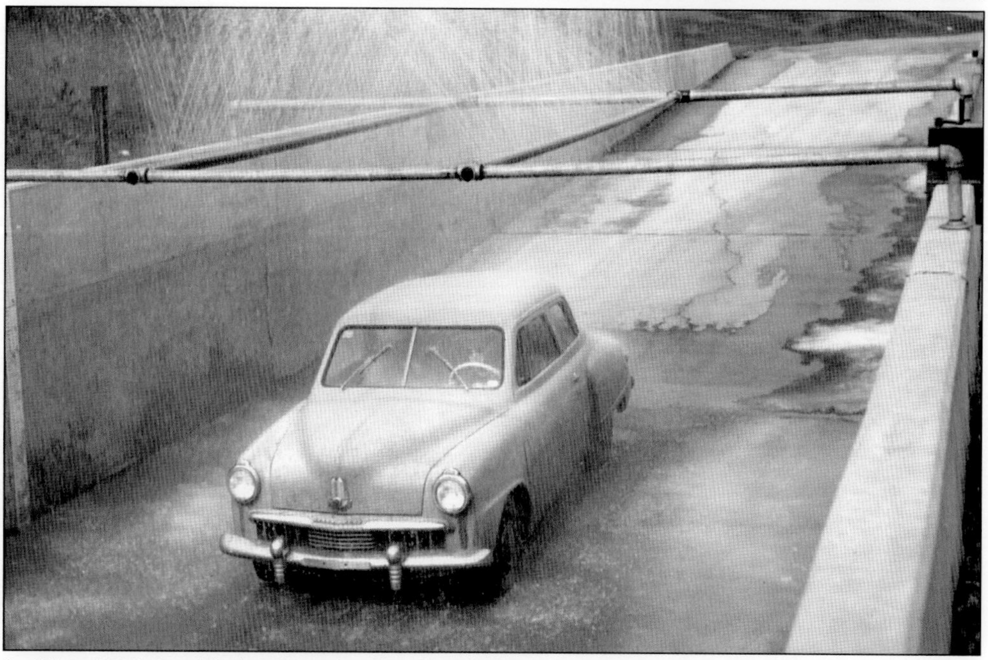

In May 1946, Studebaker was the first automaker to introduce all-new cars following World War II. Here a radically styled 1947 Studebaker Champion is shown splashing into the water bath at the Studebaker Proving Ground near South Bend. The facility combines a "tub bath" with a "shower," an unusual testing feature for the time. (N.)

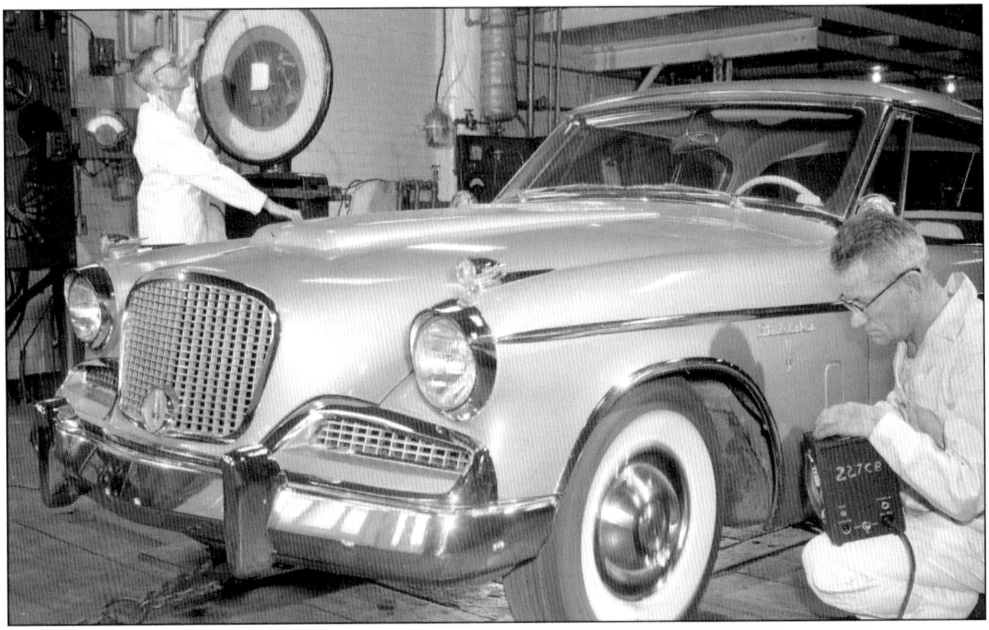

In this photograph, a 1958 Studebaker Hawk is subjected to extensive testing in laboratories at the Studebaker Proving Ground. The front wheels are mounted on a chassis roll dynamometer that rotates them from an external power source. Little investment was wasted in updating styling of the popular Hawk coupes for several years, but it was the sawed-off Lark models of 1959 that extended the life of Studebaker until 1966. (N.)

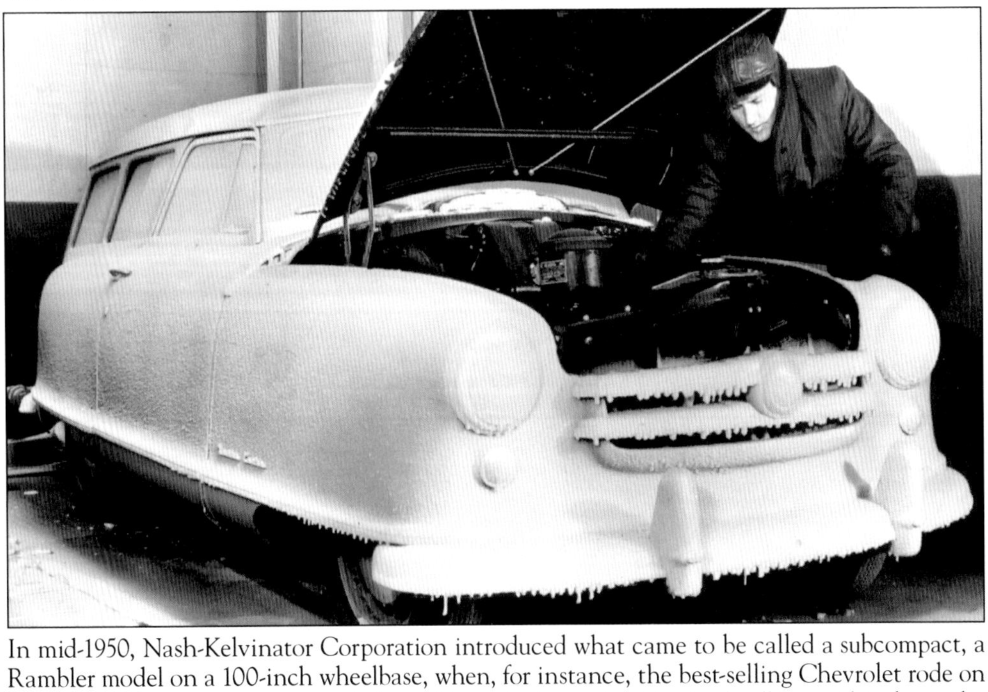

In mid-1950, Nash-Kelvinator Corporation introduced what came to be called a subcompact, a Rambler model on a 100-inch wheelbase, when, for instance, the best-selling Chevrolet rode on a 115-inch wheelbase and other Nash models had 112- and 121-inch wheelbases. This shows the somewhat familiar view of a Rambler station wagon that has been subjected to wetting down in an engineering laboratory cold room. (N.)

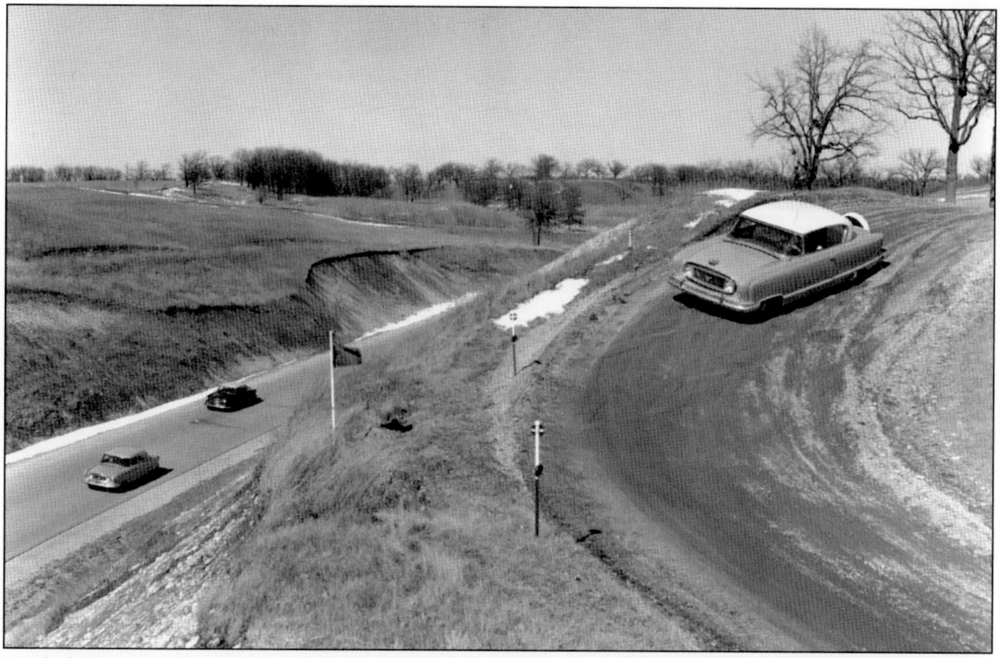

Nash began building its proving ground near Burlington, Wisconsin, in 1944 and finished it in 1947. In this scene, a restyled 1955 Nash is shown rounding one of the durability roads, while below and to the left, other Nashes pass swiftly on either a straightaway or one side of a high-speed oval. (N.)

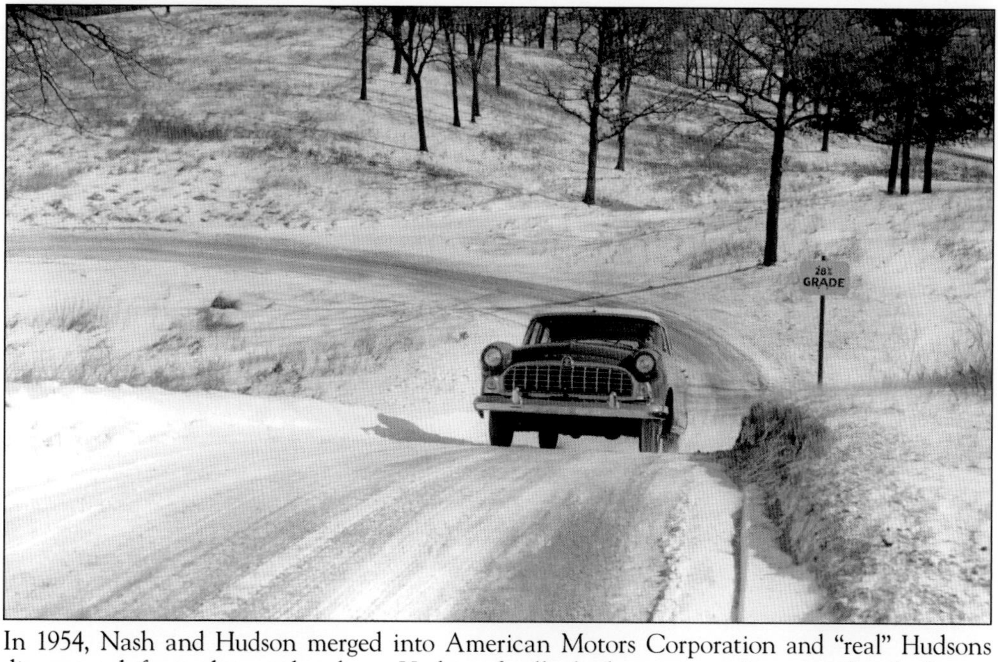

In 1954, Nash and Hudson merged into American Motors Corporation and "real" Hudsons disappeared from the marketplace. Hudson finally had a test track, even if only for its short-lived Nash-based models of 1955–1957. Here a 1955 Hudson is shown on the Burlington Proving Ground. After Chrysler acquired American Motors in 1987, the track was sold to MGA Research Company, which rents it out to various users. (N.)

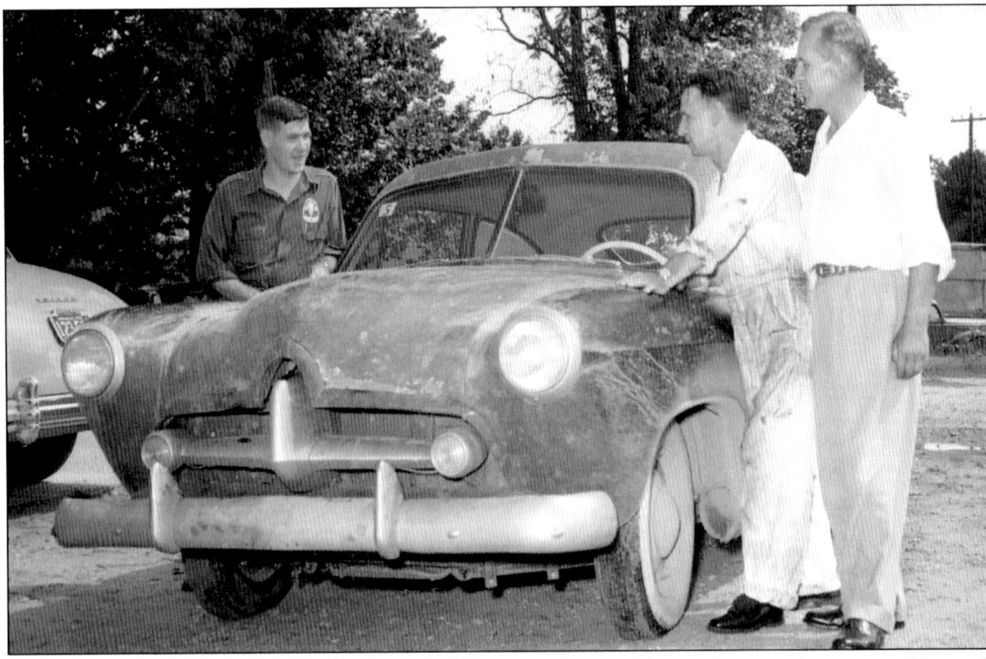

Kaiser-Frazer followed Nash to the U.S. small car market in 1951 with the subcompact Henry J, shown here after a test run over muddy Michigan back roads. For 1952, a spin-off was produced for sale by Sears, Roebuck and Company department stores, called the Allstate, which differed slightly in styling. Both cars, like the Nash Rambler, shared a 100-inch wheelbase. (N.)

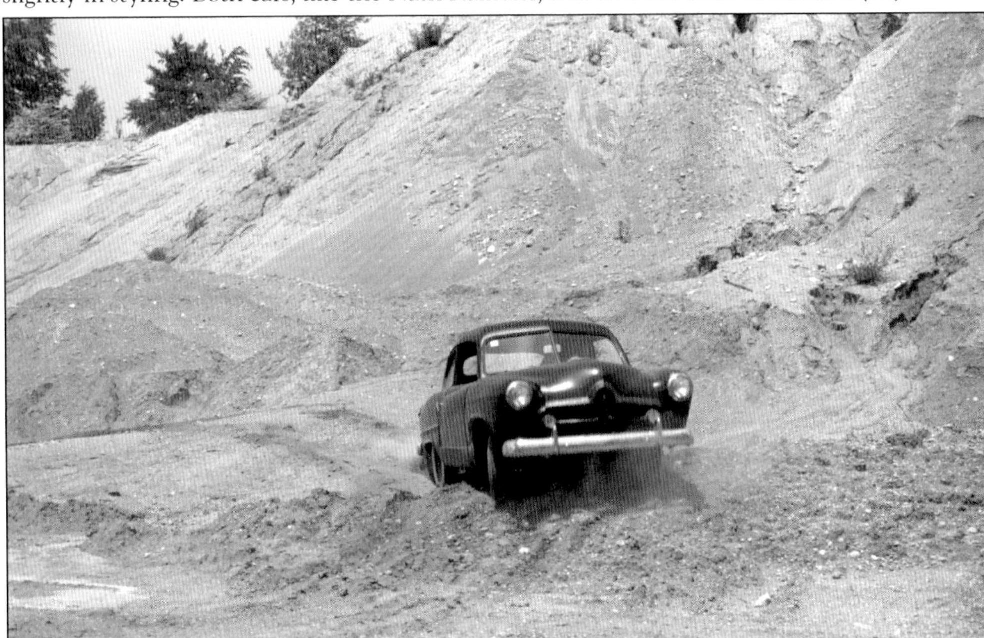

Somewhere in Michigan, Kaiser-Frazer engineers found a lonely gravel pit where they could wring out their prototype Henry J without interference from other motorists or the merely curious. The Henry J was offered with both four- and six-cylinder engines (supplied by Jeep maker Willys-Overland of Toledo) and in only one body style, the two door shown in these pictures. (N.)

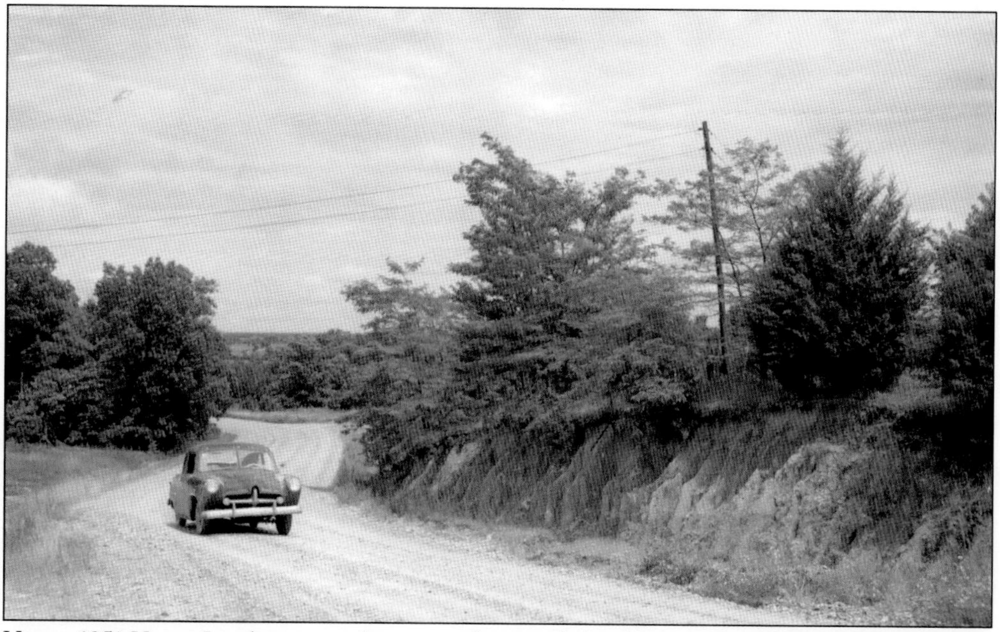

Here a 1951 Henry J is shown winding around a graveled public road, probably in the Irish Hills area of southern Michigan. With the four-cylinder engine, the car reportedly could obtain 25 miles per gallon highway fuel mileage. But with cheap gasoline and a list price of $1,363, the car could not compete. The industry leader, Chevrolet, sold a larger, six-cylinder sedan for $1,540. The last year for the Henry J was 1954, when only 800 were built. (N.)

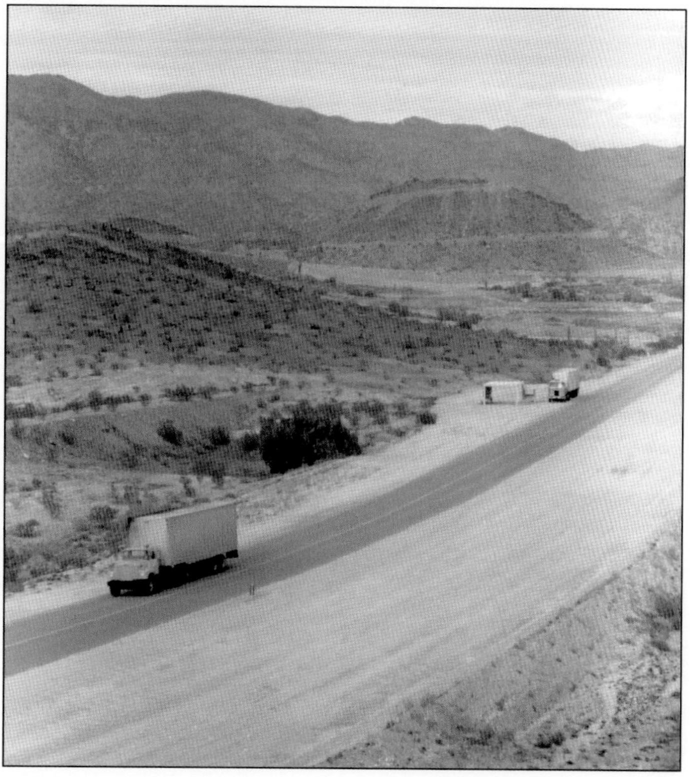

Now known as Navistar, the International Harvester Company of Chicago and Fort Wayne, Indiana, established an Arizona proving ground in the mountains near Phoenix for development and testing of its heavy truck models, shown here. International Harvester spent five years road testing a new V-8 diesel engine, running up nearly seven million test miles before introduction to fleet operators. (N.)

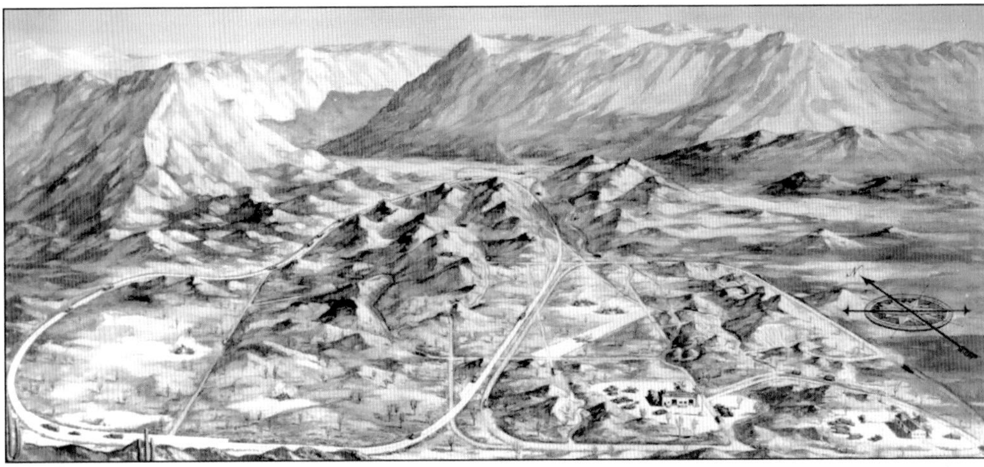

This is an artist's rendering of the mountainous International Harvester proving grounds, as the company termed it. It did not have as extensive test facilities as those of Detroit's big three automakers. The twisting, paved durability route stretched out seven and a half miles. Climbing steep mountains was particularly demanding of trucks carrying heavy highway loads, testing engines, transmissions, axles, and cooling systems. (N.)

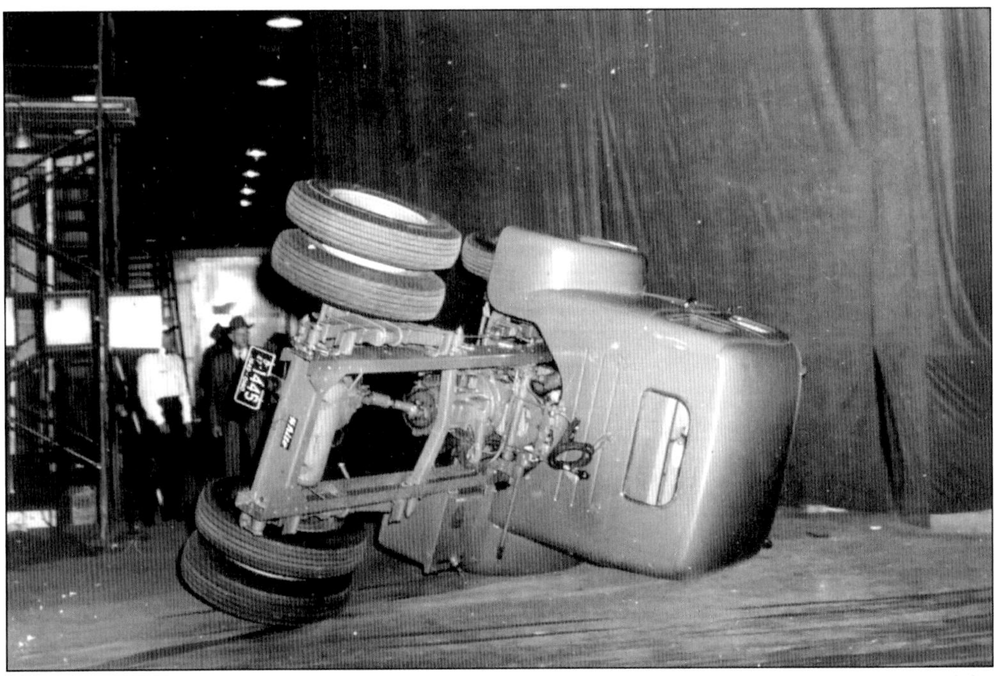

The White Motor Company of Cleveland specialized in medium trucks, such as those used for garbage collection, as well as heavy highway tractors for pulling cargo trailers long distances. Here in a safety test, a White medium-truck chassis cab has overturned after being driven off a ramp at a White engineering test facility. The location and date are unknown. (N.)

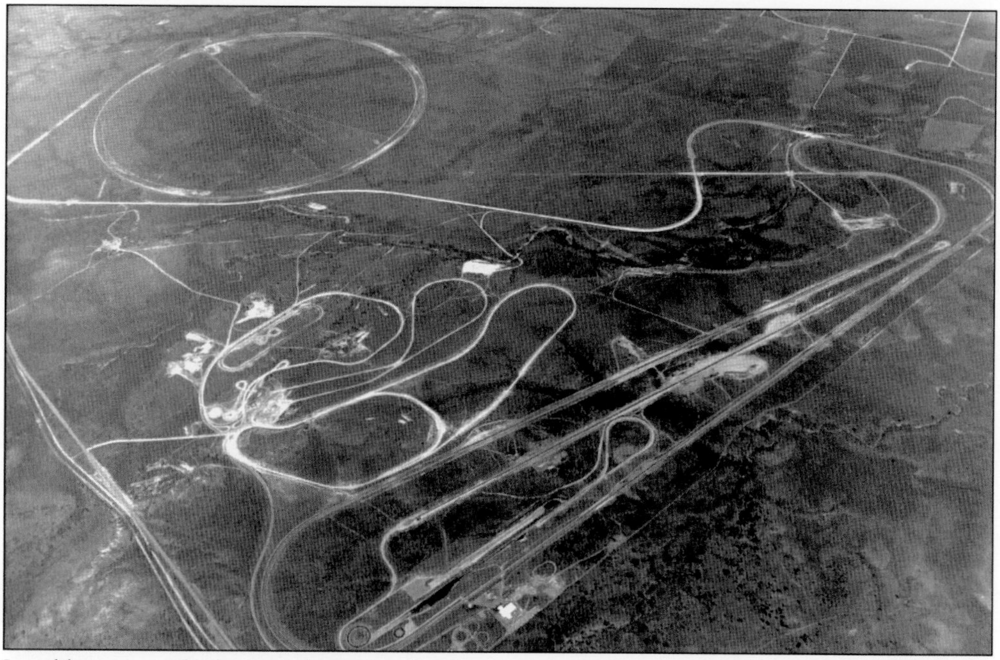

In addition to vehicle manufacturers, the tire companies also operated test tracks. This is an aerial view of the Goodyear Tire and Rubber Company proving ground in Texas. High speed and durability roads are shown where the huge variety of passenger car and truck tires are tested for puncture resistance, tread life, braking, and skid performance. (N.)

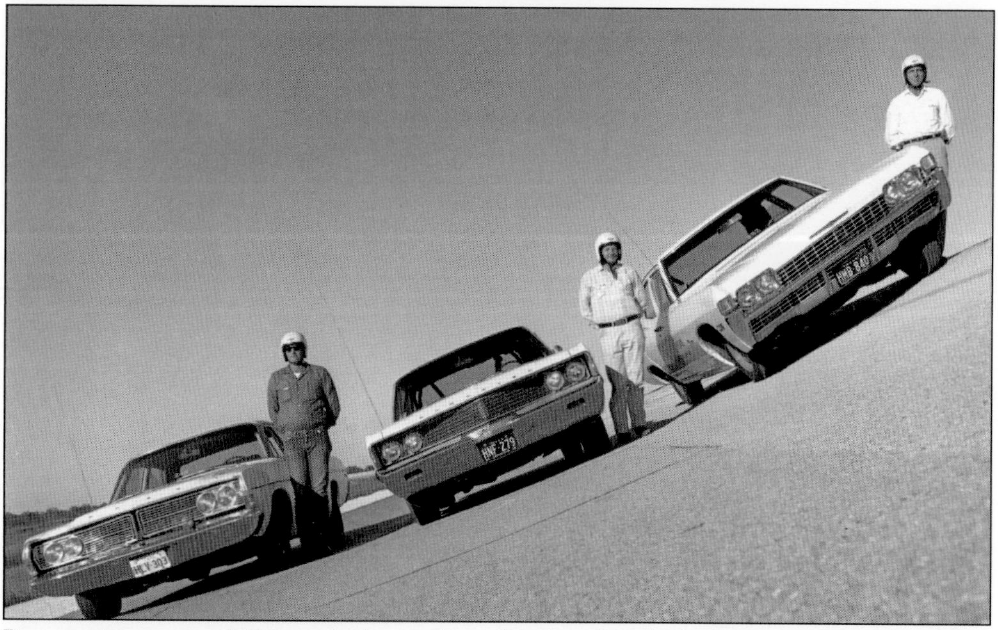

Because tires are carefully matched to each model of car for which the automakers select them, the tire manufacturers must test their products on the same type of vehicles. This photograph at Goodyear's Texas test track shows a line up of 1968 models. From left to right are a Ford Custom, a Chrysler Newport, and a Chevrolet Biscayne. The attitude of the erect-standing drivers shows how steep the high-speed track curves were graded. (N.)

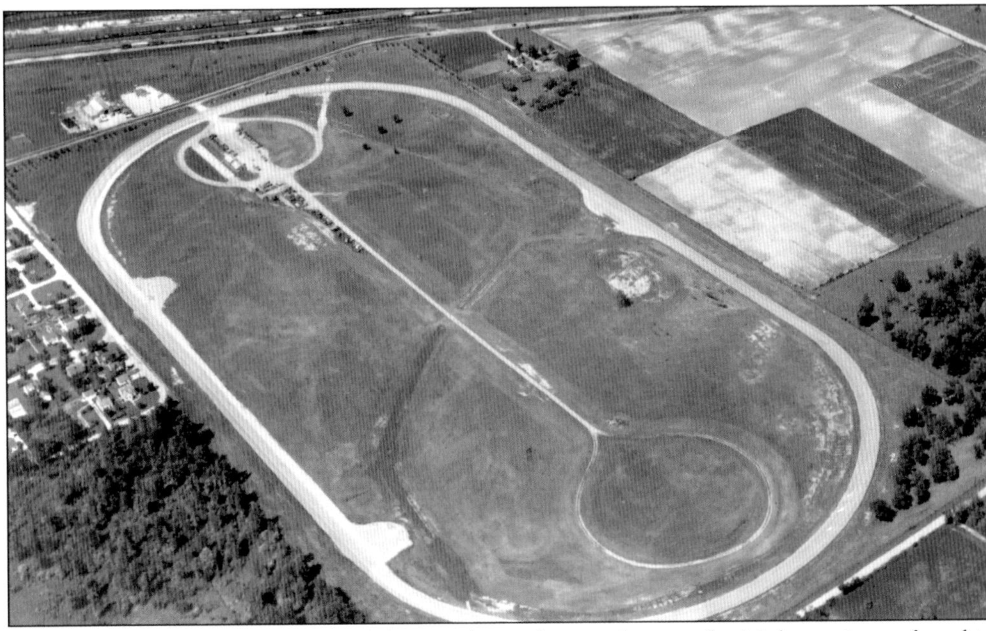

This proving ground is unidentified, but it is located somewhere in the Midwest. It was found in the National Automotive History Collection files without labeling. It may have belonged to a truck manufacturer such as International Harvester/Navistar or to one of the major automotive suppliers. It presents the usual high-speed oval, as well as garage/laboratory buildings and possibly a skid pad. (N.)

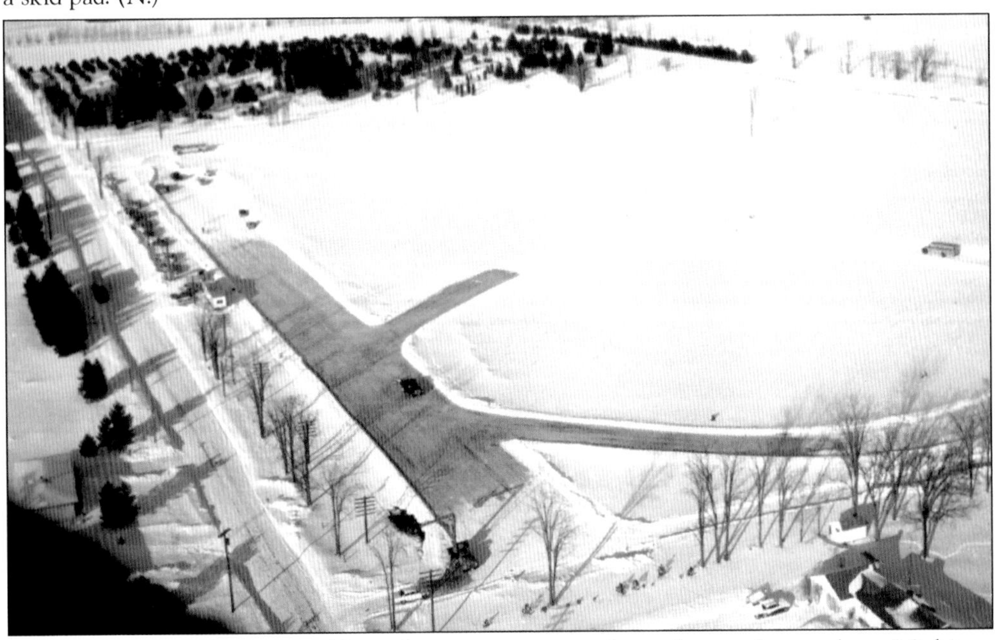

This winter scene depicts a cold-weather testing station located near the northern Michigan town of Gaylord, amid a popular year-round vacation area. The facility is small, and because it is snow covered, only a few roadways can be discerned. A school bus is seen at right, plowing along a snowy straightaway. The private facility may have been rented by a variety of manufacturers for evaluating traction on ice and snow. (N.)

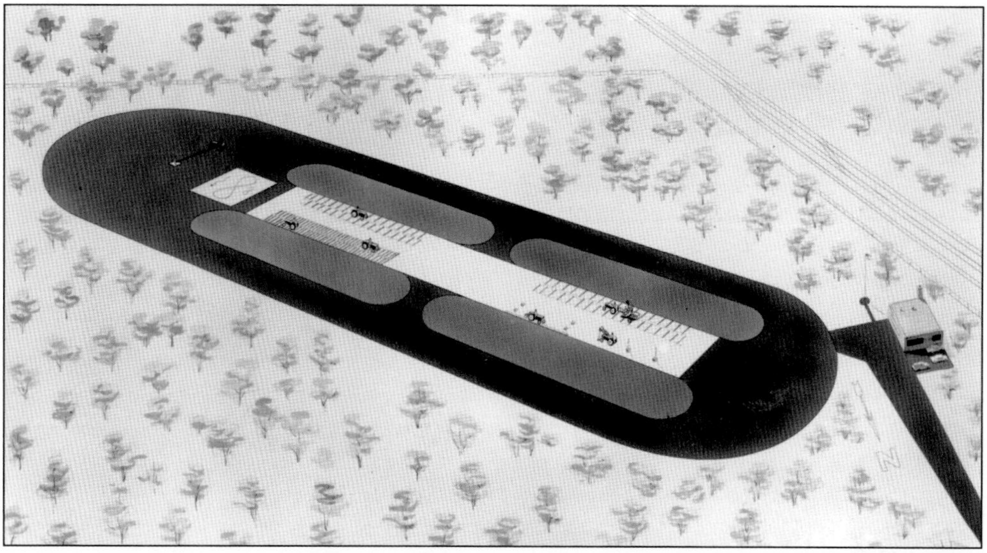

This rendering illustrates a different kind of test track, located in 1955 in upscale Birmingham north of Detroit, for Ford Tractor Operations. It was used by tractor and implement engineers to develop their products near their offices and was readily visible from nearby roads and the adjoining railroad line. Ford closed the facility, which is now a shopping center, after merging its tractor operations with a foreign tractor maker in the 1980s. (N.)

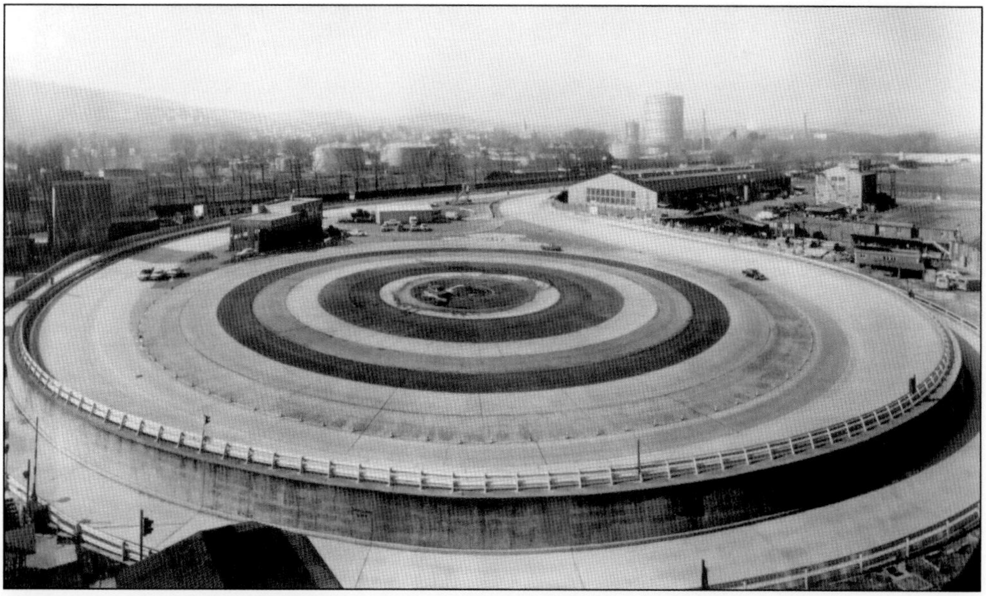

Foreign manufacturers also have their home proving grounds, often squeezed into urban areas because of lack of available land in centuries-old jurisdictions. This photograph depicts a skid pad at Daimler-Benz's testing ground at Stuttgart, Germany. Foreign manufacturers with extensive North American sales also found it necessary to establish desert test tracks in the American Southwest or California or rent facilities in the United States. (N.)

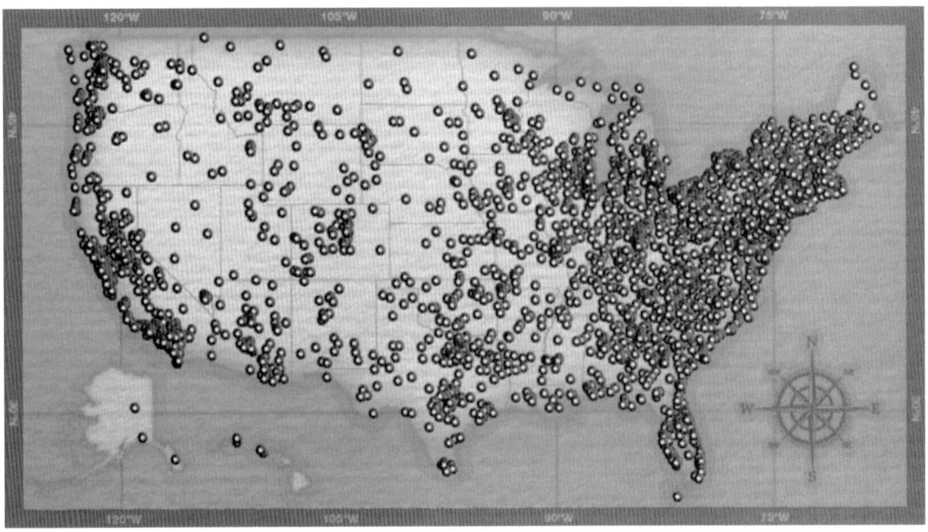